D1499617

Political Traditions in Foreign Policy Series

Kenneth W. Thompson, Editor

The values, traditions, and assumptions undergirding approaches to foreign policy are often crucial in determining the course of a nation's history. Yet, the interconnections between ideas and policy for landmark periods in our foreign relations remain largely unexamined. The intent of this series is to encourage a marriage between political theory and foreign policy. A secondary objective is to identify theorists with a continuing interest in political thought and international relations, both younger scholars and the small group of established thinkers. Only occasionally have scholarly centers and university presses sought to nurture studies in this area. In the 1950s and 1960s the University of Chicago Center for the Study of American Foreign Policy gave emphasis to such inquiries. Since then the subject has not been the focus of any major intellectual center. The Louisiana State University Press and the series editor, from a base at the Miller Center of Public Affairs at the University of Virginia, have organized this series to meet a need that has remained largely unfulfilled since the mid-1960s.

THUCYDIDES'
THEORY OF
INTERNATIONAL
RELATIONS

A Lasting Possession

EDITED BY

LOWELL S. GUSTAFSON

LOUISIANA STATE UNIVERSITY PRESS
Baton Rouge
MM

Designer: Melanie O'Quinn Samaha

Typeface: Body text Bembo, display Trajan

Typesetter: Coghill Composition Co., Inc.

Printer and binder: Thomson-Shore, Inc.

Library of Congress Cataloging-in-Publication Data

Thucydides' theory of international relations : a lasting possession / edited by
Lowell S. Gustafson.

    p.   cm.—(Political traditions in foreign policy)

    Includes bibliographical references and index.

    ISBN 0-8071-2538-5 (alk. paper)—ISBN 0-8071-2605-5 (pbk.: alk. paper)

    1. International relations—Philosophy.   2. Greece—Foreign relations—Philosophy.

    3. Thucydides—Contributions in international relations.   I. Gustafson, Lowell S.

    II. Political traditions in foreign policy series.

JZ1305.T48 2000

327.1'01–dc21   99-087375

Chapter 4 is reprinted from *The American Scholar,* Volume 53, Number 3, Summer 1984.
Copyright © by the author.

It will be enough for me, however, if these words of mine are judged useful by those who want to understand clearly the events which happened in the past and which (human nature being what it is) will, at some time or other and in much the same ways, be repeated in the future. My work is not a piece of writing designed to meet the taste of an immediate public, but was done to last forever.

—Thucydides
The Peloponnesian War
book 1, chapter 22
(Warner translation)

Those who want to look into the truth of what was done in the past—which, given the human condition, will recur in the future, either in the same fashion or nearly so—those readers will find this History valuable enough, as this was composed to be a lasting possession and not to be heard for a prize at the moment of a contest.

—Thucydides
The Peloponnesian War
book 1, chapter 22
(Woodruff translation)

But he that desires to look into the truth of things done, and which (according to the condition of humanity) may be done again, or at least their like, he shall find enough herein to make him think it profitable. And it is compiled rather for an EVERLASTING POSSESSION, than to be rehearsed for a prize.

—Thucydides
The Peloponnesian War
book 1, chapter 22
(Hobbes translation)

CONTENTS

Thucydides' Theory of International Relations

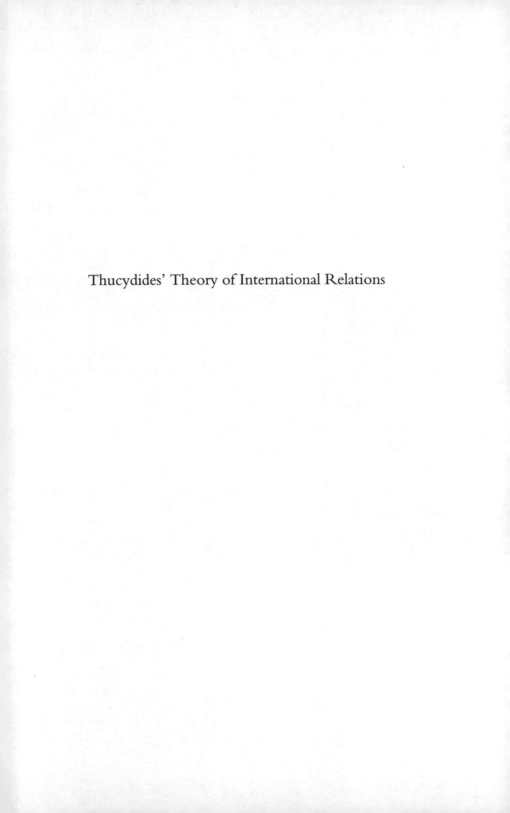

INTRODUCTION

LOWELL S. GUSTAFSON

LONG SEEN AS A FATHER OF
history and sometimes as one of political thought, Thucydides is
also one of the first analysts of international relations whose writings continue to help us understand our contemporary condition.[1] In the *History of the Peloponnesian War*, Thucydides presents
his theory of international relations and political philosophy, the
relationship between international politics and the regime or type
of government, various understandings of realism and pluralism,
and the role of ethics in international relations. His inductive,
descriptive, and dialogic method requires his readers to carefully
and attentively cull this theory from the book.

1. A classic commentary on Thucydides describes itelf as an "historical commentary
on a historian." Arnold Wycombe Gomme, *A Historical Commentary on Thucydides* (Oxford: Oxford at the Clarendon Press, 1945), 1:1; see also 84. One work that sees the
Peloponnesian war as having stimulated political thinking is Ulrich von Wilamowitz-
Moellendorff, *Aristoteles und Athen* (Berlin: Weidmann, 1893), 1: 171–85.

I

The rich and evocative theory of international relations presented over twenty-four hundred years ago by Thucydides in a world torn by conflict is important in its own right and as a historical document, as well as for the light it casts on our contemporary condition. Thucydides considered the Peloponnesian War in ancient Greece, or Hellas, to be a great war that was worth writing about. He produced a great book that remains worth reading in part because it challenges its reader to understand greatness and what that war can show to the careful observer about human affairs.

Though the book's title is usually rendered in English as the *"History* of the Peloponnesian War," the Greek word usually translated as *history* meant inquiry rather than description, account, or an explanation of caused events. Thucydides' inquiry leads Michael Palmer to see him as more a political philosopher thinking about human nature than a chronicler giving an account of events.[2] The way that Thucydides conducted his inquiry did have a great influence on the development of what we now mean by *history*. His choice of topic was primarily human nature and secondarily a war between great powers. Some have lamented that the latter choice has had much influence on the subject matter of many subsequent accounts, perhaps to the neglect of other worthy topics. His approach has been influential in that it was not merely a chronology, nor was it filled with anecdotes and social customs. It was not poetry and held little if any place for the gods and mythology, distinguishing him from Homer, Herodotus, and many others before him.[3] His inquiry was primarily based on observations of events and the record of speeches and debates, at least as well as he could re-create them. He would not inquire into the nature of humans by imagining republics in order

2. Michael Palmer, *Love of Glory and the Common Good: Aspects of the Political Thought of Thucydides* (Lanham, Md.: Rowman & Littlefield, 1992).

3. For a comparison of Thucydides and Herodotus, see Simon Hornblower, *Thucydides* (Baltimore: Johns Hopkins University Press, 1987), 13–33.

to answer how people should be, but by observing how they acted throughout his adult life in order to answer how they are. In this, the ancient Greek inquirer has found resonance in readers from the ancient and modern periods.

Still, the particular examples of human actions may be representative of their forms. The Peloponnesian War was the quintessential war, in which human nature clearly showed itself. It was the archetype, perhaps a perfect example of what is universal. With its debates and speeches, all in a context of dramatic action, it is a great conversation with great consequences. It is a precursor to the Platonic dialogues.

Thucydides believed that human nature was essentially the same across time and place. As David Cartwright writes, Thucydides "did not see 'history' as straightforward record of fact, a source of amusement, a medium for moralizing, or an instrument of propaganda. He wrote to offer his reader an opportunity to come to understand something permanent and profound."[4] He is asking questions of what he observes, inquiring into a major conflict between the two great powers of his time to understand his own era's condition in ways that will help others in the future understand theirs. As Margaret Hrezo shows in chapter 2, Plato later responded to Thucydides, however different Plato's approaches and ideas were from those of the historian.[5] The *History of the Peloponnesian War* is one of the great influential texts of the ancient period.

In medieval Europe, Plato and Aristotle admittedly had more influence than Thucydides. However, Thucydides found an attentive audience in the West starting again in the Renaissance. Francesco Guicciardini (1483–1540) sought understandings from

4. David Cartwright, *A Historical Commentary on Thucydides: A Companion to Rex Warner's Penguin Translation* (Ann Arbor: University of Michigan Press, 1997), 4.

5. Dionysius of Halicarnassus was another ancient to respond to Thucydides, although it was primarily as a critic of Thucydides' style. See Dionysius of Halicarnassus, *On Thucydides*, trans. W. Kendrick Pritchett (Berkeley: University of California Press, 1975).

histories of alliances, diplomacy, and wars to better comprehend his own era.[6] His reading of Thucydides led him to ideas about balance of power and equilibrium, and the influence of character, in international systems. Guicciardini reintroduced the West to Thucydides after a thousand years, and the modern period he helped interpret became a powerful filter through which this ancient historian has been subsequently understood. The more famous author of modernity, Machiavelli, read Thucydides and commented on some of his stories, but the Florentine preferred Livy. Still, the two authors share a secular attitude towards politics, a desire to learn through historical example more than by abstract principle, a regard for calculated self-interest, a preference for the combination of virtue with greatness and honor rather than with meekness, and similar estimations of the role of fortune or chance in politics and the role of military force.

Thomas Hobbes is famous for his reading and translation in 1629 of *The Peloponnesian War*, which taught him about the search for regularities in society, the problems of democracy, and the need for an overwhelming power to maintain order and security. Hobbes's interpretation has been another major filter through which Thucydides has influenced subsequent eras. Laurie M. Johnson has demonstrated, however, just how different Thucydides and Hobbes are on the issues of human nature, justice, leadership, and regimes. Hobbes, she argues, reduces human thought and action to one motivation or cause, while Thucydides expands the view to a more rich and rounded picture.[7]

Thucydides has attracted the attention of Americans no less than Europeans. Basil Lanneau Gildersleeve, a classics professor at

---

6. Francesco Guicciardini, *Maxims and Reflections of a Renaissance Statesman*, trans. Mario Domandi (New York: Harper & Row, 1965), and *The History of Italy* (London: Collier-Macmillan, 1969).

7. Laurie M. Johnson, *Thucydides, Hobbes, and the Interpretation of Realism* (DeKalb: Northern Illinois University Press, 1993), x, 205, 212. See also Peter R. Pouncey, *The Necessities of War: A Study of Thucydides' Pessimism* (New York: Columbia University Press, 1980), 151–57.

the University of Virginia who had served in Robert E. Lee's army thirty years earlier, published a piece in 1897 entitled "A Southerner in the Peloponnesian War."[8] Gregory Crane finds that William Tecumseh Sherman's "attitude toward the use of power and the practice of warfare owes much to the tradition that Thucydides inaugurated." Crane traces "a line from Melos, where the Athenians annihilated the entire population of a small island, to Sherman's devastating march through the heart of the Confederacy to the firestorms caused by Allied bombing in Dresden and Tokyo that incinerated tens of thousands of children, women, and noncombatants: military necessity, coolly articulated, served to justify ancient and modern actions alike."[9]

Crane may be inaccurate in much of this. If Thucydides was primarily recording the actions of politicians and soldiers of his period, then they rather than he began the tradition alleged by Crane. The Athenians did kill the men and enslave the women and children of Melos, but they did not annihilate the entire population. Sherman did not do what was done in Dresden and Tokyo; the Union general limited his use of force to fighting enemy combatants and destroying buildings, infrastructure, livestock, and crops. However, inaccurate or not, Crane continues the common assumption that somehow Thucydides sanctions and advocates the unlimited use of force to achieve foreign policy objectives.

In 1929, after the Great War, Charles Norris Cochrane saw in Thucydides not the ceaseless struggle for power, but the genesis of scientific analysis of international relations. He wrote that the "truth is that Thucydides had the assured faith of a scientist because he was scientist, because, in fact, he was inspired by contact with a department of positive science which in his day had suc-

8. B. L. Gildersleeve, "A Southerner in the Peloponnesian War," *Atlantic Monthly* 80 (1897): 330–42.

9. Gregory Crane, *Thucydides and the Ancient Simplicity: The Limits of Political Realism* (Berkeley: University of California Press, 1998), 23.

ceeded in extricating itself from the coils of cosmology." He continues that unlike Herodotus, Thucydides does not introduce religious or metaphysical principles to explain human behavior, and unlike Homer, he writes scientific history rather than imaginative literature. Indeed, he is the father of political science as much as of history.[10]

Before Cochrane, F. M. Cornford had contended that there was indeed a good deal of myth in Thucydides' account.[11] The book can be read as a "prose tragedy," as the "Tragedy of Athens" and its decline. He wonders how scientific it is to make up speeches the way an author thinks they should have been. More recently, post-modernists could see in Thucydides an account of passion more than myth or reason. Crane notes that Pericles calls for Athens as an object of love and adoration in erotic terms.[12] During the Cold War between the United States and the Soviet Union in the late twentieth century, the book was often read as a case study of bipolarity between an authoritarian land power and a democratic sea power.

The contemporary reader of Thucydides often comes to his book with the accumulation of millennia's worth of interpretations of those who have read him in order to understand better their own eras and human beings in all periods. If one considers the beginning of the international system to have been in 1648 with the Peace of Westphalia, our own international period has lasted just over a mere three hundred and fifty years. The post– Cold War period has been a scant decade or so. Our situation now is different from what it was during the Cold War and much different from what it was before the world was organized by the principle of sovereign nations. Still, the effort to read a book from 2,500 years ago, and other writings by those who have tried to

10. Charles Norris Cochrane, *Thucydides and the Science of History* (New York: Russell & Russell, 1965), 3, 14, 25, 33.

11. F. M. Cornford, *Thucydides Mythistoricus* (London: Arnold, 1907).

12. Crane, *Thucydides and the Ancient Simplicity*, 318–20.

understand it since, helps us understand our own time—and perhaps become greater people as a result.

The authors of this volume reconsider Thucydides' theory of international relations in the post–Cold War world in which the United States is the single greatest military power. We find lessons in Thucydides' writing that must be incorporated into our own understanding of greatness. Misunderstanding it could bring the United States in a period of military unipolarity and economic multipolarity to grief.

THUCYDIDES AS THEORIST OF INTERNATIONAL RELATIONS

We begin our discussion by recognizing the importance of Thucydides, which is not always done. Some recent scholarship takes a cavalier or arrogant attitude toward ancient wisdom, Laurie M. Johnson Bagby observes in chapter 1. She argues that a scientistic approach to the study of international relations is incapable of using two important tools: judgment and the moral sense. She suggests that a return to the "classical" approach to international relations scholarship might now be fruitful, considering the limited success of the scientific-behavioral approach. Considering also the dramatic changes in world politics since the fall of the Berlin Wall, and the international complexity unveiled at the end of the Cold War, perhaps it is time to reevaluate classical ways of analyzing international politics. Thucydides' *History* can provide us with a contemporary reference for understanding many of the age-old problems and recurring situations that now dominate the international scene.

First, Thucydides' analysis of the Peloponnesian War includes multiple variables, with no attempt to reduce those variables to a single overarching and unidimensional theory. Second, Thucydides re-introduces us to the necessity of carefully exercising our own judgment in the analysis of complex situations and events. Third, Thucydides reminds us that our analysis cannot be and should not be morally neutral. Moral issues are a part of the political world which a truly realistic approach must take into account. Thucydides' approach to the Peloponnesian War can help us create some middle ground between those who are still dedicated to the scientific method and those who never left or are returning to the classical method.

In chapter 2, Margaret Hrezo places Thucydides' theory within the broader context of Greek political theory. She contends that "Thucydides was realistic, but he was an incomplete political realist. Here was a man who, although he understood the reasons behind the changes in Athenian politics and her consequent drive for expansion, was thoroughly appalled by the new morality and overwhelmed by the tragedy to which he was a witness. He saw beyond the mere facts of the war to what it meant for Hellenic society, and he made some judgments concerning those facts. This was a person who felt in the deepest part of himself that he was watching a world in chaos and who struggled for some way to make it meaningful to himself, his contemporaries, and future generations." It was concerns such as these that would have great impact on the most famous of Greek philosophers, Plato.

INTERNATIONAL RELATIONS AND THE REGIME

Thucydides argues that the real cause of the Peloponnesian War was "the growth of the power of Athens and the fear this inspired in Lacedaemon." W. Daniel Garst notes in chapter 3 that this has sometimes led to theories emphasizing the importance of international anarchy and the quest for power in international relations. He pushes the question further to ask why Athens' power grew. He finds at least part of the answer to be in the type of development of Hellenic states' character and domestic political institutions. These, more than the anarchic international structure, fostered the ways these states behaved.

Thucydides does not merely draw connections between the

distribution of power in fifth-century B.C.E. Greece and states' behavior. He is more interested in how this distribution of power came about and particularly why Athens, rather than Lacedaemon, acquired an empire. To answer this question, Thucydides concentrates on the internal attributes of states. He contrasts Spartan dullness, indolence, and conservatism with Athenian restless energy and innovation. Part of the reason for the differences in attributes of these states came from the variations in relations between the groups within them, particularly the oligarchy and the *dēmos*.

In Athens, democracy made its empire possible. Athenian imperialism helped to reconcile its own men of wealth to democracy. Its leading men profited considerably from shaking down the oligarchies of allied and subject cities, but its lower classes benefited as well. It was easier in the short term for Athens to continue to blunt its class divisions by adding to its conquests and tightening its control over subjects than to change its political system and avoid imperial overstretch, Garst argues. This means that it was not a system external to Athens, but Athens' own internal disorders, that ultimately caused the war that ruined Hellas.

In chapter 4, Clifford Orwin continues the consideration of Thucydides' theory of internal politics. Orwin carefully analyzes the Mytilenian Debate to challenge the view, "widespread among democratic theorists, that as 'community' requires 'participation,' so 'participation' breeds 'community.' Many of the advocates of participation today view it as 'transformative.' They see it not merely as a better or the only legitimate way of going about addressing substantive political problems, but as itself the solution to most of our nagging discontents. To hear the participationists tell it, in fact, our ills seem to be of two sorts: those that must be cured if participation is to 'be meaningful,' and those that meaningful participation will cure. These latter include those sentiments of distrust, powerlessness, and 'alienation' rampant in modern democratic societies. Liberty, equality, fraternity, or community: these are divined to inhere in the experience of political participation itself."

REALISMS REVISED

Thucydides is often known not as an analyst of reason in international relations or types of regimes, but as a founder of the realist view of the primacy of power in international affairs. The growth of Athenian power over other cities is the central story of Thucydides' account of the period before the Peloponnesian War. Imperialism spans the subfields of domestic and international politics in Thucydides' writing. Athens' domestic attributes of daring and innovation led it to build an empire of many city-states. With as much pessimism and perhaps even tragedy as exists in the book, Thucydides' still seems to suggest that the demands of empire built with conquest and daring, and maintained sometimes with tyranny, can be reconciled with moderation, justice, and the common good, argues Jack Riley in chapter 5. Athens' ultimate failure to do so does not disprove the theory of how this might be done. Early in the book, in the Archaeology, Thucydides inextricably connects freedom, rest, material progress, daring, and greatness with imperial domination, Riley contends. Life in early Greece was nasty and brutish until the Athenian and Spartan empires developed. However, Thucydides warns that crisis may unleash the powerful passions of the desire to rule, driven by greed, the love of honor, and the love of victory, which may rise above the law and unleash an insolent daring and violent excess. While Pericles may approve of this, Thucydides does not. Rather, Thucydides advocates a synthesis of Athenian daring with Spartan moderation in the governance of an expanding empire.

Steven Forde argues in chapter 6 that "Thucydides is clearly a 'realist' of some kind, meaning that he is to some degree skeptical about the applicability of morality to the political world, especially the world of international politics. It is the extent of his realism that is in doubt. Some have maintained that Thucydides' realism is thoroughgoing, that his only purpose in treating moral issues is to show how illusory morality is. The more common interpretation though is that moral excellence, while tenuous, is admired by Thucydides, and that when it is overturned, which is especially likely during war, he regards the loss as deplorable. In this view"—which Forde shares—"the tension between Thucydides' realism and his admiration for morality gives his work a tragic cast. Morality represents an important human achievement, but one that proves sadly vulnerable to the realist pressures of politics and war."

Jack Riley makes the important observation that it was not Alcibiades' ambition, nor even his city's imperial expansion per se, that made inevitable the ultimate disaster for Athens, but the failure to calculate what was needed for the campaign. The synthesis of daring and moderation discussed in chapter 5 is made possible not by piety or respect for ancestors, but by natural ambition governed by careful calculation of always limited resources and power. Ambition and daring bring greatness which can be undone if power is irrationally thought to be unlimited. Because power and resources are always distributed, the sense of unity from empire must always be tempered by the observation of pluralism, Thucydides argues, as I claim in chapter 7. Pluralism results from the acceptance by political actors of the need for freedom of individuals, various groups in society, cities, and nations. Actors are most rational when they desire their own freedom and accept that of others because they have accurately calculated their own and others' power. Excessive love of power, feelings of vengeance, greed, excessive ambition, wishful thinking, a loss of a sense of limits, or other factors often cause irrational estimates of relative power in one's own favor. Irrational thought or inaccurate calculation lead to overreaching one's capacity, which can cause one's own destruction as well as that of an entire political system.

Rational calculations of power are not precise and certain, but reasonably accurate. They are based on wisdom and prudence.

This is so because not everything can be calculated. Chance and fortune place limits on rational calculation. Not everything can be known and factored into calculations; hence, not everything can be predicted and controlled. There cannot be unchecked intellectual or political power, as I argue Thucydides suggests.

INTERNATIONAL ETHICS

A critique of the mistaken Athenian notion of greatness from excessive ambition is developed in chapter 8 by Craig Waggaman. He argues that Thucydides is not merely calling for accurate calculations of power; the theory of *The Peloponnesian War* includes the observation that sustained greatness must incorporate virtue, goodness, and justice. "The question of what defines national greatness is central to the study of international relations." What makes *The Peloponnesian War* such a fascinating work is the continuing debate over the meaning of Athenian greatness. Because Athens and the United States seem to have so much in common, Thucydides' "possession for all time" remains a pond in which we see constant glimpses of our own reflection as we strain to see under its surface.

"The 'problem of Pericles,' " says Waggaman, "is about much more than an interpretation of what Thucydides thought about the events he was describing. Thucydides seemed to recoil from the decline of behavior, character, and rhetoric that he witnessed during the war. Yet he doesn't go nearly as far as Socrates did in laying the blame for what he saw at the feet of the Athenian 'heroes' who built 'ships and walls and dockyards and many other such things,' but left no room for virtue or moderation." A society that left no room for virtue or moderation, and made "the madness of empire the measure of goodness . . . would see politics as simply a struggle among competing interest groups for advantage. It would bring forth a political science that called such a view of politics empirical. It would create citizens who would criticize and despise such a politics, but nevertheless adopt its methods in their own lives, calling such behavior appropriate to 'real world.' Such a culture would create institutions of higher education that cared nothing about the souls of their students, only about providing them with the requisite and measurable competencies that would ensure them and their city material success. Such a society would preach tolerance and equality while the hearts of its citizens became increasingly hardened from lack of contact with the good and the beautiful."

In chapter 9, Nick Pappas draws on his experiences in the Vietnam War and his observations of contemporary America to discuss when power is real and when it is an illusion. He examines the eerie parallel between the deformation of reality and its public policy results in ancient Athens and twentieth-century America. In Athens the collapse of the personal and public order found in the paraenetic myth of Homer was followed by the triumph of the murderous "Athenian thesis" as described in *The Peloponnesian War.*

This is as much a lesson for the twenty-first century of the common era as it was for the fifth century before the common era. Thucydides' message remains relevant. The nature of man does not change. Although some individuals and societies may have clearer conceptions of just existence, there is no clear line of progress from "primitive" to "advanced" modes of existence. Material progress does not equal spiritual progress. As societies attempt to find their way towards transcendence, the possibilities for deformation are as great as the possibilities of grace and salvation. Human beings will as often confuse their own selfish desires for those of God or the Good as they will achieve a genuine understanding of the demands of transcendence.

The parallel to America is seen in the ascendancy of "political realism" to a position of authority among American policy-making elites. The reduction of human life to the search for power resulted in an inability on the part of Athens to make rational calculations between means and ends in the field of pragmatic action, and even about rational ends themselves. The result was "imperial overstretch," military disaster, and eventual defeat. Could it be that the power upon power that is the United States is immune to such miscalculations? It is left for the reader to decide whether the parallel is well-taken or goes too far in explaining the nova-like blossoming of the American version of the nightmare Athenian maritime empire.

In the nine following chapters, Thucydides is shown to be a sophisticated theorist of international relations. His theory of international relations and political philosophy, the relationship between international politics and the regime, understandings of realism and pluralism, and international ethics challenge our understandings of him and of contemporary international relations.

PART I

THUCYDIDES AS THEORIST OF
INTERNATIONAL RELATIONS

1

FATHERS OF INTERNATIONAL RELATIONS?
THUCYDIDES AS A MODEL FOR THE
TWENTY-FIRST CENTURY

LAURIE M. JOHNSON BAGBY

THIS ESSAY WAS INSPIRED
by Kenneth Thompson's book *Fathers of International Thought,* not
the particulars of it but rather its basic purpose. Thompson has
put together a small, very readable volume, dealing with great
philosophers who have had a direct or indirect impact on how
we view and study international relations. He starts with Plato
and Aristotle and ends with Hegel and Marx, and though he does
not devote a chapter to Thucydides, he does provide the student
of international relations with an overview of classical political
thought as it relates to international politics. Thompson, and apparently many others in this discipline, believe that there is still
much to be learned from these men, things that should still be

learned by anyone who professes to have some expertise on the subject. Perhaps as we move into the twenty-first century we are coming to grips with the fact that modern learning is crippled by a cavalier or arrogant attitude toward ancient wisdom.

But wasn't the "classical" approach to studying international relations rejected as unrealistic, impractical, out of touch with the times, imprecise, even moralizing? Wasn't the revolution of the sixties and seventies (at least in this field) about moving forward from mere speculation and philosophic ramblings to a truly scientific program, in which concrete evidence concerning human behavior and the behavior of states would be gathered, empirical theory formulated, and knowledge be truly cumulative? Remember Morton Kaplan's famous criticism of traditionalism and defense of his systems approach: "The humanist who wants to substitute in human events a verbal process called reason or understanding for a verbal and/or mathematical process called science has confused intuition with the articulation of communicable knowledge."[1] Kaplan did acknowledge that the human sciences are likely to be more uncertain than the natural sciences, but as much as possible they should emulate the natural sciences nonetheless. In other words, for Kaplan there was no difference in kind between the two subjects. Intuition, introspection, these were the tools of traditionalists. These tools were not to be trusted, because the human senses and human perceptions were not trustworthy conveyers of empirical truth.

In the face of these types of assertions, Hedley Bull made "the case for a classical approach." Those who advocate the scientific or behavioralist approach, he wrote, "aspire to a theory of international relations whose propositions are based either upon logical or mathematical proof, or upon strict, empirical procedures of verification." From the sixties to the seventies, this approach had become the "orthodox methodology" within the United States,

---

1. Morton A. Kaplan, "The New Great Debate: Traditionalism vs. Science in International Relations," *World Politics* 19 (October 1966): 4.

whereas in Bull's Britain it had "virtually no impact at all."[2] Obviously, Bull felt that the British position was superior, and not only because it was understandable instead of "tortuous and inelegant."

In Bull's opinion, there were several reasons why the advocates of the scientific method would be disappointed. By confining themselves to what can be proven empirically or logically, the advocates of the scientific approach rejected two very important tools for analysts of international relations: judgment and the moral sense. Also, whenever they made a meaningful contribution to the subject matter, advocates of the scientific approach had to abandon that approach in favor of classical methods. The number of hard-to-measure or control variables in international relations made the prospect for cumulative knowledge aspired to by advocates of the scientific approach unlikely, and if they stuck to the measurable and controllable, they tended to remain at the periphery of the important questions. Their love of model-building removed them ever more from political reality, with all of its exceptions to the rule. Perhaps most critical of all was Bull's claim that the advocates of the scientific method, "by cutting themselves off from history and philosophy, have deprived themselves of the means of self-criticism, and in consequence have a view of their subject and its possibilities that is callow and brash."[3]

Bull predicted that, contrary to the aspirations of the American school, the field of international relations would "remain indefinitely in the philosophical stage of constant debate about fundamentals."[4] Nevertheless, the American school disregarded Bull's warning and proceeded down the promising path of truly scientific analysis. No more "mere speculation," no more competing philosophies for modern scholars. Like Machiavelli, they

2. Hedley Bull, "International Theory: The Case for the Classical Approach," *World Politics* 18 (April 1966): 362.

3. Ibid., 375.

4. Ibid., 370.

were determined to not write about things that had never been proven to exist.

While we have moved considerably beyond the early systems and models, we still have many of the problems Bull predicted we would have, including a certain disconnect from practitioners. Have we become "new scholastics, who have sought refuge in a world of intellectual constructs essentially in order to escape from political reality"? Some scholars believe we have. John Garnett reminds us that it has been quite possible from the 1960s forward for graduate students in international relations to obtain Ph.D.'s but have very little knowledge of political history, political theory, or particular governments. He believes that this imbalance needs to be corrected.[5] Now we find the prominent scholar Kenneth Thompson devising a volume to acquaint those thirsty for a more classical background with the basics of what those classics might mean for our studies.

We also have a growing number of textbooks which emphasize the so-called fathers of international thought, from Charles Beitz's *Political Theory and International Relations* (1979) to Paul Viotti's and Mark Kauppi's *International Relations Theory* (1987), or their newest *The Global Philosophers: World Politics in Western Thought* (1992). A new reader, *International Relations and Political Theory* (1993), devotes sections to Plato, Aristotle, St. Augustine, Machiavelli, Hobbes, Kant, and Hegel, before getting to latter-day fathers such as Morgenthau, Bull, and Keohane and Nye.[6] It is not too much of a stretch to say that there is a trend in the direction of reassessing the importance of the classics for a good

5. Ibid., 365, 12.

6. Charles R. Beitz, *Political Theory and International Relations* (Princeton: Princeton University Press, 1979); Paul R. Viotti and Mark V. Kauppi, *International Relations Theory: Realism, Pluralism, Globalism* (New York: Macmillan, 1987); Mark V. Kauppi and Paul R. Viotti, *The Global Philosophers: World Politics in Western Thought* (New York: Lexington Books, 1992); Howard Williams, Moorhead Wright, and Tony Evans, *A Reader in International Relations and Political Theory* (Vancouver: University of British Columbia Press, 1993).

education in international relations. Why is there this growing interest in the classical as opposed to modern, scientific approach to international relations? Perhaps one reason for the increasing interest in the classics is that our current circumstances more resemble the distant than the recent past. In politics and philosophy it may be fair to say that there is really nothing new.

BEYOND THE TWENTIETH CENTURY

Louis Halle wrote in 1952, "What is remarkable about Thucydides is that he is less obsolete, today, than the chronicles of our most recent past." Halle felt that there was a remarkable resemblance between America after the First World War and Athens after the Persian wars; both were "called upon to assume the leadership of the free world." Part of Halle's point, of course, is that history tends to repeat itself in a general manner, and that one can therefore fruitfully search it for fairly concrete parallels. The parallels in Thucydides are especially worthwhile because Thucydides was such a remarkable analyst. This is what Louis Lord was trying to do in 1945 when he noted that the Germans had rightly compared themselves to the Athenians in character, while the Spartans, comparable with the British, were "protectors of liberty," but "slow to action and imperturbable." He found parallels between Persia and America, both "a little bit aloof and at first undecided as to which side [they] should favor, and possessed of almost unlimited resources."[7]

At another level, for Halle, Thucydides was and is relevant because his history demonstrates that, despite changing circumstances, human nature remains the same. Thucydides' teachings about the causes of war, the flaws of democracy and the slide from statesmanship into demagoguery, the deterioration of morals during hardship, and the domestic impact of a lengthy, and espe-

7. Louis Joseph Halle, Jr., *Civilization and Foreign Policy* (New York: Harper & Brothers, 1952), 262; Louis Lord, *Thucydides and the World War*, Martin Classical Lectures, vol. 12 (New York: Russell & Russell, 1945), 231, 229.

cially an ideological, conflict, all relate to a universal and timeless human condition. In other words, Thucydides' work is both valuable in relaying information about parallel circumstances, and in imparting timeless lessons of use to anyone interested in politics. For Halle, the lesson of Athens was that of a Shakespearean tragedy: "The tragedy of Athens, as Thucydides saw it, lay in her inability to live up to the moral responsibility that had come to her as a result of her moral excellence. She had achieved, by sheer character, the prosperity that corrupts character."[8]

Quite a powerful and timeless lesson for the West, and especially for America, who could easily be corrupted by her post–World War II power, just as the Athenian empire succumbed to hers. As we entered the Cold War period, however, a different vision of Thucydides emerged. Due to the predominance of realist thought, this was the Thucydides of power balance and power transition, the Thucydides of bipolarity. Athens was often likened to America, while Sparta was compared to the Soviet Union, although for Peter J. Fliess, the comparison was reversed, with the Soviets appearing more like the Athenians. According to Fliess: "The period's characteristic distribution of effective international power between two superpowers bears a striking resemblance to the bipolarization of power which has occurred on a global scale since 1945 and which has relegated all nations other than the United States and the Soviet Union to a different and inferior status."[9]

This comparison emerged around the same time that models of polarity were being heavily discussed, and one of the most important questions for international relations scholars concerned which system was most stable, the multipolar or the bipolar. Two schools of thought emerged, with men like Kaplan arguing for multipolarity, and men like Kenneth Waltz arguing for bipolarity.

8. Halle, *Civilization and Foreign Policy*, 266.

9. Peter J. Fliess, *Thucydides and the Politics of Bipolarity* (Nashville: Parthenon Press, 1966), viii.

As Carlo Santoro points out, however, the bipolarity of the Cold War period was built upon nuclear deterrence, an unprecedented factor, from which it was difficult to generalize.[10] This unprecedented factor led to a system in which there was conflict, but it was conflict of a rather predictably limited nature. The threat of nuclear war determined where and to what extent the two superpowers would confront each other indirectly. Direct confrontation seemed out of the question, and thus the international system itself was remarkably stable in its bipolarity, and promised to continue indefinitely.

That stability, along with the horrific realization of the destructiveness of modern warfare, led the academic community into a search for propositions about power and conflict that could be made and built upon scientifically. Models were constructed which attempted to quantify the elements of power and predict how much power was necessary for a certain effect. The underlying assumption seemed to be that the Cold War was brought about by the fearsome nuclear power of the United States and the Soviet Union, that post-war distrust (due to the security dilemma) had caused the arms race which resulted in these arsenals, and that now the existence of the arsenals to a large extent actually dictated events. Realist thought tended to assume that understanding the ideological clash between the two superpowers or acknowledging their respective regime differences was secondary to the importance of understanding the tension caused by their respective military might. "The role of the domestic political system can certainly influence the way in which the systemic rules are functioning, but cannot reverse them. Indeed, the life cycle of an international system is determined above all by its structural traits. It is determined by the number of actors, the historical form

---

10. Carlo Santoro, "Bipolarity and War: What Makes the Difference?" in *Hegemonic Rivalry: From Thucydides to the Nuclear Age*, ed. Richard Ned Lebow and Barry Strauss (Boulder: Westview Press, 1991), 76.

of their interaction, the spatial arrangement of the various units, and their exchange of material, energy, and information with the surrounding environment."[11]

Realists either emphasized the compelling passions inherent in human nature which made international relations a "war of all against all," or, more and more, the determining nature of the anarchical international structure. But in the 1970s a groundswell of dissent concerning these grand realist theories appeared, attempting to ascertain the influence of geography, communications patterns, functionalism, and integration. The Correlates of War Project emerged, as did models concerning deterrence, alliance behavior, bargaining, and decision-making. Models attempted to explain foreign policy decisions as products of bureaucratic or organizational processes.[12] Game theory attempted to model and predict decision-making under various circumstances in a mathematical fashion.

On the one hand, beyond his supposed characterization of Hellas as a bipolar world, and his statement that fear of Athens' growing power had caused Sparta to go to war, Thucydides seemed of little help in building grand theory in this new scholarly environment. On the other hand, because of the desire for systematic, scientific treatment of the subject, Thucydides did not seem attractive to those building middle-level theory, even when theory was concerned, as his analysis was, with such things as individual or group psychology. Thus Thucydides still claimed the title of "father" of a general way of thinking, but his more subtle and complex wisdom fell into the background. Knowledge that could be modeled or quantified, and tested, was the order of the day. The traditionalists balked at this development, but in time their voices were submerged under the prevailing American tide.

11. Ibid., 76.

12. James E. Dougherty and Robert L. Pfaltzgraff, Jr. *Contending Theories of International Relations: A Comprehensive Survey* (New York: Harper & Row, 1990), 10–11.

As we can see now, not all of the confidence with which the scholarly community embraced the social-scientific approach was justified. Garnett observes that "this kind of writing numbs our sensitivity to major moral issues" by resorting to value-neutral "jargon." The study of political philosophy and political history went into decline. "It was not that philosophical matters were deemed unimportant in principle, but that there seemed to be no way of dealing with them scientifically." Nevertheless, acknowledged or unacknowledged, our norms continued to strongly influence what we studied. Competing theories shifted between the poles of realism and idealism, with their corresponding normative assumptions and goals.[13] By the 1980s, there was a growing sense of frustration, a feeling that the search for international theory was an "elusive quest."

Most recently, world events have contradicted the structuralism upon which contemporary realist theory is often based. While we may not have fully come to grips with this, perhaps the return to an interest in classical thought is at least partly a response to these events. Simply quantifying and measuring elements power did not predict and could not explain how internal politics in the former Soviet Union would change the shape of the balance of power and global politics in ways hardly imaginable a few short years ago. Russia is becoming a regional, imperial power, and not an appreciable rival to the United States, despite the fact that its nuclear arsenal still exists.

THUCYDIDES: A CONTEMPORARY REFERENCE

In this new and seemingly more complex international environment, we can usefully look back to Thucydides for guidance.

13. John C. Garnett, *Commonsense and the Theory of International Politics* (Albany: State University of New York Press, 1984), 11; David M. Ricci, *The Tragedy of Political Science: Politics, Scholarship, and Democracy* (New Haven: Yale University Press, 1984), 145; Yale H. Ferguson and Richard W. Mansbach, *The Elusive Quest: Theory and International Politics* (Columbia: University of South Carolina Press, 1988), 79–108.

Thucydides was recognized by Hobbes as the most political historian ever, and he is characterized in many modern scholarly works
as the first scientific historian. Charles Cochrane claimed that "already in the fifth century B.C., Thucydides had grasped and applied the principles of scientific method with such success that his
work constitutes a standard of presentation."[14] This suggests that
perhaps Thucydides' goals, and even methods, are not so far removed from our own. How did Thucydides earn the reputation
for being "scientific"?

First, Thucydides rejected religious or mythical explanations
for events. Thucydides never in his own words refers to supernat-
ural causation, either for human decisions or for human or natural
disasters. When his characters rely on the gods to decide when
and where to act, they look foolish and are prone to failure. Nicias, who fatally delayed the removal of his army from danger during the Sicilian Expedition, was "somewhat too much given to
divination" (7.50), according to Thucydides.[15] This is not to say
that Thucydides was an atheist or held no mythical beliefs, but
only to say that he tried to explain events as much as possible in
terms of natural causation, that which could be proven, or at least
reasoned about.

Second, Thucydides was fairly thorough in his presentation of
the facts. He reported a multiplicity of variables which led to the
initiation of hostilities in the Peloponnesian War, for instance. He
reported the facts with little elaboration or sentiment, unlike the
poets, who "put into song, adorning and amplifying their theme"
(1.21). Thucydides stated his concern for factual and accurate reporting. While he reconstructed speeches that he heard himself

14. Charles Cochrane, *Thucydides and the Science of History* (New York: Russell &
Russell, 1965), 166.

15. See Leo Strauss, *The City and Man* (Chicago: Rand McNally, 1964), 160–61;
Thucydides, *The Complete Writings of Thucydides: The Peloponnesian War*, trans. Richard
Crawley (New York: Random House, 1951), book 7, chapter 50 (all subsequent references to *The Peloponnesian War* in this chapter are to this edition and are by conventional
book and chapter).

or were reported to him, "according to the sentiments most befitting the occasion," he also "adhered as closely as possible to the general sense of what was actually said." And as for the deeds of the war, he thought it his duty to report them "only after investigating with the greatest possible accuracy every detail" (1.22). As we will see, he was not morally neutral in his presentation, but neither did his presentation disarm the reader's judgment. By taking into account the moral dimensions of the war, Thucydides may have been more of a realist than many modern realists.

Third, Thucydides' method involved taking those facts he gathered and drawing from them "generalizations about human action which constitute the usefulness of history and give to it the character of science."[16] He took the diversity of evidence at his disposal and attempted to give it order and function. While he knew that the events of the Peloponnesian War would not repeat themselves exactly, he nonetheless claimed that his work would remain useful, a "possession for all time" (1.22). It would yield general principles which would prove useful in understanding, evaluating, and even perhaps predicting future events.

Yet Thucydides' "science" is not our science, and is considered by some to be primitive at best, due to the fact that he does evaluate and can be said to be selective in approaching the data of history.[17] Can Thucydides' science in any way claim to be superior to our own? What, specifically, does his work say to contemporary students of international relations?

THUCYDIDES' ATTENTION TO MULTIPLE VARIABLES

Thucydides manages to report a variety of factors that resulted in a particular decision or event without giving the reader the impression that he is simply reporting the chaos of the war. Far from it, his presentation gives us a sense of order and purpose.

16. Charles Cochrane, *Thucydides and the Science of History* (New York: Russell & Russell, 1965), 16.

17. See Virginia Hunter, *Thucydides the Artful Reporter* (Toronto: Hunter Rose, 1973).

How does he do this? The contemporary realist reading of Thucydides' *History of the Peloponnesian War* often tends to focus heavily on Thucydides' statement at 1.23, that the war was caused by Sparta's fear of Athens' growing power. But Thucydides did not stop at this system-level observation. Certainly Thucydides must believe that relations among independent states (or empires) are characterized by anarchy, that is, the absence of an overarching power to control them. Also, Thucydides certainly does say that fear of Athens' growing power caused Sparta to declare war. But focusing on Thucydides' statement that Sparta was compelled to war by fear of Athens' growing power ignores the question of what choices and decisions each country's successive leaders made to get themselves into such a situation.[18]

Thucydides thinks these choices and decisions, represented by him as products of free will and not simply as products of structural constraints, are important enough to discuss at length. For example, he tells of how, immediately after they had led the successful effort against the Persian invasion, the Spartans decided to retire from the field (1.89). They did this even though they were acknowledged as the strongest city in Hellas.[19] The Athenians decided to remain, took the town of Sestos, and then went about rebuilding their city and its walls. Themistocles put off Spartan

18. The Corinthians at the Spartan war congress think Sparta is to blame for the situation precisely because Sparta did *not* react in the predictably realistic way towards Athens' growing power, instead encouraging it at one point, and looking the other way at a later point (1.68–69).

19. Orwin makes the strongest recent argument for the influence of the Spartan fear of a Helot uprising in explaining Sparta's conservative behavior. But he does not wish to go so far as to say that this fear produces necessity. See Clifford Orwin, *The Humanity of Thucydides* (Princeton: Princeton University Press, 1994), 85–86. As in most cases, Thucydides produces a layered explanation, including the Helots (1.101, 4.55, 4.80, 5.14), but also individual idiosyncrasies and choices (1.84, 1.94–95), and what we might call national character, often in accounts of Spartan battle tactics, on which the influence of the Helots would seem secondary. Yet there is no evidence that Thucydides thought that national character or culture constituted necessity. (1.68–71; see 3.29, 3.31, 3.89, 4.55, 5.54, 5.55, 5.82, 5.113, 5.115, 5.116, 6.93, 6.95, 8.24, 8.96).

questions concerning the walls until he presented the Spartans with finished Athenian fortifications, to which they acquiesced. Even after the Athenian walls were built, the Spartans continued to hold joint military exercises with the Athenians. The idiosyncrasies of the Spartan commander Pausanias made the Hellenes look to Athens for leadership. But rather than replace Pausanias with a better representative, the Spartans simply recalled him, satisfied that the Athenians would handle the allies (1.95). Indeed, Thucydides often demonstrates the influence of individual personalities on the course of the war. Take, for examples, the violent demagogue Cleon, the statesmanlike Pericles, the ambitious Alcibiades, the Athenian-like Hermocrates, and the overly pious Nicias.

Thucydides' account of the war shows that he would not agree with any entirely structural explanation, such as that Sparta's fear of Athens' growing power was alone the cause of the war. To see Thucydides' statement about Sparta's fear as his final word on what caused the war would be to "encourage an attitude toward history not uncommon among scholars of many kinds: an unconscious disdain for it, a disregard of its complexity . . . an unexamined assumption that its lessons and insights lie on the surface for anyone to pick up, so that one can go at history like a looter at an archeological site, indifferent to context and deeper meaning, concerned only with taking what can be immediately used or sold."[20]

The fact that Thucydides felt it necessary to write the *History* in the way he did, with all its details, all its analyses of cultural differences and decision-making processes, belies the notion that he would agree with any unidimensional theory. Many scholars have demonstrated the inadequacy of strictly structuralist assumptions and predictions when measured against the historical record, and structuralism has been criticized for being too general or ab-

20. Paul Schroeder, "Historical Reality vs. Neo-realist Theory," *International Security* 19 (summer 1994): 148.

stract to easily relate to particular circumstances. Thucydides demonstrates that the type of theory we call structuralism must necessarily be accompanied by other forms of analysis in order to accomplish the task of "political education."[21] Thucydides points the way toward a practical, if less elegant, use for such system-level theories within the overall project of description, explanation, problem-solving, and prediction.

Thucydides' narrative suggests that he thinks the structure must be taken into account as one variable, but there is much left to know and analyze which may even interfere with initial conclusions drawn from the given structure. The authors of *The Logic of Anarchy* seem to be moving in this direction, though they would characterize what they are doing as redefining or broadening the definition of structure.[22] They claim that it is only when other variables are brought into the analysis that change in the international structure can be accounted for.[23] But rather than try to integrate disparate variables into one grand and consistent theory, international relations scholars may have more to gain by turning their focus from theory-building and toward using, in different combinations depending on the need, the many theories they have already developed. These theories, if understood more as Thucydides might have understood them, as "generalizations" and not as iron-clad formulae, when used in combination, may offer us more concrete and useful information.

21. See Schroeder, "Historical Reality vs. Neo-realist Theory," 108–48; see Robert O. Keohane, ed., *Neorealism and Its Critics* (New York: Columbia University Press, 1986); Clifford Orwin, "Thucydides' Contest: Thucydidean 'Methodology' in Context," *The Review of Politics* 51 (summer 1989): 358.

22. For instance, they claim that political rhetoric should be incorporated into a theory of structure: "Language, and its use both by statesmen and publicists in deliberations about foreign policy, was put forward as one manifestation of power: a structure, like the balance of power or the market." Barry Buzan, Charles Jones, and Richard Little, *The Logic of Anarchy: Neorealism to Structural Realism* (New York: Columbia University Press, 1993), 234.

23. Ibid., 66–80. See also R. B. J. Walker, "Realism, Change, and International Political Theory," *International Studies Quarterly* 31 (March 1987): 65–86.

JUDGMENT

What does this inclusion of multiple variables, some of which are not conducive to empirical measurement, mean for the analyst? Obviously, he or she cannot arrive at one single cause for any event, a conclusion which seems to make devising a "grand theory" very difficult, if not impossible. No theory based on many levels of causation will ever be simple or elegant. Indeed, one could argue that in the absence of such simplicity or elegance, there can be no theory at all. This is probably true, if we define "theory" narrowly. But if we cannot find an overarching theory in our modern sense in Thucydides, and yet we think we are satisfied upon reading Thucydides' explanation of and extrapolations from events, what replaces theory and still provides us with a satisfactory explanation? What allows us to make and apply to any particular set of circumstances the types of generalizations Thucydides might make regarding the impact of individual personalities, national character, decision-making processes, as well as systemic influences?

As soon as many variables come into play, judgment must also. Judgment is not, as Kaplan may have thought, the same thing as intuition. Intuition is a feeling, a hunch. Intuition comes as a result of the unconscious dealing over time with information at its disposal; all of a sudden we just "feel" that we are right. Judgment, on the other hand, is based on experience and keen observation, processed and applied consciously to the current situation. This, according to Strauss, is political science in its original sense. "It consists of careful and judicious collections and analyses of politically relevant data," some of which may be quantified, but much of which cannot. Furthermore, "it is only when the Here and Now ceases to be the center of reference that a philosophic or scientific approach to politics can emerge."[24]

It is difficult to chart or quantify the process which culminates

24. Leo Strauss, *What Is Political Philosophy?* (Glencoe, Ill.: Free Press, 1959), 14, 16.

in judgment, because of the very complexity of the calculations involved, as well as the type of information or knowledge that might be part of the calculus. It would be impossible to quantify or scientifically describe character, and yet an individual leader's character defect can be a real and very significant variable in explaining an outcome. The "headstrong" nature of the Spartan Pausanias, whose "behavior seemed an aping of despotic power" (1.95) and who consequently was unpopular with the allies, was a key factor in Sparta's decision to retire from leadership of the alliance in favor of Athens. Nicias's extraordinary attention to things divine at a moment when hesitation in the name of piety could be lethal could be blamed (among other things, of course) for the failure of the Sicilian Expedition (7.50). Alcibiades' grandiosity, which led the Athenians to reject his leadership, might also be blamed for that failure (6.15). Also, no amount of statistical information can substitute for direct knowledge of political culture which can lead to an accurate prediction about how a particular people will react to a particular event. Thucydides often alluded to the pious and conservative nature of Sparta as an explanation for everything from grand strategy to decisions on the field of battle.

Thucydides applies his own judgment throughout in his selection, ordering, and treatment of events. But by introducing us to the many different factors involved in the war, he is also allowing his readers to develop their own sense of judgment. This development of human wisdom is indeed a kind of "cumulative knowledge" which allows the reader to analyze the events of his time with a better understanding of human nature, especially human nature under these types of pressures. This type of teaching frees us from the need to examine only what is measurable or somehow controllable. Since most of what happens in domestic and especially international politics is uncontrollable, and much is not measurable, we cannot dismiss Thucydides' claim that his history, despite not measuring up to today's scientific standards, would not only explain the Peloponnesian War but would be "a possession for all time."

A MORAL SENSE

In the quest to be scientific, political scientists have become dedicated to the ideal of value-neutrality put forth by positivism. Bull felt that holding fast to this distinction led to a disregard of much relevant information, while Strauss believed that the more seriously we strived for value-neutrality "the more completely we develop within ourselves a state of indifference to any goal, or of aimlessness and drifting, a state which may be called nihilism."[25] Are these and other similar objections to the fact-value distinction just sentimentalism?

As stated above, Thucydides' teaching is not morally neutral, but neither do we get the sense that he is passing summary moral judgment for us. How does Thucydides manage to traverse this sensitive area and still leave us with the impression that he has indeed not followed in the footsteps of the poets? Perhaps it is because Thucydides knew that ignoring moral issues in the name of objectivity was really not dealing with the totality of the relevant evidence. In other words, dismissing the impact of values on societies is neither scientific nor objective. A look at the Melian Dialogue and the Mytilenaean Debate will give us a sense of how Thucydides dealt with moral issues within his overall analysis of the war.

Concerning Thucydides' Melian Dialogue, Paul Viotti and Mark Kauppi state: "This classic contains the essential ingredients of the realist perspective as stated in perhaps its boldest and most extreme form." But they also point out: "Thucydides is sometimes unfairly criticized as an advocate of harsh and brutal wartime policies, one who rationalized such events as he described in the famous Melian dialogue. Thucydides, however, favored

25. Ibid., 19.

the democracy of the Golden Age of Pericles. In fact, the second half of *The Peloponnesian War* is a description of the degeneration of Athenian democracy and the resulting fanaticism that turned the war from a defensive effort to a war of conquest. The Melian dialogue reflects the latter phase of the war and should not be viewed as a personal preference on the part of Thucydides."[26]

The Athenians at Melos express what has come to be known as the "Athenian thesis," that they and all other human beings are *compelled* by fear, honor, and interest to rule wherever they can. This is the justification for either subduing or destroying the rather harmless island city Melos. If through this thesis the Athenians at Melos express the essential elements of realism in "its boldest and most extreme form" and yet the Melian Dialogue is not to be taken as Thucydides' preference, then what is Thucydides saying about the realism used by the Athenians in the Melian Dialogue?

Is the dialogue representative of Thucydides' thought? Not if by this we mean that Thucydides fully agrees with the Athenians' position in the dialogue. However, the dialogue may be representative of Thucydides' thought if by this we mean his analysis of the impact of a particularly harsh realism when it is used in practice. Such "thoroughgoing realism,"[27] used as it was at Melos, as an ideological justification for political and military actions, could then be seen as Paul Schroeder sees the idea of balance of power, as a "historical variable, changing over time, conditioned by historical circumstances, and freighted with ideological assumptions."[28]

From this perspective, part of Thucydides' teaching can be seen as an exposition of the danger inherent in Athenian realism or any other "immoral" idea when it is used as an ideology or

26. Viotti and Kauppi, *International Relations Theory*, 79, 36.

27. Steven Forde's terminology. See Steven Forde, "Varieties of Realism: Thucydides and Machiavelli," *Journal of Politics* 54 (May 1992), 384.

28. Schroeder, "Historical Reality vs. Neo-realist Theory," 148.

justification for actual policy. Perhaps this explains the inevitable conclusion to be drawn from Viotti and Kauppi's statement that realism in its most extreme manifestation becomes a form of "fanaticism."[29]

It is easy to conclude that the Melians foolishly refused the Athenians' offer, naively trusting in divine or Spartan intervention. One can accuse the Melian oligarchs of irresponsibly deciding the fate of so many of their countrymen "behind closed doors." But even if these conclusions and accusations were to be largely accurate, the Melians' assessment of the Athenians might still be seriously considered. The Athenians easily reduced the remaining Melians to slavery, with no immediate consequences to themselves. Yet the Athenians were soon to experience grave political and strategic reversals due to their increasingly extreme ideology.[30] The Sicilian Expedition, launched with such grandiose hopes and hubristic impulses, is placed by Thucydides immediately after the Melian Dialogue. The Melians' disaster is followed by the internal political chaos and the eventual military defeat of Athens. As Steven Forde puts it, "The primacy of self-interest over justice, proclaimed for a generation or more as the basis of the city's policy, came eventually to infect the city's domestic life. When the community declares itself free from moral restraints in international politics, individuals conclude eventually that those restraints have no claim on them either."[31]

In other words, while international relations may remain out-

---

29. [Thucydides' warnings about excessive daring and ambition are discussed also by Jack Riley in chapter 5. *Ed.*]

30. E. H. Carr translates this position toward realism into the language of international theory when he writes: "The utopian who dreams that it is possible to eliminate self-assertion from politics and to base a political system on morality alone is just as wide of the mark as a realist who believes that altruism is an illusion and that all political action is based on self-seeking." Carr, *The Twenty Years' Crisis, 1919–1939* (New York: Harper Torchbooks, 1964), 97.

31. Steven Forde, "Varieties of Realism: Thucydides and Machiavelli," 384. [Craig Waggaman argues in chapter 8 that Pericles' positions lead with disastrous consequences to those of Cleon and Alcibiades. *Ed.*]

side of the sphere of true morality to a larger extent, domestic community is the sphere of genuine morality and citizenship. The two, however, are inextricably linked, and Thucydides, in order to truly understand and relate the cause of Athens' demise, had to acknowledge the role of moral issues in that demise. Is this not more objective and scientific than trying to remain "value-neutral" by ignoring these issues? These issues cannot be ignored when they have a practical impact on domestic and international policy, as they did in the case of Melos and subsequent events.

The Mytilenaean Debate provides us with another example of Thucydides' analysis of moral issues and provides us with a glimpse of the moral lessons he intended to impart. Diodotus is a character who seems to have been created by Thucydides for the purposes of demonstrating moral prudence and statesmanship under trying conditions. His arguments are juxtaposed to the "violent" Cleon's (3.36) in the Mytilenaean Debate (428 B.C.). Cleon's arguments are fashioned to be characteristic of the violent and hubristic attitude that Thucydides very much disliked.

The Mytilenaeans were an independent ally of Athens who had openly revolted and attempted to persuade other Lesbian cities to do the same. Like the Melians later, the Mytilenaeans hoped for Spartan aid, but they received none and were subdued fairly easily. The Mytilenaean commons had helped the Athenians in this project. Thus the Athenians faced a not unusual problem of whom to punish for the rebellion and how. Initially, the choice seemed easy. Cleon took advantage of the initial rage of the Athenian people to convince them to mete out the punishment the Melians were to later receive. But the next day, perhaps moved by a sense of honor, certainly by a sense of guilt, the Athenians felt "repentance" for their earlier decision. This feeling of guilt precipitated the call for another vote and the ensuing debate between Cleon and Diodotus. Thucydides' treatment of the situation thus far indicates that Diodotus came to the debate with an advantage: the Athenians were already feeling the pangs of their conscience.

Paul Rahe writes, "Thucydides nowhere suggests that Diodotus' appeal to self-interest was effective. He traces the Athenian change of heart to the very sense of decency that both speakers expressly abjure (3.36), and he makes it clear that the rowers of the first dispatch-trireme shared their compatriots' sense of dismay at what had initially been decided (3.49)."[32]

Cleon spoke first, again attempting to inflame the anger of the demos. Anyone who, like Diodotus, urged calmer reflection was to be suspected of some form of treachery. Cleon noted that, contrary to normal expectations, in the case of the Mytilenaeans, justice and expediency did coincide. The Mytilenaeans committed the gravest crime—they voluntarily revolted instead of remaining true to their promises. The Mytilenaeans were not forced to commit this crime, therefore they should be punished more severely than those who switch allegiances due to outside pressures. The punishment is expedient because it will deter others from such voluntary acts.

Diodotus attacked Cleon's argument at its most vulnerable point, at least considering the mood of his audience. He questioned Cleon's assumption that acts such as this rebellion can ever be fully voluntary. Diodotus employed the Athenians' own realistic view of human nature to convince his audience to be lenient with the Mytilenaeans.

"In a word, it is impossible, and a mark of extreme simplicity, for anyone to imagine that when human nature is wholeheartedly bent on any undertaking it can be diverted from it by rigorous laws or by any other terror" (3.45).

Diodotus then took another realistic assumption, that justice and expediency often do not coincide, and turned that assumption in favor of leniency. Justice might demand a harsher sentence, but expediency must take precedence over justice, and expediency called for moderation in this case. Having warned the audience that there are times when a good citizen who hopes to

---

32. Paul A. Rahe, "The Moral Realism of Thucydides," *Security Studies* 5.

lead must lie in order to be believed, Diodotus went on to claim that he was disregarding justice in the name of Athenian interest alone. Diodotus argued that the death penalty did not deter rebellion, because human nature was always prone to unfounded hopes. He indicated that the only thing that would prevent people from acting on such hopes was the presence of overwhelming force, which might prevent such hopes from forming in the first place.

Clifford Orwin points out that Diodotus's position on human nature sounds close to that of the Athenians at Melos, but in a very important way it is different. It is realism at a deeper level, realism that recognizes not that human beings are rational calculators of self-interest, but very often are held in the sway of their irrational passions and hopes (3.45). These irrationalities often destroy the possibility of a true understanding of what is expedient. Such an understanding of human nature necessarily councils moderation. True rationality would have to take into account the high incidence of irrationality.[33]

"Confusedly in the envoys to the Melians, more clearly in the thought of Diodotus, Athenian rationalism implies political moderation—even as it comes to grips (confusedly in the envoys, clearly in Diodotus)—with the imposing obstacles that our nature poses to such moderation."[34]

Diodotus's argument thus indicates a way in which justice and expediency coincide after all. By acknowledging our common human frailty, an acknowledgment that was already taking place in the Athenian people before the debate began, Diodotus recommended the harshest punishment for the oligarchs who initiated the revolt, but he recommended that the people go unpunished. This action was expedient, for it would encourage the people in other cities not to hold out against Athenian forces

33. [As I argue in chapter 7 of this book, for Thucydides, reason must include consideration of the unknowable: chance, fortune, even the gods. *Ed.*]

34. Orwin, *The Humanity of Thucydides,* 204.

to the bitter end. But the unspoken theme that resonated with Diodotus's audience was that this recommended sentence was also just, or at least more just than Cleon's recommendation, because it recognized our common human frailty, a mitigating factor in the Mytilenaeans' guilt that the Athenians could understand. Diodotus's argument succeeded because it wedded outward expediency with the Athenians' natural feelings of repentance.

What Diodotus's performance in the Mytilenaean Debate proves is that the statesman in a society used to thoroughgoing realist rhetoric can still appeal to that society's innate moral sense, but that appeal will always be a balancing act that few leaders can perform. Perhaps this is why Thucydides often seems to approve of the more conservative Sparta, whose sensibilities are less susceptible to such sophistication.[35] Through the Mytilenaean Debate, Thucydides teaches that this innate moral sense is a political reality which (in order to be truly realistic or "scientific") must be taken into account by both participants and observers.

CONCLUSION

Is it possible to create some middle ground between those who are still dedicated to one version or other of the scientific method and those who either never left or are returning to the classical approach? Obviously, one way in which a rapprochement might be accomplished would be by a reevaluation of our attitudes toward and our expectations of the theories we have created in the past few decades. By viewing the essential ideas of these theories, whether they are theories of structure, decision-making, political culture, or communications, as generalizations that we can combine and recombine based on the situation we are dealing with, we can break through the strictures we have artificially imposed upon ourselves in the name of emulating the natural sci-

35. Ibid., 195.

ences. If we do this we will at one and the same time be lowering and elevating our expectations of theory. We will be lowering our expectation for any one theory, but we will be elevating our expectations, in practice, of what insights into contemporary events we can derive from our theories. Thucydides' approach provides us with a model for this process.

Following the Thucydidean model requires a reevaluation of the importance, not to say the necessity, of judgment in analysis. No formula can tell us when and where to apply a particular theory or generalization. We have not found a way around the need for judgment, and rather than try to find an escape through some ultimate grand theory or airtight model, perhaps we should begin to ask the question, What kind of training and education is necessary to develop good judgment?

John Garnett, for one, suggests that the study of philosophy and, even more, history, is a better training ground than abstract theory for developing such judgment. As we have seen, part of the reason for our discipline's obsession with theoretical consistency is the quest since the 1950s for a "scientific" theory. Any such theory must make certain blanket assumptions about state behavior, but as Garnett points out, state behavior is actually the behavior of discrete human beings, and not all human beings are motivated alike. No "elegant" theory explains the idiosyncrasies of individuals and societies, and so no such theory can account for "the importance of the accidental, the contingent and the unpredictable in human and state affairs." Another commentator, Michael W. Doyle, observes that "Thucydides seemed to disapprove of all the simple formulas."[36]

When trying to decide why country X decided to act in the way it did, Garnett recommends that the scholar must engage in "imaginative reflection," putting himself or herself into the shoes of the leader or leaders of that country, just as Thucydides did. As

---

36. Garnett, *Commonsense*, 5; Michael W. Doyle, "Thucydidean Realism," *Review of International Studies* 16 (July 1990): 228.

Thucydides did in the case of the Melian Dialogue, the scholar must try to understand "not what the world is really like, but what people *think* the world is like."[37] No matter how naive, violent, or hard-bitten, no matter how *unrealistic* these thoughts may be, they are what cause actors to act, and so the scholar must attempt to understand them in their own terms.

Finally, can rapprochement be found between those who insist on value-neutrality and those who consider such neutrality either unproductive or dangerous? Is there a way to account for moral issues without losing all objectivity? Thucydidean realism is concerned with the ramifications of immoral actions both at home and abroad. Thucydides recognizes the impact of immoral policies because of the type of politics such policies will foster within a country. Therefore he recognizes the value of the type of prudent moderation urged surreptitiously by Diodotus.[38] At least in this respect, then, values become facts that we as scholars ignore at our peril. While values may not be amenable to empirical analysis, they oftentimes are of such importance that without an understanding of moral issues at stake, we are at a loss to adequately explain very important events. Faced with events such as the fall of the Berlin Wall and the demise of communism in the former Soviet Union and Eastern Europe, the ethnic and religious strife if Yugoslavia, and the improbable continuance of peace initiatives in the Middle East, we may usefully look back to the example of Thucydides, who provides us with a much-needed example of how to deal reasonably with the immeasurable.

37. Garnett, *Commonsense*, 18.

38. See Laurie M. Johnson [Bagby], "Rethinking the Diodotean Argument," *Interpretation* 18 (fall 1990): 53–62.

2

THUCYDIDES, PLATO, AND THE KINESIS
OF CITIES AND SOULS

MARGARET HREZO

"BUT THE RACE OF BIRDS
was created out of innocent light-minded men, who, although
their minds were directed toward heaven, imagined, in their simplicity, that the clearest demonstration of the things above was to
be obtained by sight." Such is Plato's evaluation in *Timaeus* of
Thucydides. It is too harsh. Yes, Thucydides was a Sophist, and
he did seek empirical explanations for the Peloponnesian War.
He did want his work to be both realistic and useful. His piety
was conventional and qualified. However, this was no "light-
minded" man. His "sight" told him that this war was not merely
"a series of battles and campaigns that had a formal beginning
with a declaration of war and a formal end with a treaty of
peace." This was a tearing out, root and branch, of a previous
way of life, sense of morality, and political culture. Such an up-

heaval, he believed, could not be studied by the usual methods. It was unique and did not fit into the cycles of such historiographers as Herodotus. So he adopted the methodology Hippocrates had developed for the study of disease. He would catalog the symptoms and reach the essence or "idea" of the disease from which Greece suffered. He called what he saw a *kinēsis* (a movement or upheaval) in order to describe its breadth and intensity. And, since the nature of man remains unchanged, he thought that if his study of the symptoms was thorough, the future scientist of politics might even be able to predict the outbreak of a *kinēsis* before it occurred.[1]

Thucydides was realistic, but he was an incomplete political realist. Here was a man who, although he understood the reasons behind the changes in Athenian politics and her consequent drive for expansion, was thoroughly appalled by the new morality and overwhelmed by the tragedy to which he was a witness. He saw beyond the mere facts of the war to what it meant for Hellenic society, and he made some judgments concerning those facts. This was a person who felt in the deepest part of himself that he was watching a world in chaos and who struggled for some way to make it meaningful to himself, his contemporaries, and future generations.

In so doing, Thucydides did give us "a possession for all time." The image of disease was aptly chosen and provided a powerful metaphor for comprehending both the suicide of Athens and the link between its spiritual disintegration and its loss of prestige and power. *The Peloponnesian War* gave us the paradigm of social disorder. Thucydides experienced the reality of mundane exis-

---

1. Plato, *Timaeus*, paragraph 91, in *The Dialogues of Plato*, trans. B. Jowett (New York: Random House, 1920) (all subsequent references to *Timaeus* in this chapter are to this edition and are by paragraph); Eric Voegelin, *The World of the Polis* (Baton Rouge: Louisiana State University Press, 1957), 358; Thucydides, *The Peloponnesian War*, trans. Richard Crawley, revised and with an introduction by T. E. Wick (New York: Modern Library, 1982) book 3, chapter 82 (all subsequent references to *The Peloponnesian War* in this chapter are to this edition and are by conventional book and chapter).

tence and the vicissitudes of power politics without losing a connection with man as part of some sort of moral order. But
Thucydides could go no further. He offered an insightful diagnosis of the disease; he was not a healer. He did not possess the right
tools for healing, because without the concept of the soul it is
almost impossible to grow beyond observation of the political
disease to the prescription of some remedy. Thucydides could
not move beyond piety and obedience to religious forms to a
philosophic understanding of virtue and the place of the soul in
the cosmos.

In *The Republic, Timaeus,* and *Gorgias,* Plato seems to reach
a similar diagnosis of Athenian social and moral disintegration.
However, Plato's vision of reality has a broader scope, which enables him to move beyond diagnosis to the prescription of a cure.
He can give us the tool that Thucydides lacked. Plato sees that a
science of politics must be supplemented by a "science" of the
soul or it will be unable to do more than either accept the political disease it sees or express moral indignation at it. Reality per-
vades the work of both Thucydides and Plato. Plato, however,
argues that "the clearest demonstration of things" may not be by
sight. Instead, he maintains, reality stretches out far beyond what
our sight can tell us, through the cosmos and to the edge of the
Agathon (Good). This essay explores the similarities between the
methods, diagnoses, and reactions to Athens' "new morality" of
Thucydides and Plato and examines how Plato reorients the Hippocratic notion of disease that we encounter in Thucydides from
the diagnosis of social disintegration and national self-destruction
to their healing.

THUCYDIDES' DIAGNOSIS OF A DISEASED ATHENS

> I must go down to the seas again, to the lonely sea and the sky
> —John Masefield, "Sea Fever"

Thucydides uses the metaphor of "going down" in *The Peloponnesian War* as he describes Athenian preparations for the expedition to Syracuse:

The Athenians themselves, and such of their allies as happened to be with them, went down to Piraeus at daybreak, upon a day appointed and began to man the ships for putting out to sea. With them also went down the whole population, one may say, of the city, both citizens and foreigners, the inhabitants of the country each escorting those that belonged to them, their friends, their relatives, or their sons, with hope and lamentation upon their way, as they thought of the conquests which they hoped to make, and of the friends whom they might never see again. (6.30)

The reader, who already knows the fate of the expedition, is borne down by the weight of the Athenian juxtaposition of hope and fear and is finally crushed by Thucydides' almost jejune observation that, in spite of the fears of the Athenians, "the strength of the armament, and the profuse provision which they remarked in every department, was a sight that could not but comfort them" (6.31). It is the power of the Piraeus that has made Athens an imperial power admired for her art, theater, and riches. It also is the power of the Piraeus that has made Athens ill.

The metaphor of illness seems to summarize Thucydides' description of the degeneration of Athenian virtue and civic life that began with the formation of the Delian League. Athens is a sick city because, as her empire expanded, she replaced friendship with faction and, thereby, lost contact with the heart of what had made her the leader and school of Hellas. To Thucydides, Hippocrates offered the perfect method for a scientific study of this sickness. Hippocrates based his method on the collection of symptoms and the assignment to them of the *idea* of the disease or its name. This methodology offered doctors a reliable way of recognizing, treating, and even predicting human ailments. Speculative hypotheses that claimed to understand the ultimate causes of disease could be rejected. Both the source and the treatment could be deduced from the observable symptoms.

Throughout *The Peloponnesian War* the entire universe seems to be out of sorts and without harmony, as if stricken by some kind of plague. The political world is chaotic. City-states are faithless to one another without either justification or compunction. The same lack of faith characterizes relationships among different parties within the city-states. Treaties are made but not kept. Never has there been a war like this in terms of duration, and never have so many cities fallen or been laid desolate. No one can remember such bloodshed and banishing both on the field and in the strife of revolution. Genuine leadership focused on some common good is nonexistent. Control of the social order, such as it is, shifts from oligarchs to democrats and back again, sometimes overnight. The natural world mirrors this disorder in occurrences of earthquakes, eclipses of the moon and sun, droughts, and plagues that exceed anyone's memory (1.23). Human relationships fare no better. As there is no faith among cities, there is no faith among men. The self-interest and passion of the moment rule all, as Thucydides shows in his description of the massacre of the men, women, children, and even beasts of the town of Mycalessus by some derelict Thracians who had missed the movement to Sicily. He calls this "a calamity, for its extent, as lamentable as any that happened in the war" (7.30). From Thucydides' perspective "the whole Hellenic world is convulsed" (3.82). The list of symptoms seems endless and, perhaps, applying Hippocrates' method to the study of politics would help in understanding and treating this convulsion.

Thucydides believed that the source of the convulsion existed further back than the outbreak of hostilities in 432. In fact, he traces the symptoms to 479 B.C. and the policies of Themistocles after the war with Persia, especially the fortification of the Piraeus. During the Congress at Lacedaemon, Athenian envoys argue that the Medean War gave their city "fair title to our possessions" and "claims to consideration" (1.73). It was not Athens, they maintain, "who set the example, for it has always been the law that the weaker should be subject to the stronger" (1.75). For Thucydides, however, this hasn't always been the law. Instead, Athenian imperialism and the fear it engendered broke down all relationships, made friendship impossible, and maybe even affected the order of the world. What he describes is a set of conditions and events which affect the physical and political world in much the same way a fever affects the body.

Fever breaks down the harmony of the body. In 2.49, Thucydides describes the symptoms of the plague. In these symptoms one sees a body at war with itself. There are violent heats of the head, redness and inflammation of the eyes, and discharges of bile. Victims could not quench their thirst and thrust themselves into rain barrels for relief, "though it made no difference whether they drank little or much." They suffered "violent spasms." Overall, "the disorder first settled in the head, ran its course from thence through the whole of the body, and even where it did not prove mortal; it still left its mark on the extremities" (2.50).

In a similar fashion, faction breaks down the harmony of society. Because faction thrives on self-interest, it makes impossible friendship between individuals and within political communities. To Thucydides, it is evident that self-interest is the motivation of all actors in the war. Faction is the social disease that eats away at the health of Athenian society. In the symptoms of faction one sees a society at war with itself, and faction, too, often begins with the head and works its way out through the extremities.

Thucydides' description of the various Athenian leaders bears this out. Thucydides makes it clear that appeals to justice, friendship, honor, or the morality of the last generation in formulating or carrying out policy are considered worthless and are overtly ridiculed. Only self-interest is worth consideration. In the debate over the fate of the Mitylenian rebels, for example, Cleon maintains that if Athens "determines to rule, you must carry out your principle and punish the Mitylenians as your interest requires; or else you must give up your empire and cultivate honesty without danger" (3.42). This, by the way, is the advice offered Sparta by the Corinthians before the war begins (1.69). In Cleon's eyes, sparing the Mitylenians would be equal to inviting the dismantling of the empire. Do not, he says, "be traitors to yourselves."

This is stereotypical political realism. But does Thucydides agree with it or condemn it? After all, he describes Cleon as the "most violent man in Athens" and as genuinely interested solely in his own self-promotion and enrichment. Thucydides makes it clear that this is no courageous, prudent patriot (3.37).

Diodotus, when he argues against condemning the Mityleni-ans, must mask his real intentions because it is no longer possible to discuss justice in Athens. In the debate he too will coolly appeal to the *interest* of the Athenians. However, he will also say that in his Athens the "best counselor" must "lie in order to be be-lieved." "The city and the city only, owing to these refinements, can never be served openly and without disguise; he who does serve it openly being always suspected of serving himself in some secret way in return" (3.44). It is a diseased and disordered city in which good advice "is as suspect as bad," cynicism concerning any leader's commitment to the common good prevails, and it is thought that "butchery" (3.48) will keep the subjects of its em-pire under control.

So, too, must Nicias speak in terms of self-interest in urging against the Sicilian Expedition. He must argue that even if the campaign were successful, Athens would "leave many enemies behind you to go yonder and bring back more with you" (6.10) and that it is folly to conquer territory she cannot control (6.11). He will not speak against his conviction, but he will change the way in which he argues because "against your character any words of mine would be weak enough" (6.10). But Nicias also seeks to serve his own self-interest. He desires very much to stay at home and be comfortable. Nicias expresses the sensibility of the older Athens much as does Cephalus in *The Republic.* Theirs is an easily understood moral order of custom and law. Justice is paying one's debts, being patriotic, showing proper respect for statues and holy places of the gods, and offering the correct sacri-fices to them. It is a ritualistic moral order, but it is a recognizable one. It is also a moral order with which Thucydides seems very comfortable.

Alcibiades, however, seems to represent for Thucydides the logical extreme of Athenian sickness. This man cares only for self-interest and is ready to destroy the city to achieve his own ends. Thucydides maintains that Alcibiades supported the expedition for purely selfish reasons: (1) to "thwart" Nicias; and (2) because he was "exceedingly ambitious of a command" by which he could gain personally "in wealth and reputation" (6.15). Achievement of his goals requires Athens to remain in a perpetual motion that sounds suspiciously like the "great movement" or *kinēsis* Thucydides uses to describe the war as a whole. "Men do not rest content" (6.18). Let the rest of the Greeks see how "little we care for the peace" (6.19) and let Athens attempt to become the master of all of Hellas, for "we must not be content with retaining but must scheme to extend it [i.e., the empire], for, if we cease to rule others, we are in danger of being ruled ourselves. Nor can we look at inaction from the same point of view as others, unless you are prepared to change your habits and make them like theirs" (6.18). Further, friendship among citizens also is nonexistent in Sicily and will assist Athens in achieving her goals. Is it any wonder Thucydides describes Alcibiades as a man who bore great responsibility for the ruin of the Athenian state? Alcibiades is not the only Athenian, or Hellenic, leader with such beliefs. If it is slightly hyperbolic to blame the loss of the war on Alcibiades alone, it is quite accurate to blame it on his type of leadership.

Even Pericles, the leader of whom Thucydides speaks most highly, does not seem to escape his censure. Pericles still speaks of honor, but it is an honor thoroughly infused with the city's self-interest. "The admiration of the present and succeeding ages will be ours, since we have not left our power without witness . . . whether for evil or for good" (2.41). And those who died defending expansion of the empire are redeemed, since "his merit as a citizen more than outweighed his demerits as an individual" (2.43). By the second year of the war, when the plague devastates Athens and "fear of gods or law of man there was none to restrain them," Pericles is even more blunt. The city must stand firm out of self-interest. Its empire is a tyranny which it may have been wrong to take, but which it would be unsafe to free (2.64). Pericles is a leader of moderation and prudence, but Thucydides seems to indicate that present in Pericles are the seeds of Cleon and Alcibiades and, therefore, the germs that caused the current disease.

The feverish activity of the city-states sounds very much like the course of the fever brought by the plague. Nowhere do these symptoms appear more clearly than in Thucydides' description of events on Corcyra. There is no comity here. Instead there are all the symptoms of the disease. In the course of the fight between democrats and oligarchs, power within the city will change hands several times—each time with more bloodshed than the last. In describing the revolution on Corcyra, Thucydides uses language straight out of visions of the apocalypse or the Day of God in Hesiod and the Old Testament. "During the seven days that Eurymedon stayed with his sixty ships, the Corcyraeans were engaged in butchering those of their fellow-citizens whom they regarded as their enemies. . . . Death thus raged in every shape and, as usually happens at such times, there was no length to which violence did not go; sons were killed by their fathers and suppliants dragged from the altar and slain upon it; while some were even walled up in the temple of Dionysus and died there" (3.81). This description is not very different from Thucydides' explanation of the effects of the plague on individuals and on Athens (2.50, 2.54).

After the revolution, "every form of iniquity took root in the Hellenic countries" (3.83). In chapters 82–85 of book 3, Thucydides is doing more than explaining and applying the doctrine of political realism. Words like "excess," "butcher," "atrocity," "iniquity," and "massacre" tend to remain outside the vocabulary of even refined realists. He speaks of these as "symptoms" of a "lust for power arising from greed and ambition"(3.82). Further, he attributes these symptoms to faction or party and seems to regard them as something akin to a disease. This is not a healthy society.

Instead, it is one where "words had to change their ordinary meaning and to take those which were now given," and where "reckless audacity came to be considered the courage of a loyal ally; prudent hesitation, specious cowardice; moderation was held to be a cloak for unmanliness; ability to see all sides of a question, inaptness to act on any. Frantic violence became the attribute of manliness; cautious plotting, a justifiable means of self-defense." Here is the fever's violent spasms, bile, and phlegm. The disease has progressed so far that it endangers the core of social life— traditional notions of honor and piety. "The ancient simplicity into which honor so largely entered was laughed down and disappeared; and society became divided into camps in which no man trusted his fellow. To put an end to this there was neither promise to be depended upon, nor oath that could command respect" (3.82–83). In such a time, life had to appear as a dream in which it was impossible to tell what was real and what was nightmare.

These passages appear to be a takeoff on the kind of grim apocalyptic future we find in the poets and prophets. For example, Hesiod describes the "days of doom" in the following manner: "Men will dishonour their quickly aging parents, finding fault with them and abusing them with bitter words, monstrously overbearing, not knowing the vengeance of the gods. . . . Neither will be in favor the man who keeps his oath, or the lawabiding, or the man of excellence; men will rather praise the evil-doer and the works of hybris. Right will lie with brute strength, and shame will be no more."[2]

And, in an Israelite parallel to the Hellenic fear of falling out of the order of the gods, we see Hosea's portrayal of the terrible Day of God.

> No truth, nor mercy, nor knowledge of God in the land.
> By swearing, and lying, and killing, and stealing, and committing adultery, they break out, and blood toucheth blood.

2. Hesiod, *Works and Days*, as cited in Voegelin, *World of the Polis*, 159–160.

Therefore shall the land mourn, and everyone that dwelleth therein shall languish, with the beasts of the field, and with the fowls of heaven; yea, the fishes of the sea also shall be taken away.[3]

The words of visions and dreams must have seemed to Thucydides to have become reality in a world that partook of a societal and moral disintegration as severe as the wrath of any god.

Thucydides' strongest description of this disintegration is the Melian Dialogue, in which the Athenians reduce even the gods to creatures of interest who deny any justice other than the will to power. When the Melians reject the command of the Athenians to join the Athenian empire, they appeal to the fortunes of war, possible Spartan help, and finally to the gods, who will be on the side of the just. In response the Athenians pour scorn on the first two hopes and *then*

When you speak of the favor of the gods, we may as fairly hope for that as yourselves, neither our pretensions nor our conduct being in any way contrary to what men believe of the gods, or practise among themselves. Of the gods we believe, and of men we know, that by a necessary law of their nature they rule wherever they can. And it is not as if we were the first to make this law, or to act upon it when made: we found it existing before us, and shall leave it to exist for ever after us; all we do is to make use of it, knowing that you and everybody else, having the same power as we have, would do the same as we do. (5.105)

Every relationship, indeed all of life, is to be dictated by calculations of self-interest. There can be no friendship, no harmony in a city where promises and alliances are made only for the moment and are dropped as soon as they become inconvenient or another party offers a better deal. Order cannot exist in such a place—only disorder and disease.

From this sketch we have a picture of a Thucydides who knew

3. Hosea 4:1–3 Authorized Version.

that something dreadful had happened to Athens. He also was aware that the same forces that lead to national greatness, creative outburst, and imperial exuberance can also result in imperial tyranny, civic corruption, and the death of the spirit. But, as Eric Voegelin points out, what does it mean when the stuff of visions and dreams become the substance of "reality"? Is it the nightmare of the apocalypse or the nihilism of the Athenians? "These," says Voegelin, "are the questions from which the science of politics has sprung with Plato and Aristotle."[4] Thucydides understands well the nature and causes of what he sees, but in politics, as in medicine, that is not enough. Understanding cancer does not mean one can cure it. In *Timaeus*, Plato argues that it is easier to prevent disease than to treat it. Doctors are either helpless or may do actual harm (*Timaeus* 89). Thucydides may even recognize this himself. When plague strikes Athens, the doctors are helpless in the face of its power, and, in fact, are its first victims. And so let us now turn to Plato for an understanding of not only the psychic forces that drove the Athenians on the path to the destruction of their spirit and their empire, but also of the elements required for a cure.

PLATO, HARMONY, AND THE HEALTH OF CITIES AND SOULS

And all I ask is a tall ship and a star to steer her by.
—John Masefield, "Sea Fever"

The Republic, like *The Peloponnesian War*, contains a downward movement to the Piraeus. And again that descent is a metaphor for the health of Athens. Socrates, like Thucydides, views Athens as a diseased city. To him, the abandonment of the demands of righteousness is the disease. In *The Republic* he will poke and probe at his patient relentlessly as he attempts to isolate the symptoms and draw forth the idea of the disease at both the individual

---

4. Voegelin, *World of the Polis*, 164.

and societal level. Finally, in the Myth of Er, Socrates will engage in his own personal "going down" and return, in the concept of the soul, with the star Thucydides needed to guide his thought from a description of disorder to its healing.[5]

Thucydides was caught between two worlds, and try as he might, he was never able to find the logic that would make him feel at home in either one. On the one side beckoned the old Athens, with its stability, order, political comity, and comfortable moral code—the Athens of Nicias and Cephalus. On the other side lay the Athens of the younger generation of Cleon and Alcibiades, which seemed to Thucydides to be cut off from all the qualities he considered admirable. He could find no safe harbor and no standard of measurement. The older Athens is gone. The new one is abominable. And Thucydides' method of categorizing symptoms, instead of breaking down the Herodotean hypothesis of history's cyclical nature, actually reinforced it. He may have isolated symptoms and classified them into their *idea*, but history remained the rise and fall of power relationships with no criteria to determine whether a regime was a better or a worse one. Thucydides, like Nicias, had no recourse but to step back and hope that the younger generation would acquire prudence. As *The Peloponnesian War* demonstrates, however, prudence had disappeared from the Hellenic world.

Plato argues that the idea of an immortal soul linked to transcendence provides the logical connection missing in Thucydides because only the idea of a soul engaged in a loving search for the Good can act as a counter both to refined realism and to the ritualism of a Cephalus that constantly threatens to degenerate into realism. His message will be that human beings are responsible for their actions. Any fault is ours, not the gods. Once he has

5. [In chapter 8, Craig Waggaman gives evidence that Thucydides' salutary judgment on the character of Pericles is a clue to the inadequacy of the method of Thucydides and the need to incorporate the science of politics as developed by Plato into our analysis. *Ed.*]

made his diagnosis, the prescription for a return to health becomes clear. Cities and souls, just as human bodies, degenerate
from lack of balance, harmony, and self-discipline. And renewed
health for the city and the soul, just as for the body, will depend
on creating or restoring those qualities. This can only be done,
Plato maintains, by participating in that which "is connected with
something always the same, immortal, and true."[6] The standard
will be friendship on the individual, social, and political levels.
And the key to friendship is the harmony of a musical soul. At
the end of book 9 Socrates summarizes his prescription for a
healthy soul: " 'Next,' I said, 'he won't turn the habit and nourishment of the body over to the bestial and irrational pleasure
and live turned in that direction, nor look to health, nor give
precedence to being strong, healthy, or fair unless he's also going
to become moderate as a result of them; rather he will always be
seen adjusting the body's harmony for the sake of the accord in
the soul.' 'That's entirely certain,' he said, 'if he's going to be
truly musical' "(*Republic* 591d). In music, sounds become beautiful when they are combined with balance, harmony, proportion,
and passion. Notes become friends and each individual sound is
better because it attends to the "good" of the music as a whole.
The healthy soul and the healthy city exist in the same kind of
friendship that is inspired by a kind of divine *mania* or passion.

In *Timaeus*, Plato gives us a beautiful image of the prescription
for health described above. Cosmos is *psychē* (soul). The healthy
soul and the healthy city are part of the cosmos because they
partake of the soul that is the universe and by which everything
ultimately was created. "For the original of the universe contains
in itself all intelligible beings, just as this world comprehends us
and all other visible creatures" (*Timaeus* 31). The Creator "compounded" the world out of fire, water, earth, and air, "leaving no
part of any of them nor any power of them outside" (*Timaeus*

---

6. Plato, *The Republic*, trans. Allan Bloom (New York: Basic Books, 1968), 585c. All
subsequent references to *The Republic* in this chapter are to this edition.

33). He did this so that his work could be as perfect as possible and as unified as possible. The Creator wanted "no remnants out of which another such world might be created" (*Timaeus* 33). If the Creator fashioned everything out of one soul and if His goals were perfection and unity, then all aspects of life and each piece of creation will be in health and peace when it is in harmony with the one soul that unifies it all. "And for these reasons, and out of such elements which are in number four, the body of the world was created, and it was harmonized by proportion, and therefore has the spirit of friendship; and having been reconciled to itself it was indissoluble by the hand of any other than the framer" (*Timaeus* 33). Health is harmony; that is, friendship achieved through proportion. Attention to proportion will mean attention to the balance between motion and rest. A recurring theme in Plato is that "motion never exists in what is uniform" (*Timaeus* 58). Wherever there is uniformity there is rest; wherever there is lack of uniformity, motion. That is why the city in speech that Plato describes in *The Republic* cannot exist. If it lacked motion it would be outside of time, beyond time, eternal. However, this idea forms an interesting contrast to Alcibiades' contention that the city must either remain in motion or die.

And, just as health is harmony, disease is lack of harmony, or motion. What is the opposite of friendship? Faction. Plato argues that "everyone can see whence diseases arise" (*Timaeus* 82). The first possibility is that some excess or defect or disproportion has disturbed the balance of air, earth, fire, and water in the sick individual. For, "a thing can only remain the same with itself, whole and sound, when the same is added to it, or subtracted from it, in the same respect and in the same manner and in due proportion; and whatever comes or goes away in violation of these laws causes all manner of changes and infinite diseases and corruptions" (*Timaeus* 82). Each part of the city strives for its own advantage. It is as if the body is being torn apart by faction, and there is no balance or proportion among its elements.

But a second, and worse, source of disease is when the generation of marrow, bone, and flesh out of the four elements proceeds in the wrong order. Every piece and process in the body has a natural sequential order, and "when each process takes place in this order, health commonly results; when in the opposite order, disease" (*Timaeus* 82). In this way, also, a body can be out of "friendship" with itself. The result will be "all sorts of bile and serum and phlegm" carried through the body by the blood. Then "things go the wrong way" and become corrupted: "first they taint the blood itself, and then ceasing to give nourishment to the body they are carried along the veins in all directions, no longer preserving the order of their natural courses, but at war with themselves, because they receive no good from one another, and are hostile to the abiding constitution of the body, which they corrupt and dissolve" (*Timaeus* 82). There is no possibility here for uniformity, harmony, rest. All is raging in a motion that is detrimental to the body's health.

Souls and cities experience the same need for friendship, for they, too, are part of the one soul that forms the universe. The soul "is"; it does not become. It has no motion, and is at rest. And because the city is built of souls, it also must follow the pattern. Souls and cities, like bodies, are subject to faction and can lose friendship. Again and again in *Timaeus* and *The Republic* Plato associates disease and decay with faction and loss of friendship. And again and again, he ascribes the cause to lack of an education that nurtures harmony, balance, moderation, and self-discipline.

The body becomes ill through a lack of balance among the four elements or when "things run backward." This usually occurs from bad nourishment of the body. Perhaps, the food was rancid, or self-discipline and moderation were not exercised in consumption. Maybe there was no thought to balancing a diet, or some external stimuli upset the body's uniformity and set it in motion.

Souls also become diseased from "sensations" which create "a very great and mighty movement" that stirs up and violently shakes "the courses of the soul" (*Timaeus* 83). Unguided, sensations result in too much slavery and/or too much freedom, and "when these two come into being in any regime, they cause trouble, like phlegm and bile in a body" (*Republic* 564b). Then, as with a diseased body, there is no harmony, order, or friendship in the soul. In *The Republic* Plato identifies those sensations with the Great Beast (*Republic* 493b) that upsets the soul with its insatiable demands to pursue pleasure and avoid pain. That image reappears in book 9's description of the tripartite soul: "the pleasant and the painful, when they arise in the soul are both a sort of motion" (*Republic* 583e).

There is a similar image in *Phaedrus* that helps explain why souls become disordered. It is as if the soul journeys in a chariot pulled by two horses. One horse is "noble and handsome and of good breeding, while the other is the very opposite so that our charioteer necessarily has a difficult and troublesome task."[7] Each soul tries to proceed to the "divine banquet," but the horse with the evil nature, unless well-trained, is constantly pulling the chariot off course and "heavily toward the earth." Here "the extremity of toil and struggle awaits the soul" (*Phaedrus* 247). Sometimes, with great difficulty, a soul is able to control both horses, follow the path of the gods' chariots, and see Reality. Other souls see part of Reality. And others fail altogether; "their circuit is far below where they jostle and trample on one another, each trying to outstrip his neighbor. So there is confusion and rivalry and the sweat of desperate competition in which many are lamed and many have their wings broken through the incompetence of their charioteers. And, for all their struggle, not one of them is able to gain a glimpse of Reality; and so they go away and feed on the food of illusion" (*Phaedrus* 248). This is the food of the realists and of Athens. It looks very much like Thucydides' *kinēsis* applied

---

7. Plato, *Phaedrus*, trans. W. C. Helmbold and W. B. Rabinowitz (New York: Macmillan Library of Liberal Arts, 1956), paragraph 246. All subsequent references to *Phaedrus* in this chapter are to this edition and are by paragraph.

to the human soul. Again the cause of the motion or upheaval is faction. The two horses have different interests and pull in different directions. If the soul is ordered toward friendship, balance, and proportion, and if the experienced sensations are combined "in him with any true nurture or education, he attains the fullness and health of the perfect man, and escapes the worst disease of all; but if he neglects education, he walks lame to the end of his life, and returns imperfect and good for nothing to the world below" (*Phaedrus* 44).

Plato applies the image of disease caused by faction to the city as well. According to *The Republic*, the city in health, in friendship, is a perfect union of private and public good (*Republic* 463e). Disease enters when private good and public good no longer exist in harmony and friendship and factions seek to promote their own self-interest. There is never any direct condemnation of Athens in *Timaeus* or *The Republic*. In fact, *Critias* praises Athens as "first in war and in every way the best-governed of all cities, and is said to have performed the noblest deeds and to have had the fairest constitution of any . . . under the face of heaven."[8] The citizens harmonized perfectly. Athens had no factions and was at rest. But what Athens is this? To Critias, it is the ancient Athens of Solon. Once upon a time and long ago, it seems, Athens was the city in speech.

This is not the Athens of *The Republic*. The Athens represented in the arguments of Thrasymachus and Adeimantus, even though indirectly, is a feverish city, rife with faction, and undergoing massive *kinēsis* (*Republic* 369b–373e). We become spectator to the decay of the "city in speech" in books 8 and 9. We watch as the founding principle of each type of regime, when out of balance or flowing backwards, generates the bile and phlegm that will accelerate its decay to a lower type. There is no place for rest and friendship here. And Plato says "a man is like his city."

---

8. Plato, *Critias*, in *The Dialogues of Plato*, trans. B. Jowett (New York: Random House, 1920), paragraph 24. All subsequent references to *Critias* are to this edition and are by paragraph.

In *The Republic*, Plato makes it clear that a city's leaders have a special responsibility for the quality of its soul. The degeneration of regimes and the transformation from ruler or servant of the city to drone occurs "as a result of want of education, bad rearing, and a bad arrangement of the regime" (*Republic* 552e). In *Timaeus*, he writes that in the body "the oldest part of the flesh which is corrupted, being hard to decompose, from long burning grows black, and from being everywhere corroded becomes bitter, and is injurious to every part of the body which is still uncorrupted" (*Timaeus* 83). Leadership plays this role in the city. It should be the source of reason and education for citizens. And Plato's standards are very high. According to *Gorgias*, not even Pericles can meet them. When the leadership promotes faction rather than harmony, disease will filter through the city as it does through the human body and destroy its heart.

However, the source of friendship in the city, as in the body and the soul, is the love of the Good. Reason is important in the search and in balancing each soul's, and each city's, two horses. But passion, almost a certain kind of madness, also is required (*Phaedrus*, 244). Just as no one wants to be ill, "no man is voluntarily bad." Instead, the "bad become bad by reason of an ill-disposition of the body and bad education, things which are hateful to every man and happen to him against his will" (*Phaedrus* 63). In a city the leaders are the source of reason and education, but no quantity of laws will redeem a city with a sick soul, and the health of a city's soul is a direct reflection of the health of its citizens' souls" (*Republic*, 425e–427a). "Isn't it charming in them that they believe the greatest enemy of all is the man who tells the truth—namely, that until one gives up drinking, stuffing oneself, sex and idleness, there will be no help for one in drugs, burning, or cutting, nor in charms, pendants, or anything of the sort" (*Republic* 426a).

Thus, in the city, prudent political leadership is not sufficient either to achieve the common good or to be realistic. Alone it can only inform the inevitable rise and fall of power relationships.

True leadership also must rest on a passionate commitment to the Good that reaches beyond mere adherence to the strictures of the old moral order. Reality is founded in transcendence and, thus, in order to be realistic, politics too must be grounded there. The philosopher's madness is required—a love of wisdom that would seem excessive to many. But without that love, disease will always overcome the souls of individuals and cities. The Great Beast can be controlled only through reason, persuasion, and divine *mania*. Those, like Thucydides perhaps, who learn "by heart" how to approach the beast and take hold of it and walk with it prudentially—those who study its symptoms and try to apply them— have learned little. They cannot genuinely teach because they do not genuinely know. They cannot genuinely know because they have chosen not to study so much of the real world. "Knowing nothing in truth about which of these convictions and desires is noble, or base, or good, or evil, or just, or unjust, he applies all these names following the great animal's opinion—calling what delights it good and what vexes it bad. He has no other argument about them but calls the necessary just and noble, neither having seen nor being able to show someone else how much the nature of the necessary and the good really differ" (*Republic* 493c). This is the bird who, although well-intentioned, wrongly thinks the things of heaven can be grasped by observation, understood by categories, and taught through expression of moral indignation. Plato seems to see Thucydides as such a bird, and, therefore, to believe that Thucydides, the prudent collector of what can "be obtained by sight," cannot teach us anything. Only the philosopher, the passionate seeker of wisdom, can see "through" the observable world clearly and deeply enough to give us "a possession for all time." The genuine possession for all time is *dikē* (righteousness).

CONCLUSION: WHAT IS SIGHT?

But in heaven perhaps, a pattern is laid up for the man who wants to see and found a city within himself on the basis of what he

sees. It doesn't make any difference whether it is or will be somewhere. For he would mind the things of this city alone, and of no
other.

—Plato, *The Republic*

Our comparison of Thucydides and Plato raises a serious problem
about the structure of a political science which makes a distinction between "realism" (Thucydides) and "idealism" (Plato). For
example, Hans J. Morgenthau, the author of *Politics among Nations*
and an important teacher of international relations to America's
post–World War II political elite, claims Thucydides as a champion of the realist school by citing his "identity of interests is the
surest of bonds between states or individuals." Likewise, Donald
Kagan, in his *On the Origin of War*, writes that there are many
theories concerning the reasons people in states fight wars, but
that Thucydides had already grasped the problem more clearly
in fifth-century B.C. Athens than anyone has since. Thucydides
certainly anticipated the modern realists in the famous Melian
Dialogue, where he presents the Athenian spokesman trying to
persuade the Melians to yield to the might of Athens.[9]

But as this analysis suggests, Periclean Athens and its foreign
policy was the stuff of the worst visions and nightmares of an
apocalyptic future of the poets and prophets. Thucydides seemed
to sense this, but his limited methodology prevented him from
seeing and describing the psychic forces underneath the *kinēsis*.
On the other hand, Plato, borrowing the terminology of the *ideas*
from the same medical science of Hippocrates used this concep-
tual language to describe the order and disorder of the soul, now
differentiated to mean the metaphor of the place where the
human-transhuman mediation takes place. From this perspective
Plato is able to sweep aside the bright, but empty, beauty of Athens' exterior and see the mania in its soul working its way out as

9. Hans J. Morgenthau, *Politics Among Nations: The Struggle for Peace and Power*, 6th ed.
(New York: Alfred A. Knopf, 1985), 10; Donald Kagan, *On the Origins of War* (New York:
Doubleday, 1995), 8.

the *erōs tyrannos* rather than the Socratic *erōs philosophos*. Maybe the message of both Plato and Thucydides is that the health of a city depends on friendship between politics and *dikē*. The question then becomes what does the use of Thucydides as an illustration for a realist teaching of politics or for a typology of the causes of war suggest? Is the implication that *America too* is blind and groping, as pneumapathological as the Athenians at Melos and Syracuse? As Eric Voegelin writes, if we understand the "reality" described by Thucydides as an apocalyptic nightmare, we gain a first approach to Plato's much misunderstood "idealism" as the attempt to overcome a nightmare through the restoration of reality.[10]

We also gain a first approach to an understanding of the relation of imperial Athens to the teaching and practice of politics in twentieth-century America. As Critias says of the Atlantians, to those who could not see clearly, they looked most glorious and blessed. But for those who could see, they "being unable to bear their fortune, behaved unseemly . . . and visibly debased, for they were losing the fairest of their precious gifts," their divine portion. *Critias* ends with a counsel of the gods as Zeus, who rules by law and is able to see into such things, seems to want to inflict some punishment on Atlantis for its unseemliness. "And when he had called them together, he spake as follows: . . . ." (121). *Critias* ends with a deliberate stop in the dialogue. The rest of Plato's life was spent filling in that blank by perfecting the dialogues that were the continued encomium of a good man, Socrates. The inference may be that the gods punished Athens because Athens had killed Socrates and, by doing so, had deliberately destroyed the chance to heal its soul. Thucydides reported the wrath of the gods and the destruction of the old order; Plato traced the destruction down into the souls of the Athenians and up to the heights of the source of order.

10. Voegelin, *World of the Polis*, 164.

PART II

INTERNATIONAL POLITICS
AND THE REGIME

3

THUCYDIDES AND THE DOMESTIC
SOURCES OF INTERNATIONAL POLITICS

W. DANIEL GARST

NEOREALIST THEORIZING
has focused on the systemic sources of state behavior. The so-
called Third Image—the anarchic structure of international politics—leads all states, regardless of their internal characteristics, to
behave in certain uniform ways. All states engage in a constant
quest to increase their relative capabilities and, on occasion, fight
wars in order to safeguard their external security.[1] Thus, Thucydides' celebrated judgment on the "real" cause of the war between
Athens and Sparta—"the growth of the power of Athens and the

1. For the most influential statement of the neorealist perspective, see Kenneth Waltz,
Theory of International Politics (Reading, Mass.: Addison-Wesley, 1979); for the controver-
sies surrounding neorealism, see Robert Keohane, ed., *Neorealism and Its Critics* (New
York: Columbia University Press, 1986).

fear this inspired in Lacedaemon"[2]—is customarily invoked in arguments emphasizing the timeless role of international anarchy and the quest for power in shaping the relations between states.[3]

This essay will argue that Thucydides departs from neorealist thinking on the *Primat der Außenpolitik*. None of this is to deny the importance Thucydides accords to insecurity and the quest for power in driving state action. However, a close reading of Thucydides' history shows that the internal structures of states, particularly their political institutions, are equally, if not more, important in determining states' behavior. I will argue that this is evident in Thucydides' account of the outbreak of the conflict, the intensification of the war, and the Athenian decision to invade Sicily. I conclude by comparing Thucydides' "Second Image" arguments with recent theorizing on the relationship between state behavior and regime structures.

The Outbreak of the Peloponnesian War

At first glance, Thucydides' account of the origins of the conflict between Athens and Sparta resonates strongly with neorealist arguments on the importance of insecurity and the quest for power in motivating state action. This is apparent not only in the celebrated judgment on the "truest cause" of the conflict, but in the speeches given in the crucial Congress of the Peloponnesian Confederacy at Sparta.

The verbal exchanges in this meeting are used by Thucydides to draw out the psychological implications of the growth of Athenian power and the range of choices Sparta and her allies have, or feel they have, in dealing with it. In his response to the Corinthian speech, King Archidamus counsels waiting for at least two more years before entering into war, arguing that while con-

---

2. Thucydides, *The Peloponnesian War*, trans. Richard Crawley, revised and updated by T. E. Wick (New York: Modern Library, 1982), book 1, chapter 23. All subsequent citations in this chapter are to this edition and are by conventional book and chapter.

3. Waltz, *Theory of International Politics*, 66.

flict with Athens is inevitable, the Athenian threat is not immediately pressing (1.82). This address strongly affirms the particularly Spartan virtues of caution and moderation; however, it is the simple bullheaded appeal for war made by Sthenelaides that carries the day. This outcome can be seen as supporting neorealist claims on the primacy of the Third Image in driving state behavior, even if Sthenelaides' appeal is as much based on simple notions of justice and irritation over the patronizing Athenian tone, as it is with the threat Athens poses to Spartan allies. The Spartans are driven by the growth of Athens' power to go to war, despite their innate caution and habitual slowness in acting.

The insecurity associated with international anarchy and consequent necessity of states to obtain power is also present in the Athenian defense of their empire. The Athenians argue that they have done nothing "contrary to the common practice of mankind" in refusing to give up their empire "under the pressure of three of the strongest motives, fear, honour and interest" (1.76). Confronted by Spartan hostility, the Athenians must hold on to their empire: "when you had ceased to be the friends you once were, and had become objects of suspicion and dislike, it appeared no longer safe to give up our empire, especially as all who had left us would come to you" (1.75). This view is echoed by Pericles in his first speech. This address urges the Athenians not to make concessions to Sparta and its allies; giving in will only lead to further demands, and the war is necessary to properly demonstrate Athenian resolution (1.140).

However, Thucydides is not content simply to draw connections between the distribution of power in fifth-century B.C. Greece and the behavior of states. What most interests Thucydides and is more fundamental to his history is the question of how this distribution of power came about, particularly why Athens rather than Sparta acquired an empire. In dealing with this question, the focus of Thucydides' history shifts from the anarchic Third Image to the internal attributes of states.

This is evident first in the Corinthian speech which opens the crucial debate at Sparta. This rhetorical tour de force contrasts "Spartan dullness and indolence, old-fashioned respectability and narrow-minded conservatism" with Athens' "restless energy, marvelous élan in acting and planning" that makes the Athenians "capable of meeting any situation."[4] The Athenians are "addicted to innovation," and are "born into the world to take no rest themselves and give none to others" (1.70). The Spartans, on the other hand, are "old-fashioned" in their habits. While the Athenians move swiftly, the Spartans "wait until the power of the enemy is twice its original size" (1.69). And while the Athenians have unlimited desires, the Spartans "ideal of fair dealing is based on the principle that if you do not injure others, you need not risk your fortunes in preventing others from injuring you" (1.71).

These differences, the Corinthians argue, stem from the failure of the Spartans to emulate Athens' spirit of innovation. Thus, when the Corinthians pointedly tell the Spartans that their habits are "old-fashioned," they state that in politics, as in art, "improvements ever prevail," and that "constant necessities of action must be accompanied by constant improvements in methods." "The vast experience of Athens," they claim, "has carried her further along the path of innovation" (1.71).

That Thucydides shares the Corinthian view of the Spartan character is evident throughout his narrative of the war. Rather than preparing for naval operations, the Spartans begin the war in time-honored fashion by ineffectually ravaging Attica, even though Archidamus himself had pointed out that such action was pointless (1.80, 2.18–22). This strategic incompetence is even more evident in the first overseas adventure, the effort to aid the revolting oligarchy in the Mytiline. The Spartan admiral, Alcidas, completely botches this operation; he fails, through his slowness, to assist the revolt in the Mytiline and then makes no effort to

---

4. Werner Jaeger, *Paideia: The Ideals of Greek Culture*, trans. Gilbert Highet (New York: Oxford University Press, 1945), 395.

incite unrest against Athens in Ionia. All Alcidas does is murder some islanders whom he has taken at sea (3.26–33).[5]

The speeches of Pericles which follow the Pentecontaetia and Spartan ultimatum elaborate on the Corinthian depiction of Athens' character. The Corinthians note that because of their restless energy, the Athenians are "daring beyond their judgement" and are propelled to "adventures beyond their power" (1.70). These traits are reflected in the ambitious expedition to aid Egypt's rebellion against Persia. The Athenians undertake this venture even though they continue to face serious threats to their security in Greece (1.104–112).

Pericles' acute awareness of the dangers posed by the Athenian tendency to "take no rest themselves and give none to others" is evident in the strategy he adopts to fight the war. In calling upon the Athenians to stand firm against Spartan demands, Pericles warns them that their lack of moderation is the one thing which can bring about defeat. He explains that victory is certain as long as they refrain from undertaking further conquests and avoid superfluous campaigns (1.144). To make this passive strategy acceptable to the Athenians, Pericles is careful to frame it in the context of action and movement. Even if Attica is lost, Athens will retain its navy, which it can use to maintain links with its overseas empire and harass the Peloponnese with sudden blows on the coastline.

Pericles is confident of a successful outcome to the conflict because of the far greater experience of the Athenians in seafaring naval operations (1.142–143). In making this point, he alludes to the broad differences between Athens and Sparta reviewed earlier in the speeches at Sparta. Because the navy requires rowers and

5. The envoys from Samos who meet Alcidas at Ephesus pointedly tell him that "he was not going the right way to free Hellas in massacring men who had never raised a hand against him" (3.32). Alcidas's behavior foreshadows the Spartan mock trial and execution of the Plataeans shortly afterwards (3.52–68).

rowers mean democracy, Athens' maritime empire follows directly from its political innovations. This connection between Athenian naval power and democracy is made explicit by Thucydides in his account of the defeat of the oligarchic coup mounted in 411 against democracy in Athens. This effort fails because of the resistance by the armed forces, above all the navy based in Samos (8.72–79).[6] Thus, writing nearly a century after Thucydides, Aristotle observed that the "naval element are wholly democratic" and their numbers enabled them, despite being lightly armed, to usually overcome the oligarchy in political struggles.[7] The maintenance of naval power is largely incompatible with oligarchic rule.

Pericles' next speech, the well-known Funeral Oration, addresses in detail this relationship between Athens' democratic political institutions and its activity and empire. The expressed purpose of this address is to strengthen the Athenian determination to pursue the war and bolster support for the cautious and difficult strategy adopted by Pericles against the growing discontent caused by the loss of homes and property (2.21).

Pericles responds to such criticism by arguing that Athens' existence is not defined by specific material possessions. Rather, it rests on the unique nature of Athenian democracy, which makes Athens' empire and material wealth possible. By providing each citizen with the opportunity to participate in public life, in debate and deliberation, Athenian democracy produces a unity of will among its citizens that is far stronger than that resulting from blind obedience to the state (2.37–40). Thus, Athenian enterprises are described as a "singular spectacle of daring and deliberation," and those who fail to participate in civic affairs are not merely "unambitious" but "useless" (2.40). Pericles contrasts the

6. Indeed, the emissaries sent by the oligarchic plotters in Athens to Samos to reassure the navy "feared, as it turned out justly, that the mass of seamen would not be willing to remain under the oligarchic constitution" (8.72).

7. Aristotle, *Politics*, trans. Benjamin Jowett (New York: Modern Library), book 6, chapter 7, p. 271.

bravery of the Spartans, which results from a "painful discipline" inculcated from childhood, with the self-conscious patriotism of Athenian citizens, who are able to live as they please and are just as ready to act bravely when they must. While the Spartans invade only after securing the backing of their allies, the "Athenians advance unsupported into the territory of a neighbor, and fighting upon foreign soil usually vanquish with ease men who are defending their homes" (2.39).

Pericles' comments in these addresses echo those made by the Athenian emissary in the debate at Sparta. While the Athenians argue that necessity—"fear, honor and interest"—motivated them to hold on to their empire, this defense is not the only justification they offer for Athens' behavior. In claiming that refusal to give up an empire "under the pressure of the three strongest motives, fear, honor and interest" is "not a very remarkable action or contrary to the common practice of mankind," the Athenians tell the audience that other states would have done the same and their behavior should thus not be viewed with envy and spite. But in addition to making this claim, the Athenians contend that they are indeed different from other human beings and different in a better way, not in a worse way, as the Corinthians implied.

The latter line of argument is first evident in the Athenian insistence that they have "fair title" to their possessions because of the "daring patriotism" of Athens during the Persian invasion of Greece. If Sparta provided formal leadership of the Greek coalition against the Persians, then it was the Athenians who made the unique contribution to victory by having the courage to take their ships and fight on even after their city had been lost and property destroyed. The Athenians remind the audience that the "acknowledged salvation of our cause" was the destruction of the Persian fleet at Salamis. Athenian naval power, combined with the sagacity of Themistocles in commanding it, was decisive in turning back the invasion (1.74).

In making these claims, the Athenians argue that they displayed the greatest courage, strength, and above all intelligence. It was the Athenians, not the Spartans, who realized that the military needs of the Persian War were unique and required new and innovative strategies. This view is shared by Pericles, who asks in his first address: "Did not our fathers resist the Medes not only with resources far different from ours, but even when those resources had been abandoned? and more by wisdom than by fortune, more by daring than by strength, did they not beat off the barbarian and advance their affairs to their present height?" (1.144).

The Athenians go on to argue that the services they performed in defeating Persia made it possible for their empire to come into being without the use of force. They tell the Spartans that their empire acquired "by no violent means, but because you were unwilling to prosecute the war against the barbarians and because the allies spontaneously asked us to assume command" (1.75). In making this claim, the Athenians argue that because of their actions and deeds, it is Athens, not Sparta, which can claim to exercise hegemony over Greece.

Finally, the Athenians argue that they differ in the manner in which they rule over their empire. The Athenians state they are "not so superior to human nature as to refuse domination" and yet, at the same time "respect justice more than [their] situation compels them to do" (1.76). The long chapter on judicial relations is designed to show that Athens does unnecessarily impose limits on itself in dealing with allies over whom it has complete control (1.77). This emphasis on the unique generosity of Athens is also present in the Funeral Oration. Here Pericles states, "We throw open our city to the World, and never by alien acts exclude foreigners any opportunity for learning or observing, although the eyes of an enemy may occasionally profit by our liberality" (1.39).

It could be argued at this point that the Athenian speeches are merely an effort to excuse Athens' drive for domination and can be dismissed as propaganda bearing little relation to actual reality.

Such a case can certainly be made with respect to the manner in which Athens controls its empire at the outset of the war. In reviewing the transformation of Athens' supremacy into empire in the Pentecontaetia, Thucydides describes how the Delian League, established by Athens to continue the war against Persia, became an extortion racket. The Athenians, Thucydides observes, were no longer the "old popular rulers they had been at first" (1.98–99).

But Thucydides' narrative dovetails with the other ways in which the Athenians defend their conduct. This is especially the case with respect to Athens' role in defeating the Persian invasion. Thucydides anticipates the Athenian emphasis on their unique contribution to victory in the Median War in the first pages of the *Peloponnesian War*. Here he describes how Sparta assumed command of the Greek Confederation opposing Persia because of its land power, while the Athenians "having made up their minds to abandon their city, broke up their homes, threw themselves into their ships and became a naval people" (1.18). This passage introduces the basic motif in Thucydides' history, the contrast between conservative Sparta, which clings to old-fashioned ways of waging war, and innovative Athens, which embraces naval warfare. Its placement in the sketch history which opens Thucydides' work is highly significant. This section, the so-called Archeology, lays prime stress on the development of navies, particularly on their role in tying the world together and making possible the greater concentration and use of power. The basic claim set forth here is that ships are a uniquely good way to get things from one place to another, giving naval powers a distinct edge in creating wealth and warfighting.

The same can be said for the Athenian claims on how their empire first came into being. Thucydides notes that even Sparta's allies recognized the valor the Athenians displayed in the Median War; this behavior and Athens' naval power led the allies to urge the Spartans to oppose Athenian efforts to fortify their city (1.90). And nowhere does Thucydides dispute the claim that, initially at least, Athens held hegemony through the free wishes of its allies. The Athenians "succeeded to the supremacy by the voluntary act of the allies." Athens' "supremacy commenced with independent allies who acted on the resolutions of a common Congress" (1.96–97).

This voluntary allegiance was not simply a product of the "hatred" generated by the violent behavior of Pausanias, the Spartan general still in command of the Greek Confederation against Persia. It fundamentally reflects a broader rejection of Sparta's leadership and the transfer of hegemony (*hēgemonia*) over to Athens. Even after Pausanias is replaced with a new commander, Dorkis, the Spartans "found the allies no longer inclined to concede to them supremacy." This development leads Sparta to withdraw from the conflict against Persia, giving Athens undisputed leadership in this struggle (1.95).

Thucydides states at the outset of his history that the complaints over Epidamnus and Potidaea were merely pretexts for the war, which mask its underlying cause, "the growth of the power of Athens and the fear this inspired in Lacedaemon" (1.23). This discussion has tried to show how this oft-cited judgment itself masks a deeper and more fundamental cause of the conflict, the marked contrast in the domestic structures of Athens and Sparta and the impact this had on their behaviors. Sparta's conservatism, rooted in its highly stable oligarchic constitution, makes it slow to act and unable to adopt a naval strategy and grasp the advantages offered by this new form of warfare. Democratic Athens, on the other hand, embraces activity and innovation. And the egalitarian nature of Athens' democratic constitution is bound up with the development of its naval power, which enables the Athenians "to take no rest themselves and give none to others."

It is thus the Athenians who make the unique contribution to victory in the Median War and use it to take the mantle of hegemony away from Sparta. And it is Athens which converts the traditional form of supremacy, *hēgemonia*, involving leadership over autonomous allies, to empire (*arkhē*), in which the imperial power treats its dependents as it wishes.[8] The systemic imperatives which lead Sparta to discard its habitual caution and join its allies in going to war therefore grow out of the very different domestic structures and characteristics of the conflict's two main antagonists.

THE INTENSIFICATION OF THE CONFLICT

In the first sentence of *The Peloponnesian War*, Thucydides states that he wrote his history of the war "beginning at the moment it broke out, and believing that it would be a great war and more worthy of relation than any that preceded it" (1.1). This belief stemmed not only from the unprecedented amount of power amassed on both sides, but from the wide involvement of states in the conflict. Thucydides declares that "he could see the rest of the Hellenic race taking sides in the quarrel, those who delayed doing so at once having it in contemplation" (1.1).

As is the case with the origins of the Peloponnesian War, Thucydides' comments on the bipolar division of Greece during the conflict at first glance concur with neorealist arguments on how the systemic imperatives of power balancing drive state behavior. Thucydides claims that the good will (*eunoia*) of Greece was largely on the side of Sparta and against Athens. By going beyond *hēgomonia* and introducing the new phenomenon *arkhē* in Greece, the Athenians enabled Sparta to pose as the liberator and claim that its objective was to free Greece from the tyranny of Athens (2.9). Waltz argues that this observation provides an excellent example of power balancing, whereby "secondary states, if they are free to choose, flock to the weaker side, for it is the stronger side which threatens them." Thus, Thucydides shows "a nice sense of how the placement of states affects their behavior and even colors their characters."[9]

8. For an acute discussion of the requirements for hegemony and empire and the behavior of Athens and Sparta in conforming to these models, see John Wickersham, *Hegemony and Greek Historians* (Lanham, Md.: Rowman & Littlefield, 1994), chapter 2.

9. Waltz, *Theory of International Politics*, 127.

Once again, however, a close reading of Thucydides' history eviscerates this superficial and self-serving reading of *The Peloponnesian War*. While Thucydides casts the stronger Athens as the tyrant and weaker Sparta as the liberator to whose side the weaker cities rallied, his narrative of the war provides little backing for this view. Indeed, a striking feature of this narrative is the absence of any concerted rush by Athens' dependent cities to break away from its empire. This failure can only be partially explained by Athens' military power. Athenian control of the sea and isolation of island cities from each other certainly hindered effective revolts against Athenian rule. But the Athenians did not maintain garrisons in dependent cities, which made it easier for their allies to secede from the empire if they wished to do so.[10]

In any case, Thucydides clearly views Athens' military might as largely irrelevant in the decisions of cities to revolt or remain loyal. One of the main motifs of his history is how actors—be they the revolting oligarchs in the Mytiline or the Melians determined to remain outside of Athenian control—overestimate their ability to succeed in the face of heavy odds. As Diodotus observes in the Mytiline debate, belief in fortune "tempts men to venture with inferior means; and this is especially the case with communities, because the stakes played for are the highest, freedom or empire, and, when all are acting together, each man irrationally magnifies his own capacity" (3.45). This view is echoed by Pericles (2.62) and the Athenians at Melos and is surely shared by Thucydides. Thus, had the subject cities wished to free themselves from Athens, they would have attempted to do so, even if Athenian military power made their chances of success remote.

All of this directs attention to a striking feature of Athens' imperial rule. In marked contrast to modern-day imperial powers, the Athenians did not aim to secure the loyalty of the upper classes among the people they ruled. The Athenian empire is

10. Donald Kagan, *Pericles of Athens and the Birth of Democracy* (New York: Free Press, 1991), 112; Russell Meiggs, *The Athenian Empire* (Oxford: Clarendon, 1972), 206–207.

unique in relation to past empires known to us in that it relied very much on the backing of the lower classes (*dēmos*) in the subject states. Thus as G. E. M. de Ste. Croix observed in a seminal article published four decades ago, "The general mass of the allied (or subject) states, far from being hostile to Athens, actually welcomed her dominance and wished to remain in her Empire."[11] A vivid, if crude, contemporary description of the class basis of Athenian imperial rule is provided by an anonymous oligarch's short pamphlet on Athens' empire and democracy written while Thucydides was collecting material for his history:

> The Athenians who are sent out bring charges against the good men among the allies and hate them. They know that the ruler must be hated by the ruled and that if the rich and good grow strong in the cities, the rule of the Athenian *dēmos* will last a very short time. That is why they strip the good of their rights, confiscate their property, exile them and put them to death, while they uphold the bad.[12]

Thus, if incorporation into Athens' empire led to the loss of political autonomy and ever greater demands for payment of tribute, then this was a price which the *dēmos* in the subject and dependent cities were willing to pay in order to maintain popular rule. Retribution by oligarchic factions restored to their original ruling position was a far worse fate than continued subservience to Athens in foreign policy. And "liberation" by Sparta promised to bring about restoration of oligarchic government. As Thucyd-

11. G. E. M. de Ste. Croix, "The Character of the Athenian Empire," *Historia* 7 (1954): 1–41. The unique nature of Athenian imperial rule and its marked contrast to modern empires is stressed by de Ste. Croix in *The Origins of the Peloponnesian War* (Ithaca: Cornell University Press, 1972), 34–43.

12. Statement cited in Meiggs, *The Athenian Empire*, 390. For Athens' promotion of democracy in other cities, see G. E. M. de Ste. Croix, *The Origins of the Peloponnesian War*, 34–43, and *The Class Struggle in the Ancient Greek World: From the Archaic Age to the Arab Conquests* (Ithaca: Cornell University Press, 1980), 294, and Meiggs, *The Athenian Empire*, 204–33.

ides notes in the Archeology, "The policy of Lacedaemon was not to exact tribute from her allies, but merely to secure their subservience to her interests by establishing oligarchies among them" (1.19). For the democratic parties, then, domination by Athens was preferable to the possibility of greater political autonomy under Sparta. This loyalty of the *dēmos* to Athens remained consistently strong throughout the war. The alliance ties of the smaller cities underwent little change and did not, as neorealist theory would predict, shift in accordance with alterations in balance of power between Athens and Sparta.[13]

Democratic Syracuse, Athens' most formidable foe, is the exception which proves this rule. Due to its strength and distance from the Greek mainland, Syracuse could remain outside of the Athenian empire and still avoid being drawn into Sparta's orbit. Thus, when faced by a more brutally imperialistic Athens, Syracuse chooses to resist and avoid losing its independence. In addition to making them more enterprising opponents, Syracuse's democratic institutions made it impossible for the Athenians to resort to the old tactic of setting democratic against oligarchic factions in order to extend their rule (8.55). But while Syracuse's democratic constitution enables it to deal the first decisive setback to Athens, it also makes it an uneasy ally of Sparta. Indeed, joint military operations between Sparta and Syracuse during the fighting in Ionia after the victory in Sicily were marked by considerable friction, particularly between the ordinary seamen in Syracuse's navy and Spartan commanders (8.78). In his effort to build up Sparta's naval power, Lysander turns not to democratic Syracuse but to autocratic Persia for support.

Although Thucydides does not discuss in any detail how the class struggle between oligarchy and democracy influenced state behavior prior to and during the war in the first two books of his history, he does allude to it a number of times. The promotion

13. Meiggs, *The Athenian Empire*, 306–39, and de Ste. Croix, "The Character of the Athenian Empire," 1–41.

of oligarchy by Sparta has already been mentioned. Near the end of book 1, Thucydides reviews how the Athenians backed the democratic faction in their effort to capture Samos and in doing this precipitated a civil war between the *dēmos* and oligarchy (1.115). Finally, in the debate at Sparta, the Athenian emissary alludes to the indirect rule practiced by Athens and Sparta. When the Athenians tell the Spartans that "your life at home [is] regulated by rules and institutions incompatible with those of others" (1.77), they issue a warning on the difficulty of imposing oligarchic rule in cities under popular rule and where the sympathy of the *dēmos* is on the side of Athens. And in emphasizing Athens' use of arbitration law courts, the Athenians obliquely refer to the practice of setting the *dēmos* against the oligarchy in ruling their empire. In addition to protecting ordinary Athenians from the depredations of the rich, the People's Law Courts were used to shake down oligarchs from Athens' allies and dependent states.[14]

While the impact of internal politics on the course of the war and behavior of states is given only brief mention by Thucydides in the first two books of his history, it becomes the central theme of book 3. Book 3 opens with the revolt of the Mytiline. The Mytiline was one of the few cities in Athens' empire where oligarchic rule was tolerated.[15] This however did not stop the oligarchy in the Mytiline from revolting, and their uprising was defeated not only by the failure of expected assistance from Sparta to materialize, but by the resistance of the *dēmos* as well (3.26–27).

The famous Mytiline debate between Cleon and Diodotus is over the harsh punishment—death to all males and enslavement of all women and children—which the Athenians initially decide to mete out to people of the Mytiline. In defending this decision, Cleon denies that a link exists between democracy and empire. "Democracy," he bluntly argues, "is incompatible with empire

---

14. Meiggs, *The Athenian Empire*, 208–209, 322, and de Ste. Croix, *The Class Struggle in the Ancient Greek World*, 290.

15. Meiggs, *The Athenian Empire*, 208.

because you forget entirely that your empire is a despotism and subjects disaffected conspirators, whose obedience is insured not by your suicidal concessions but by superiority given you by your strength and not their loyalty" (3.37).

Diodotus, Cleon's foil in the debate, seeks to reestablish the link between Athenian democracy and empire. Diodotus emphasizes that, like Cleon, he has no desire to be "influenced" by "pity or indulgence" (3.48). Following an elegant sophistic on human nature, which uses Cleon's premise, that human nature is incorrigible, to show that harsh reprisals will never deter rebellions, Diodotus turns to his main argument for leniency. This is the contention that the Athenians must recognize the different sympathies of the *dēmos* and oligarchy in the subject states. Only the revolting oligarchy should be punished, while the *dēmos* should be rewarded for displaying loyalty in order to maintain its *eunoia* toward Athens in the Mytiline and elsewhere (3.47). This long-standing Athenian policy is reaffirmed, albeit by a narrow margin, in the vote taken in the assembly following the debate.

After reviewing the mock trial and execution the Plataeans, Thucydides turns to the Corcyraean revolution. This uprising of the *dēmos* against the ruling oligarchy is the first example of the bloody revolutionary class warfare (*stasis*) which sweeps through Greece. Its spread is fueled by the efforts of Athens and Sparta to aid democratic and oligarchic factions. Thucydides describes how the "whole Hellenic world was convulsed, struggles being everywhere made by the popular chiefs to bring in the Athenians, and by oligarchs to introduce the Lacedaemonians" (3.82). In this highly charged ideological environment, "moderation was held to be a cloak for unmanliness" (3.82). And with the elimination of moderate men, "society became divided into two camps in which no man trusted his fellows" (3.83). These statements constitute a clear recognition by Thucydides of the bitter class antagonism between the *dēmos* and oligarchy that was endemic to ancient Greece.[16] This awareness is even more explicit in the opening sentence of the chapter, which concludes Thucydides' review of the events in Corcyra:

> Corcyra gave the first example of most of the crimes alluded to; of the reprisals exacted by the governed who had never experienced equitable treatment or indeed aught but insolence from their rulers—when their hour came; of the iniquitous resolves of those who desired to get rid of their accustomed poverty, and ardently coveted their neighbors' goods. (3.84)

Thucydides' discussion of these events and the different forms of indirect rule practiced by Athens and Sparta suggests that the neorealist definition of hegemonic war, a conflict which redistributes power in order to restore equilibrium in the interstate system,[17] fails to fully capture the essence of the Peloponnesian War. This is not to deny that the effort to limit the growth of Athens' power and restore equilibrium in the ancient Greek interstate system was an essential element of the Peloponnesian War. But this struggle was also fundamentally an ideological conflict, which was rooted in the domestic political divisions of Greek city-states. This conflict pitted democracy against oligarchy, and its extreme bitterness made it impossible for both individual men and states to avoid taking sides. This is underscored by Sparta's murderous treatment of the Plataeans and Athens' ruthless denial of the desire of oligarchic Melos to remain neutral.[18]

In detailing all of this, Thucydides goes beyond simply claim-

16. For the best discussion of this, see de Ste. Croix's magisterial work, *The Class Struggle in the Ancient Greek World*.

17. For this definition, see Robert Gilpin, *War and Change in World Politics* (New York: Cambridge University Press, 1981), 197.

18. In fact, the Melians, though technically neutral, sympathized with Sparta and covertly contributed to its war funds; see Meiggs, *The Athenian Empire*, 344.

ing, as does Waltz, that power balancing will occur under conditions of international anarchy. Thucydides uses the internal attributes of states—the outcome of the political class struggle between democracy and oligarchy—to analyze *which* balances will take form.[19] The opposition of the *dēmos* to oligarchic rule limits Sparta's ability to rally weaker cities against Athens, despite the latter's growing power and empire.[20] As is the case with the outbreak of the war, neorealism's insistence on according privileged status to the Third Image yields an overly simple and misleading account of the behavior and interaction of states.

Athens' Imperial Overstretch

If neorealist theory fails to provide specific predictions on the alignment of states in alliances, it does tell us that the alliances formed in the international arena will offset each other's power. According to structural realism, states above all balance power in order to maintain their relative capabilities. They do not seek to maximize their power. Aside from the fact that few states can afford to make this their goal, such behavior is self-defeating, as it prompts other states, driven by the motivation of self-help, to attempt to counteract such efforts.[21]

While this argument may describe the behavior of most states

19. Even critics sympathetic to structural realism have noted that Waltz's theory yields general but imprecise predictions: while it tells that power balancing will occur, it provides little clue as to precisely which balances will emerge. See, for example, John Ruggie, "Continuity and Transformation in the World Polity: Toward a Neorealist Synthesis," *World Politics* 35 (1983): 267–68.

20. Waltz expressly argues that the requisites of power balancing override these domestic political factors. Thus, in noting the bipolar balance at the outbreak of the Peloponnesian War, Waltz approvingly cites Jaeger's claim that "Thucydides thought this 'perfectly natural in the circumstances,' but saw 'that the parts of the tyrant and liberator did not correspond with any permanent moral quality in these states but were simply masks which would one day be interchanged.' " Waltz, *Theory of International Politics*, 127. The quotation of Jaeger is from *Paideia*, 397.

21. Waltz, *Theory of International Politics*, 105–106, 126–27.

in the anarchic realm of international politics, it fails utterly to account for the actions of states like Germany and Japan prior to 1945. Germany and Japan sought to maximize their power by pursuing wildly ambitious and unrealistic schemes of conquest. And if such actions made them exceptional, their exceptional behavior mattered a great deal in bringing about the First and Second World Wars.[22]

The Athenian expedition to Sicily, which was to be followed by campaigns on the Italian mainland and against Carthage (6.90), can certainly be seen as an instance of imperial overstretch. It is difficult to claim on any objective grounds that Athens needed to undertake this action in order to balance the power of Sparta and its allies. The Athenians had just fulfilled Pericles' basic objective of securing a stalemate and thereby demonstrating Athens' power and resolve. And the Peace of Nicias was in no way unfavorable to Athens; indeed, the treaty was seen by Sparta's allies as a sellout of their interests (5.22, 5.27).

While any objective view of the balance of power between Athens and Sparta at the end of the Archidamian War makes it hard to see the attack on Sicily as necessary to balance Sparta's power, it could still be argued that this was how the Athenians subjectively assessed their predicament. The uneasy and uncertain peace arranged by Nicias, it might be claimed, led the Athenians to see further expansion of their empire as essential in order to maintain their external security.

This is indeed one of the rationales for the expedition offered by Alcibiades during his debate with Nicias just before the decision to go ahead with the invasion is made. Alcibiades reminds the Athenians that their empire came into being because of Athens' willingness to aid allies against the Persians who had requested assistance. Athens must answer the calls for help made by its allies in Sicily against the growing power of Syracuse. Failure

---

22. For the best discussion of this overstretch, see Jack Snyder, *Myths of Empire: Domestic Politics and International Ambition* (Ithaca: Cornell University Press, 1991).

to do this will lead them to seek assistance elsewhere and thereby strengthen Athens' enemies. Thus, Alcibiades warns, "we cannot fix the point at which our empire must stop; we have reached a position in which we must not be content with retaining but must scheme to extend it, for if we cease to rule others we are in danger of being ruled ourselves" (6.18).

Yet in making these claims, Alcibiades scornfully dismisses the notion that Sparta and its allies are a threat to Athens (6.17). It is Nicias who argues that the Peloponnese can still undermine Athens' security, and this view is rejected by the assembly (6.10). And if it were indeed the case that Sparta could threaten Athens, then this threat would constitute an argument for conducting operations closer to Greece rather than directing the cream of Athenian naval and land forces to Sicily. If the Athenians do not really fear Sparta and its allies, then why do they agree with Alcibiades that they have no choice but to extend their empire by attacking Syracuse?

The answer to this question is given in the infamous Melian Dialogue. This exchange has often been noted for the brutal realism displayed by the Athenians; however, what is also striking, but less often noted, is the much greater anxiety the Athenians display about control over their allies and empire than with the external threat posed by Sparta and its allies. The Athenians state, "the fact is that the continentals generally give us little alarm"; this is because "the liberty which they enjoy will long prevent their making precautions against us" (5.99). And earlier in the Dialogue, the Athenians emphasize that the end of their empire by Sparta, "even if Lacedaemon was our real antagonist," does not concern them. This fate, they bluntly inform the Melians, "is not so terrible to the vanquished as subjects who by themselves attack and overpower their rulers" (5.91).

What the Athenians fear most, then, are "subjects smarting under the yoke, who would be most likely to take a rash step and lead themselves and us into obvious danger" (5.99). Thus, the Athenians insist on denying neutrality to Melos, the one island in the Aegean not under their control and with an oligarchic government, arguing that its incorporation into Athens' empire is essential to demonstrate Athenian strength to the allies and subject cities (5.96, 5.98).

The Melian Dialogue, Alcibiades' speech in the debate with Nicias and Euphemus's address at Camarina after the Athenians land in Sicily represent a marked change from the Athenian discourse prior to the conflict and during its early stages. The Athenians no longer bother to remind listeners of their "daring patriotism" during the Median War; such talk is now dismissed as "specious pretences" (5.89) and "fine professions" (6.84). Nor do the Athenians try to argue, as was the case in the debate at Sparta and the Funeral Oration, that in behaving like other great powers, they are unique in the moderation with which they rule. The only justifications now offered for Athens' behavior are base interest and the "law" that the strong dominate the weak.[23]

It should be emphasized that this shift does grow out of a new-found awareness by the Athenians of the envy and spite others display toward Athens and its empire. The Athenians are acutely aware of these feelings throughout Thucydides' history. For example, in his last speech, Pericles consoles the Athenians by noting how "Hatred and unpopularity at the moment have fallen to the lot of all who aspired to rule" (2.64).[24] Here and in the Funeral Oration, Pericles argues that if *arkhe* incites envy, then so be it. The praise of posterity and history will compensate for the envy of the present (2.41, 2.64). Moreover, envy is desirable because it signifies admiration and thereby indicates that you have something valuable that others would like to possess.

Thus, leaving aside the long-standing glory *arkhē* will produce for Athens, it is worthwhile in the present as a sign of Athenian

---

23. For a detailed discussion of these shifts and what they imply for Athens' power and ability to exercise hegemony, see Daniel Garst, "Thucydides and Neorealism," *International Studies Quarterly* 33 (1989): 1–27.

24. Likewise, the Athenian emissary at Sparta notes that with the growth of Athens' empire, "almost all hated us" (1.75).

power and virtue. And these qualities make Athens' unique generosity and liberality possible; because they feel more secure, the Athenians do not engage in secrecy or repressive legislation (2.39–40).[25] If envy and hatred could be used early on in the conflict to justify liberality and if, as noted earlier, Athens retained the loyalty of the *dēmos* throughout the war, then why do the Athenians display such anxiety over control of their empire and feel compelled by it to attempt new conquests?

Unfortunately, Thucydides provides only subtle clues, not clear answers to this question. One of these clues is the review of the bloody *stasis* spawned by the civil war at Corcyra which precedes the Melian Dialogue. The Athenians' curious insistence that their main foe is the subject cities in their empire, not Sparta, and their oddly sanguine attitude toward the possibility of their empire being terminated by the Spartans are easier to fathom when set against the backdrop of Corcyra. Given the savage reprisals the oligarchs and *dēmos* inflicted on one another in Corcyra and other cities, its makes perfect sense for the Athenians to state that they are most fearful of being overthrown by their subjects, especially if this happens by way of oligarchic revolts.

Other clues to the puzzle of why the Athenians believe that they have no choice but to continually extend their empire are contained in Alcibiades' address. Right after claiming that Athens must aid allies in Sicily against Syracuse, Alcibiades states, "Nor can you look at inaction from the point of view of others, unless you are prepared to change your habits and make them like theirs" (6.18). While Pericles warns the Athenians that victory is certain only if they refrain from their tendency to engage in new and ambitious schemes of conquests, Alcibiades argues "the safest rule in life is to take one's character and institutions, for better or for worse, and to live up to them as closely as one can" (6.18).

These remarks direct attention to the strong connection be-

---

25. For an acute discussion of these points, see Wickersham, *Hegemony and Greek Historians*, 69–70.

tween Athens' democracy and its aggressive imperialism. This link is especially pronounced with respect to the popular nature of Athenian democracy, as the *dēmos* were arguably the strongest backers of imperialism. Thus Nicias begins his dispirited appeal against the invasion of Sicily by noting, "Against your character any words of mine would be weak enough" (6.9). And as Thucydides himself notes, "the idea of the common people and the soldiery was to earn wages at the moment, and make conquests that would supply a never-ending fund of pay for the future" (6.24).

The popular enthusiasm for the invasion of Sicily underscores the impact of Athenian imperialism in benefiting the *dēmos*. To start with, the lower classes certainly gained from the overall affluence created by Athens' empire. As Pericles states in the Funeral Oration, "the magnitude of our city draws the produce of the world into our harbour, so to the Athenian the fruits of other countries are as familiar a luxury as his own" (2.38).[26] Imperial income also helped pay for both the many festivals which entertained ordinary Athenians and the feasts that went with them; the meat sacrificed to the gods at these events usually ended up in lower-class mouths. And the court cases which the allies were compelled to attend in Athens increased opportunities for paid service in juries to lower class citizens, who could also acquire a share of the money obtained from shakedowns of visiting oligarchs during trials.[27]

The empire provided other avenues for lower-class Athenians to enrich themselves. The Piraeus dockyards, for example, offered lucrative work for both artisans and unskilled laborers, while providing employment for five hundred citizen guards. Thus leaving aside the contentious issue of whether the building

26. See also Kagan, *Pericles of Athens*, 112, for the affluence which Athens' seaborne empire made possible.

27. Meiggs, *The Athenian Empire*, 322, and Barry S. Strauss, *Athens After the Peloponnesian War: Class, Faction and Policy, 403–386 B.C.* (Ithaca: Cornell University Press, 1986), 52.

program Pericles financed with tribute was aimed at the poor,[28] construction projects were an important source of income to ordinary Athenians. Even while under siege in 410, Athens could still afford to pay laborers working on the Erechtheum one drachma a day. And greater rewards came to the large numbers who served as sailors or soldiers; these individuals earned regular pay and, if lucky, booty. Finally, lower-class Athenians made up the bulk of the colonists given land in the empire. These grants also benefited the smaller farmers left behind, as they eased the land shortage in Attica.[29]

If the Athenian *dēmos* were uniform in their enthusiasm for imperialism, then Athens' elite were more ambivalent about conquest. This is not to deny that upper-class Athenians reaped substantial rewards from imperialism. These included profiting from the shakedowns of oligarchs tried in Athens: as Thucydides makes clear, the involvement of the Athenian elite in such actions made the upper classes in the subject cities reluctant to support the oligarchic coup in Athens (8.48). And the empire offered Athens' elite ample opportunities for securing honor and riches, through business opportunities, like foreign land purchases and contracts to maintain the fleet, or public service.[30]

But while Thucydides' well-known insistence that Athens' elite suffered the most from the war understates their stake in imperialism, it does point to a division that arose among upper-class Athenians as the war progressed. In particular, the 420s were marked by a sharp polarization between Athens' older aristocratic leaders and a new generation of demagogues. The former drew their wealth from the traditional sources of farming and mining and were therefore hurt by the Spartan invasions (1.14–17 and 7.27–28), even if Thucydides exaggerates the damage inflicted on

---

28. For differing accounts on the plausibility of this view, which goes back to Plutarch, see de Ste. Croix, *The Class Struggle in the Ancient Greek World*, 189–90, and Meiggs, *The Athenian Empire*, 132–34.

29. Strauss, *Athens After the Peloponnesian War*, 52.

30. Ibid.; de Ste. Croix, *The Class Struggle in the Ancient Greek World*, 290, 605 n. 27.

agriculture.[31] The main impetus for peace therefore came from older leaders, such as Laches and Nicias (4.118–119 and 5.16).

The second group in Athens' elite, whose ranks included the infamous Cleon, were involved in industry and trade. These new "men of the marketplace" were less affected by the damage wrought by Spartan forces in Attica and gained from the increased demand for manufactured goods associated with the war and growing importance of the import trade, especially in food. Thus, Cleon and his allies strongly opposed any move toward peace and sought to weaken the older elite by expanding state pay for public service, especially jury duty, challenging the knights' pay for state subvention, and implementing the *eisphorai*, a moderate capital levy on rich Athenians, to pay for the war.[32]

The strong popular enthusiasm for imperialism gave the demagogues the upper hand in the struggle waged within Athens' elite. These new men lacked the status of the older elite, who had monopolized public office. But the new elite had the backing of the *dēmos*, who stood to gain from new conquests. Thus, Alcibiades, whose rise to prominence was aided by his vocal backing of Cleon and opposition to the peace settlement with Sparta,[33] had no difficulty rousing support against Nicias's "do-nothing" policy. And the latter's clumsy ploy to head off the expedition by emphasizing the size of the force needed only fuels Athenian enthusiasm for the venture (6.24).

Finally, Cleon's behavior sheds further light on the urgent anxiety the Athenians display at Melos over the security of their empire and belief that it compels them to add conquests in order to demonstrate their strength to their subjects. Such feelings can be

---

31. Victor Davis Hanson, *Warfare and Agriculture in Ancient Greece* (Pisa: Biblioteca di Studi Antichi, 1983), 155–59.

32. For the best discussion of the split in Athens' elite in the 420s and disproportionate impact of the war on the Athenian upper classes, see Martin Ostwald, *From Popular Sovereignty to Sovereignty of Law: Law, Society and Politics in Fifth-Century Athens* (Berkeley: University of California Press, 1986).

33. Ostwald, *From Popular Sovereignty to Sovereignty of Law*, 293.

seen as growing out of the realization that the continual tightening of the tribute screw might alienate eventually even the loyal *dēmos* in the cities under Athenian rule. If the *dēmos* preferred subject democracy over "liberation" by Sparta and imposition of uncontrolled oligarchy, they also would have surely liked to have had payment of tribute and the supersession of their authority by Athenian judicial agreements brought to an end.[34] Thus while Pericles praises the freedom and lack of suspiciousness which was characteristic of imperial Athens, Cleon urges the Athenians to be paranoid. As John Wickersham astutely argues, "This case points to one weak point in Pericles' eulogy: the power to be generous need only be viewed a bit differently in order to become the power to be vicious and pitiless—also as a manifestation of empire."[35]

As I have argued at length elsewhere, Thucydides is not a "scientific" thinker in the commonly understood sense of the term. He does not begin by setting forth an explicit theory from which a set of deductible and falsifiable propositions follow to be subjected to empirical tests. Thucydides chooses instead to embed his theoretical arguments, such as they are, in the narrative and speeches of his history.[36] What the narrative and speeches of *The Peloponnesian War* point to is a strong connection between Athenian democracy and imperialism.

In particular, Athens' democracy underpins the rise of its empire in two ways. The first is by making it easier for the Athenians to extend their rule by informal means through alliances with the *dēmos* against oligarchy. The second and more important way democracy facilitates the growth of empire is by promoting the

---

34. The costs of the war and pressure of demagogues led the Athenians to increase tribute demands during the Archidamian War. After the disaster in Sicily, the Athenians adopted a less vindictive attitude to revolting oligarchs and tried to extract less from the subject cities. See Ostwald, *From Popular Sovereignty to Sovereignty of Law*, 293, and Meiggs, *The Athenian Empire*, 317–22 and 367–70.

35. Wickersham, *Hegemony and the Greek Historians*, 71.

36. Garst, "Thucydides and Neorealism," 4–8.

qualities emphasized in the Funeral Oration, particularly the willingness to embrace innovation and unity of will among Athenian citizens.

Thus, it is Athens, not Sparta, which builds up its naval power, the maintenance of which is incompatible with oligarchic rule. This naval power gives Athens a crucial edge in warfighting and enables it to fully exploit the greater possibilities for the creation of wealth associated with commerce. And in marked contrast to their oligarchic opponents, the Athenians were not impeded by internal political divisions from waging an aggressive imperialism. Sitting as they did on a social volcano—the restive Messenian Helots, who had only recently lost their freedom—which threatened to erupt at any moment, Sparta's leaders could not risk overextending their army. Sparta is only an extreme example of how the ever-present possibility of domestic political unrest under oligarchic rule[37] dictated caution in foreign policy.

It is important to emphasize that the success of Athenian democracy in limiting the kind of serious political unrest present in oligarchic states owed little to the wealth created by the empire. Democratic rule, including the subsidies provided to the poor to enable them to participate in politics, survived through the fourth century, despite the loss of empire.[38] Thus, while Athenian imperialism was driven by democracy, particularly the strong popular support for new conquests, the maintenance of popular rule did not depend on empire's existence. The one-sided relationship between imperialism and democratic rule underscores the main

37. For the vulnerability of oligarchic government to popular unrest, see de Ste. Croix, *The Class Struggle in the Ancient Greek World*, 287–88.

38. de Ste. Croix, *The Class Struggle in the Ancient Greek World*, part 3, and A. H. M. Jones, *Athenian Democracy* (Oxford: Blackwell, 1969), 9–10. If the Athenians behaved less aggressively after the Peloponnesian War, then it was because the losses incurred during the conflict ruled out large-scale conquests. This did not, however, prevent the Athenians from participating in the Corinthian War with the aim of restoring their former imperial position. The strong connection between Athens' democracy and its renewed imperial efforts is emphasized in Strauss, *Athens After the Peloponnesian War*.

role played by domestic political factors in Athens' overexpansion.

The compulsion which drives the Athenians to seek new conquests is therefore rooted in Athens' political institutions and, by extension, *within* its empire, as opposed to insecurity associated with international anarchy. Democratic rule and popular support for imperialism spurs Athenian expansion, which is further fueled by concern over unrest within the empire. The latter anxiety stems both from the bitter class conflict in the Greek world and consequent possibility of oligarchic revolts—a concern surely heightened by bloody *stasis* at Corcyra—and the possibility that the tightening of tribute screw threatened in the long run to alienate even lower-class supporters of Athenian rule. Thus in a passage whose importance equals that of the celebrated judgment on the "truest cause" of the conflict, Thucydides concludes that the ultimate cause of Athens' demise was not strength or efforts of its enemies but its "own intestine disorders" (2.65).

CONCLUDING REMARKS

This essay has argued that Thucydides does not share neorealist claims for the primacy of the Third Image in shaping the behavior of states in the international arena. This is not to deny that aspects of Thucydides' history conform to this thinking. However, they tend to be the less interesting and more trivial features of *The Peloponnesian War*. If neorealist theory explains why Sparta reluctantly goes to war, it sheds no light on why the Spartans voluntarily relinquished *hēgemonia* after the Median War. Even at this time, the growing power of Athens and the potential long-term threat it posed to Sparta were clearly recognized by its allies. Neorealism's emphasis on the international over domestic sources of state behavior is therefore of little use in explaining how Athens claimed *hēgemonia* from Sparta and why the disequilibrium of power between them developed. And if smaller states unable to defend themselves align, as structural realism predicts, with the great powers leading the two blocs in Greece's bipolar balance, it is stronger Athens, not weaker Sparta, whom they tend to side with.

In both these cases, focusing on domestic structures, particularly political institutions and struggles around them, sheds greater light on the behavior of states than their position in the global power structure. This is true to an even greater extent with respect to Athens' overexpansion. Neorealism's emphasis on the Third Image is no help whatsoever here; the behavior of the Athenians is a consequence of their democratic political system. Athens' democracy both promotes the growth of empire and the belief that continual conquest is essential to maintain it.

What is striking about Thucydides' arguments here is the marked difference between them and current Second Image theories of state behavior in international politics. Spurred by the recent revival of the long-standing tradition of liberal republican thought in international relations, a large body of empirical work has addressed the connection between democracy and involvement of states in warfare. Contrary to structural realist thinking, its findings strongly suggest that democracy matters in explaining the war-proneness of states. Democratic regimes are much less likely to initiate wars and do not fight against each other. Democracies are also much less prone to succumb to overexpansion.[39]

Why do Thucydides' views on democracy and imperialism differ so much from these current arguments? This is clearly not the place to address this question in any detail. But it is possible to briefly set forth an answer to this puzzle, an answer that follows from the earlier discussion of Athenian overstretch. This discussion emphasized how Athens' empire benefited both the aristoc-

---

39. Michael Doyle, "Liberalism and World Politics," *American Political Science Review* 80 (1986): 1151–69; Edward Mansfield and Jack Snyder, "Democratization and the Outbreak of War," *International Security* 20 (1995): 5–38; and Bruce Russett, *Grasping the Democratic Peace* (Princeton: Princeton University Press, 1993) and "The Democratic Peace: 'And Yet It Moves,'" *International Security* 19 (1995): 164–75; Snyder, *Myths of Empire.*

racy and lower classes. This characteristic constitutes a second striking difference between Athenian and modern-day imperialism. Every systematic study of the benefits and costs of modern-day imperialism has shown that the gains from colonies and other forms of expansion have been concentrated among narrow elites. Ordinary taxpayers, on the other hand, have not only failed to share in the gains from imperialist policies, but have borne the costs of such actions.[40]

Thus, in the most rigorous theoretical account put forward of domestic political structure and overexpansion, Jack Snyder has argued that so-called cartellized polities are most liable to succumb to imperial overstretch.[41] In "cartellized" polities political power is held by narrowly based ruling elites, while the general population is denied significant influence over the government. This regime promotes overexpansion by giving the elites sharing power a strong incentive to approve each others' pet imperial projects. This logrolling occurs because the gains from such projects flow entirely to the particular elite group supporting them, while their costs are borne by the population in general.

The gradual introduction of liberal democracy in the core imperialist powers had little impact in altering the distribution of benefits from imperialism.[42] But the growth of popular influence over the government did make it possible for imperialism to be terminated in order to eliminate the costs it imposed on ordinary

40. For examples of this work, which has focused on the late-nineteenth- and early twentieth-century British and U.S. cases, see Lance Davis and Robert Huttenback, *Mammon and the Pursuit of Empire: The Economics of British Imperialism* (London: Cambridge University Press, 1988); Jeff Frieden, "International Investment and Colonial Control: A New Interpretation," *International Organization* 48 (1994): 559–93; and Stanley Lebergott, "Returns of U.S. Imperialism, 1890–1929," *Journal of Economic History* 40 (1980): 229–52. For an important application of this analysis to older European imperialism, see R. P. Thomas, "The Sugar Colonies of the Old Empire: Profit or Loss for Great Britain," *Economic History Review*, 2nd ser., 21 (1968): 30–45.

41. Snyder, *The Myths of Empire*.

42. This, at least, can be said of Britain. See, for example, Davis and Huttenback, *Mammon and the Pursuit of Empire*.

taxpaying voters. The association between democracy and impe-rialism in Athens, then, arguably reflects the much more radical nature of Athenian democracy. In particular, the direct as opposed to representative nature of popular rule in Athens' democracy gave the lower classes much greater political influence, which included the leverage to see to it that the *dēmos* shared in the material benefits produced by Athenian imperialism. I leave it to others to take up this conjecture.

To conclude, if *The Peloponnesian War* is a possession for all time, then it is not due to its alleged affirmation of the recurring patterns and continuities emphasized in neorealism's static and ahistorical view of international politics. Its lasting value lies in-stead in telling us what was historically distinctive about Thucyd-ides' environment and how this knowledge can be used to understand better the behavior of states in present-day world pol-itics. In doing this, Thucydides underscores the limitations of neorealism's one-sided emphasis on international structures in ex-plaining the behavior of states in global politics. Properly under-stood, his history should spur scholars to bridge the disciplinary separation of international and comparative politics. Although Thucydides might not understand the contemporary power struggle, he would have no problem grasping just how artificial the current disciplinary divide between international and com-parative politics is.

4

DEMOCRACY AND DISTRUST:
A LESSON FROM THUCYDIDES

CLIFFORD ORWIN

IF THERE IS ONE THING FOR which every democracy yearns, it is more democracy. Today we often hear that "more democracy" means, above all, direct or participatory democracy, in place of the representative sort. Participation figures as a major theme in democratic theory and spurs dreams of a post-liberal world transfigured by the experience of political community.

The political community par excellence was the *polis*, or ancient city. For at least eight centuries now its memory has fired Western republicanism. Today many still look to it as a model of direct democracy. Not a sufficient model, surely, but one defective primarily in the respects in which it, too, fell short of full democracy: in holding slaves, for instance, or excluding women, or failing to abolish class distinctions. The credit for its allure here

98

and now belongs above all to Hannah Arendt. She more than anyone popularized the *polis* as the definitive "public space" and interpreted the aspiration to re-create it as the "lost treasure" of the modern revolutionary tradition. She thus revitalized the study of the ancient city from a democratic leftist perspective.

It is this perspective that I wish to question here. In particular I will challenge the view, widespread among democratic theorists, that as "community" requires "participation," so "participation" breeds "community." Many of the advocates of participation today view it as "transformative." They see it not merely as a better or the only legitimate way of going about addressing substantive political problems, but as itself the solution to most of our nagging discontents. To hear the participationists tell it, in fact, our ills seem to be of two sorts: those that must be cured if participation is to be "meaningful," and those that meaningful participation will cure. These latter include those sentiments of distrust, powerlessness, and "alienation" rampant in modern democratic societies. Liberty, equality, fraternity, or community: these are divined to inhere in the experience of political participation itself.

It is the experience of political participation that I explore in this essay. This I do by means of a single example drawn from the historian Thucydides. An example is rarely decisive. It can be suggestive, however, and this one is unusually so. For of the debates preserved for us by ancient writers who knew participatory politics firsthand, this is the only one that features a discussion about discussion. It offers us that rarity, a political deliberation that confronts the question of the limits of political deliberation.

The episode in question, the so-called Mytilenian Debate, is one of the most dramatic in Thucydides.[1] Mytilene was an ally of Athens, which revolted from her at the height of the Peloponnesian War and in collusion with the Spartan enemy. Her

---

1. Thucydides, *History of the Peloponnesian War*, book 3, chapter 36 ff. Translations are mine. All subsequent references in this chapter are by conventional book and chapter.

intention had been to instigate a general rising of the subject allies and so to cost Athens the war—this despite the fact that Athens had always treated her exceptionally well. Having with much trouble suppressed the revolt, the Athenians in their anger resolved to put to death not only the ringleaders but every adult male Mytilenian and to sell the women and children as slaves (3.36).

The debate that Thucydides re-creates is a reconsideration of this original decision. We owe it to the spontaneous qualms of the Athenian people. In the cold light of the morning after, they awaken to the reflection that it was "savage and monstrous . . . to destroy a whole city rather than the guilty." There is no time to lose: a ship is already on the way to Mytilene to enforce the decree. It may even be too late to overtake it. The reconsideration proceeds. Its foremost opponent is Cleon, "the most violent of the citizens and at that time by far the most persuasive with the people." Having carried the motion of the previous day, he most violently and persuasively defends it in the present debate. His chief adversary, now as in the first debate, is the otherwise unknown Diodotus. It is only their two speeches that Thucydides gives us. If their first go-round was no contest, this one proves closer than we would wish.

Cleon's speech is rambling, vehement, and contradictory. We may best understand it as a masterpiece of populism. Populism begins with the faith that whatever is rooted in the people is wholesome, while whatever is alien to them is corrupt. Particularly suspect are fancy words and big thoughts. Populism so conceived is a lasting feature of democratic politics. In appealing to it, Cleon overlays the issue of Mytilene with that of the loyalty of those who are soft on Mytilene. He thus foments a spirit of suspicion and mistrust, recalling—but worse than—McCarthyism in America.

Cleon begins with an attack on his listeners that is an even sharper one on his rivals (3.37). He declares that he has often reflected, and never more than now, on the incapacity of democracies for empire. Imbued as Athenians are with the trust and openness that prevail among themselves, they thoughtlessly extend these qualities to the sphere of foreign affairs as well, forgetting that their empire is a tyranny and their subject allies resentful conspirators.

We are not concerned here with Cleon's presentation of the Athenian empire. We must note, however, his characterization of the spirit of Athenian domestic life. Like much else in his speeches, it is pilfered from his immediate predecessor as leader of the Athenian people, Pericles. In the famous Funeral Oration that Thucydides ascribes to him, Pericles had praised the Athenians for the openness and lack of rancor that graced their common life (2.37). In Cleon's mouth, however, this becomes something not entirely praiseworthy. For trust is called for only where it is merited. And Cleon's point is that many whom the Athenians trust, at home as well as abroad, are nothing short of traitors.

In praising the law, and citizens who defer to its wisdom from their own, Cleon strikes a note that seems not Athenian but Spartan. In fact he here echoes an earlier speech by the decent Spartan king Archidamus (1.84). The echo falls flat, however, for the laws of Sparta, attributed to the divine Lycurgus, were thought to have been in place and unchanged for four hundred years, while the Mytilenian decree has passed yesterday at the urging of Cleon. Cleon's aim in eulogizing law is simply to discredit deliberation, by placing the result of yesterday's discussion beyond any further discussion. His praise of law thus furthers his populist attack on fast talkers.

In heaping suspicion on the orators, Cleon interprets a distinction observable in every deliberative body. It is that between those who take the lead in participating and those who are more or less content to follow, between those who advise and those who consent. This distinction between leaders and followers lends itself to several interpretations. Pericles again, in the Funeral Oration, had praised Athens for her unique ability to combine deliberation with daring, to "seek wisdom without softness." Her citizens, if not all competent to advise, were at least all competent to pass on conflicting advice (2.20). Cleon, however, describing the same city a mere three years later, presents deliberation as misleading rather than enlightening, for he recasts the distinction between speakers and listeners as that between "politicians" and "people." The former speak for reputation, and for no other reason—except where they happen to have been bribed to do so. Wit and learning dwell with the speakers; judgment and virtue with the people. As for Cleon, this speaker against speaking, he must be the strong, noisy type, the spokesman for that silent majority who have too much sense to speak.

It is, then, not only when extended to her allies that the trust prevailing at Athens is misplaced. By now, however, we have to wonder about all of this alleged trustfulness. It is, after all, *distrustful* men whom it pays to chastise for being too trusting. In democracy as Cleon knows and lives it, it is above all from distrust of others that you forge trust in yourself; that is what populism is all about.

Cleon's criticism of the people is palatable to them initially because it implies a paean to their virtues and blames them only for trusting those so much less trustworthy than themselves. But Cleon is no mere flatterer. He now proceeds to blast the people for their untrustworthiness. That corruption from which only a Cleon can save them proves in the end to be their own. For the rhetorical circus at Athens is not confined to the rings.

> For you excel at being deceived by novel arguments and at ignoring those of proven worth, and are slaves of each new absurdity and disdainers of everything familiar. What each of you wishes most of all is that he could be a speaker himself, or, if he cannot, to compete with those who do say these sorts of things by seeming not to lag behind them in wit, but to praise a saying even before it is spoken. You are as quick to anticipate what is said as you are slow to foresee its results. . . . To conclude, you are addicted to the pleasure of listening, and resemble those attending the shows of sophists rather than men deliberating in matters of state. (3.38)

It is not the politicians who corrupt the people, but almost the other way around. The speakers speak as they do because the listeners are what they are. The problem is not one of apathy: the people attend to the debates with zeal. The problem is rather their zeal. Just like the speakers—so Cleon claims—the people live to shine in the public sphere, to stand out from the crowd in the broad daylight of deliberation. They, too, therefore seize politics as a chance to display their wit: if they cannot shine as performers, they want to look like fans in the know. It is not their innocence so much as their vanity that enslaves them to the orators. If private-spiritedness is what distinguishes the politicians from the people, then Athens, as Cleon presents it, has no people, only politicians.

There is a dramatic likeness, and a no less dramatic difference, between Cleon's portrait of Athens and that of Pericles in his Funeral Oration (2.43). Both present the Athenian as freely dedicating his life to renown. For Pericles, however, this dedication unites the citizens, lifting them above all base concerns in common devotion to the public good. The renown to which they aspire is undying fame as Athenians, citizens of the noblest, strongest, freest society ever. Pursuit of fame thus seals wholehearted devotion to Athens.

That to which Pericles had exhorted, Cleon proclaims as a fact: to be an Athenian is to be devoted to fame. It is, however, a fact to be deplored. For the Athenian is a mere glory hound; there is nothing sublime in his vocation. He aspires not to undying fame but merely to glitter for the moment. His yen for celebrity, far from underwriting devotion to the city, spends itself in jockeying for position within it. It affords no basis for mutual trust, but rather makes all trust impossible, except perhaps in rogues by fools. Such a vision of democracy casts doubt on more than its capacity for empire.

But are we to take all this seriously? Cleon has his reasons for speaking as he does, and providing posterity with an accurate account of Athenian politics is not among them. His concern is to persuade his listeners and, to that end, to badger them. Still, if we cannot presume his veracity, we must respect his astuteness: he is the most effective speaker in Athens. And much of what he says about the deliberative process squares with what he must think about it—in order for it to make rhetorical sense that he says what he does.

When, for instance, Cleon harangues the people as every one a celebrity manqué, he could not expect the barb to wound unless he thought it on target. Such an interpretation of the people, moreover, would afford a plausible explanation of that mood of theirs of which Cleon's rhetoric depends absolutely, their deep distrust of those who would lead them. At the root of this distrust would lie a resentment born as much of envy as of disillusionment. Cleon is confident that in their hearts the people will accept this reprimand and, what is more, that they will thank him for it. ("We needed that: we have been much too trusting.") In this way their shame at having strayed from him will help ease their qualms over Mytilene.

For the people as Cleon presents them, there is no salvation but through Cleon. They are not, in the end, more capable of managing affairs than the clever; instead they are doomed to be managed by the clever. If Cleon establishes his kinship with them by articulating their distrust of others, he must establish their need of him by appealing to their distrust of themselves.

Cleon's position on Mytilene will be noted only briefly. Firing their hatred of their foreign foes just as of his domestic ones, he appeals now to the Athenians' fear and now to their vengefulness, two passions that unite in supporting his decree of extirpation.

The speech of Diodotus begins with a staunch defense of deliberation as the only means of reaching sound decisions (3.42). Those who would deny this, he insists, are fools or (more likely) rogues, who, "wishing to persuade of something disgraceful and doubting their ability to speak well in a base cause, . . . slander well so as to cow both their opponents and their listeners." Worst of all, he contends, are those who accuse (as Cleon has done) their adversaries of corruption. For then these adversaries, even should they prevail, are suspect and, should they fail, are reputed to be not only unintelligent, but unjust. "And such goings-on are no favor to the city, for fear deprives it of advisers."

Diodotus is commonly taken for the first recorded civil libertarian. He certainly sounds like one in stressing the blessings to society of free and fearless public debate. Yet the noted scholar A. W. Gomme could sense something in Diodotus's position which recalled that of Cleon: Diodotus in fact, according to Gomme, "comes perilously close to questioning the value of free debate." That is an understatement. Diodotus's defense of deliberation against those who would crimp it is highly misleading: it is his way of trying to crimp it.

Let us begin with the point of agreement between Diodotus and our civil libertarians. It is that deliberation is indispensable for unearthing useful truths. The difference between Diodotus and, say, J. S. Mill is over the conditions favorable to free deliberation. By a free deliberation we mean one unhampered by considerations other than those of reason: what deliberation must be freed from is the entrenched power of the unreasonable. Mill argues for effecting this by lifting almost all restraints on speech. Truth can and will triumph only through the unbridled clash of opinions. Speech is therefore to be restricted only insofar as it presents a clear and present danger to life or property. The way to the ever-less-abridged truth lies through unabridged speech.

Diodotus, however, begins where our civil libertarians leave off, with ostensibly free public discussion. He shows how the dynamic of such discussion inevitably poses a clear and present danger of its own—to the cause of truth itself.

The problem, as will appear from the lines of his speech already cited, is that so-called free debate proves a contradiction in terms. There is, Diodotus suggests, a Gresham's Law of speakers: unless the bad are silenced, they will drive out the good. They will do so by fomenting distrust; by making the good look so bad that they despair of persuading of their goodness. "The prestige of Diodotus cannot well coexist with that of Cleon," wrote Leo Strauss. The deliberative marketplace is unfree because it is bounded by considerations of trust, which markedly diverge from those of reason.

Diodotus suggests, however, that we can at least imagine a radical change in this state of things. "[The city] would prosper best if the citizens of this sort that it contains [i.e., those who intimidate by slandering] were incapable of speaking." This sounds very like a prayer, for who has ever heard of a city in which the ability to speak deserted whoever would have abused it? And given that Heaven is unlikely thus to provide for the city, is there nothing that it can do for itself? In fact Diodotus suggests that there is.

> As for the good citizen, he ought not intimidate those who speak against him, but to show himself a better speaker on the up and up; and while the moderate city will not confer additional honor on the man who advises it well, neither should it detract from what he already has; and as for him whose judgment does not happen to prevail, not only ought it not punish him, it should not even show him any disrespect. For then it would happen least that a successful speaker, in hopes of achieving still greater esteem, would speak against his better judgment and in order to please, and that an unsuccessful one would resort to these same means, he too aiming to please, so as to court the multitude. (3.42)

The course prescribed to citizens here must wait on the adoption of that prescribed to the city. For high-minded abstention from slander has proved no match for indulgence in it, or how is it that the bad citizens have managed to silence the good ones? Speaking no evil, then, cannot, under present conditions, define the part of even the best citizen, who by practicing it would endanger himself without thereby benefiting the city. (Diodotus, as will appear, is very far from practicing it.) At most, then, Diodotus is indicating how the good citizen would speak if all speakers were good citizens—that is, if the city somehow deterred bad citizens from speaking. That, as it happens, is the aim of the reform that Diodotus suggests to the city.

With Diodotus's proposed reform of the city, we reach the heart of his presentation. He offers it as dryly as if it were an amendment to the local rules of order. Upon reflection, however, it implies a radical transformation of political life. In fact it is utopian, by which I mean that it offers a spurious solution that serves to clarify a genuine problem. Here that problem is nothing less than the central one of deliberation itself, the unequal wisdom and justice of the deliberators.

There are two reasons why we must regard Diodotus's proposal as utopian. The first is the downright impossibility of putting it into use. Anyone with experience of deliberative bodies knows that to enact someone's advice is to honor him: the honor lies in the enactment. Most assemblies, indeed, observe a Diodotean etiquette: every member is equally the "honorable" (even the "distinguished") solon from wherever. This cannot obscure the fact that in every forum, when some rise to speak, the mind wanders, while for others it attends to every word. Inevitably, to persuade someone is to gain repute with him and to fail to persuade him is to lose it. The habitually persuasive enjoy great repute (which in turn enhances their persuasiveness), while those who go always unheeded get none. This is not a matter of positive law, and no law or usage can hope to oppose it.

As for tangible political honors, these are primarily offices or positions of trust and responsibility. We would be crazy not to distribute them according to perceived integrity and wisdom. Yet nothing so confirms our good opinion of someone in these regards as that we regularly follow his advice. It is, indeed, as successful speakers that most people first attract political notice and that all politicians whosoever must retain it. In this respect as in the preceding, then, it proves beyond the pale of human possibility to deny all incentive to successful speaking.

The second sense in which the proposal is utopian is this: even if it were feasible, it must prove ineffective. There are only two kinds of societies: those for which this reform would be super-fluous, and those for which it would be futile. It would be super-fluous for the wise society, and futile for all others.

The wise society would see through speakers like Cleon and so would not need this means of deterring them. Having convinced no one, they would soon subside. Such a society, in deliberating—it would be like that city sketched by Pericles in which all listeners were fully competent to judge all speakers—could always be counted on to distinguish the wheat from the chaff. It would be eager to solicit the advice even of those who spoke for the sake of reputation only—for the only way to impress it would be to advise it wisely.

Diodotus's proposal is relevant, then, only to unwise societies. This does not seem a major concession, for these include all actual societies that are or have been. We recall that Diodotus has described the city that would proceed as he advises not as a "wise" one but as a "moderate" one. It is moderate precisely in confessing its unwisdom, in seeking to deter unwise advice that it knows might persuade it if given.

On reflection, however, this "moderate" city proves an impossible halfway house. The same lack of perfect deliberative wisdom that necessitates such moderation would necessarily undo it. Let us suppose that a society, by refraining from honoring successful speakers and dishonoring unsuccessful ones, succeeded in silencing the merely honor-loving while drawing out those with pure intentions. Such a society would still have to pass on the conflicting advice before it. (We can hardly assume that all of its advisers would agree, however honorable their intentions in disagreeing might now be.) The "moderate" city, however, insofar as it fell short of wisdom itself and was therefore unable to recognize it infallibly in others, would inevitably fall back on preferring the advice of speakers it trusted. But to trust a speaker is, as we have seen, to honor him. Speakers craving honor would thus regain their incentive to speak—and to do so persuasively rather than wisely wherever the two diverged. In short, we would be back at square one. Society would be swayed by considerations of trust that it mistook for those of reason, and speakers would find some way of slipping these into the debate. They would have to—and this would be as true of the wise, patriotic speakers as of others.

For so long, then, as audiences fall short of wisdom—for so long, in other words, as they are in need of advice—wisdom will be neither sufficient nor necessary to a given speaker's success at persuading them. That is the point of Diodotus's utopian suggestion, and its ramifications are very great, both for the debate at hand and for our understanding of democracy.

The trouble with the Athenians, moreover, is not just that they cannot always recognize good advice. "What is more, if we so much as suspect someone of being out for gain, who all the same gives the best advice, we will, from envy based on the questionable assumption of his gain, rob the city of that which is clearly advantageous for it." Even where advice seems good in its own right, trust in the speaker must supplement it. We do not trust even the seemingly good advice of someone whom we distrust. Instead we suspect that something is fishy: we would rather risk ignoring good advice than have anyone put anything over on us.

From this it follows that plain good advice, in the absence of whatever it takes to foster trust, remains at the mercy of the calumnies of opposing speakers. Diodotus's advice about Mytilene, however beneficial to Athens, cannot prevail amidst suspicions that he speaks disloyally, and nothing in the advice itself can possibly suffice to dispel such suspicions. Because candor is not transparent, candor alone is never enough to lay to rest suspicions of craft. Only craft can do that, by contriving the semblance of candor.

It is likewise considerations of trust that explain the most astounding stroke in Diodotus's speech, his explicit avowal of the necessity of deception in political life. "And thus has it come to pass that good advice forthrightly spoken is no less suspect than bad, so that just as someone wishing to persuade of the most dreadful measures must win over the multitude through deception, so a man whose proposals are the very best must lie in order to get himself trusted."

You cannot persuade the city for well or ill unless you deceive it: this amounts to an admission that Diodotus is trying to deceive the city. As such it seems ill suited to dispel the distrust of him stirred up by Cleon. Such, however, must be its intention: to convey a frankness so amazing as to persuade of the honesty of the speaker. It is hard to credit the lack of candor of anyone who is so candid about it.

It is also important, of course, here as throughout Diodotus's discussion of deliberation, that he describes the situation that confronts him in such denunciatory tones. He therefore seems, as Cleon had, to be demanding of the people that they mend their ways and at last give simple honesty a hearing. He presents the way things are as so far short of what they ought to be that we are unlikely to notice that he denounces the way of the world as a means of succeeding according to it. His proclamation of his deceit thus goes as unpunished as his slur of Cleon did.

Diodotus concludes this part of the speech with one last suggestion as to how the people might decide things more sensibly (3.43). They could do so if, when matters turned out badly, they would blame themselves as much as they blame the speaker whose advice they had accepted. Perhaps then they might decide more carefully in the first place. As the adviser runs all the risks, so, on top of everything else, he bears the burden of providing what the outcome will confirm as good advice. In the long run, at least, the people learn whose advice they should have taken; because they take the long view only in hindsight, their erstwhile leader had better do so in advance. Deceit may be necessary, but is surely not sufficient, for abiding success in politics: for that, it must serve to persuade of good advice rather than bad.

The nature of Diodotus's deception? He commits at least two deceptions, both of which help to clarify just why he holds deception necessary. The first is that in assailing Cleon he stoops to the very tactics that he declares unworthy of a good citizen. For, in the course of blaming Cleon for maligning the integrity of his opponents, he maligns Cleon's integrity. In presenting such imputations of corruption as prima facie evidence of the corruption of the accuser, he manifestly engages in them—and would thus seem to convict himself of corruption. That he appears to get away with this attests not to his probity but to his cleverness: to sow distrust of someone for sowing distrust is the most ingenious way of sowing distrust of someone. (Think of Joseph Welch's famous deflation of Senator Joseph R. McCarthy during the Army-McCarthy hearings for impugning the integrity of one of Welch's legal associates: "Has it finally come to this? Have you no shame, sir?" etc. Welch simply outsmarted McCarthy, blackening his reputation—and assuring his own—while [and by] deploring the blackening of reputation. Or consider Shakespeare's Mark Antony, whose emphatic avowal that Caesar's assassins are honorable men permits him to deprive them of that reputation without cost to his own.)

Whatever Diodotus may preach, in practice he holds at most that Cleons should not malign Diodotuses. He also shows us, however, why they would be fools to desist—as opposed to merely adopting his own subtler and more effective tactics. Considerations of trust shape and limit all deliberation, and in practice Diodotus agrees with Cleon that trust accrues to those who are best at exploiting distrust.

Diodotus further agrees with Cleon that trustworthy politicians are few, Cleon being the case in point. Given that trust is paramount, that it is deserved even more rarely than it is bestowed, and that it is therefore very often misplaced, a timely redirection of it may prove of some benefit to society. Such a redirection commonly depends on fighting fire with fire. Aspersions are too important to be left to the unscrupulous.

This brings us to the second of Diodotus's deceptions. Like the first, it has succeeded not only with the Athenians but with most of the commentators. In turning to the question of Mytilene and whether the decree should be repealed, Diodotus loudly declares that though he proves the Mytilenians to be ever so guilty, he will not for that reason call for their deaths, unless this were also expedient; nor if he shows that they have some claim to pardon, will he bid the Athenians spare them, were it not for the good of Athens to do so (3.44). Cleon has argued from expediency and justice both; Diodotus rejects concern with justice as a luxury Athens can ill afford. He thus appears to have snatched the low ground from the too high-minded Cleon: his argument for sparing Mytilene is more ruthless than Cleon's for annihilating it.

In fact, however, every stage of Diodotus's stated appeal to expediency conveys a surreptitious appeal to justice. If he presents himself as harsher than Cleon to an audience once again hardened by Cleon, that is the price of his gaining a hearing—that is, of gaining their trust. His speech is a masterpiece of democratic statesmanship, an enduring example of how to appeal to a people's better selves.

Even so, the vote is very close: Cleon has persuaded more people than Diodotus has succeeded in persuading back. Still, the people do repeal the decree, thus ratifying their repentance. A second ship hastens to overtake the first. It does so just barely and only because the first crew of rowers, overtaken by the same second thoughts as the Athenian people generally, has loitered on its "horrid errand" (3.49). Were it not for their susceptibility to Cleons, the people would have less need of Diodotuses.

Distrust of their leaders, aggravated by a fear of being too trusting of them, mingled with a longing for a leader whom they can trust. Such, according to both our speakers, is the natural temper of a democratic people. Hence the permanent necessity—even in direct democracies, where decisions are in the hands of the people assembled—of what we might call image politics. The people give a hearing only to opinions of speakers they trust; their trust then does not issue from any sort of careful hearing. It follows that they are often mistaken. Participation educates, no doubt about it, but one of the things that it teaches the people is to distrust politicians, and so to doubt their own judgment, and so to distrust politicians yet more. Distrust is therefore an inevitable inconvenience of democracy.

The rift between the people and the politicians cannot be healed. At best it can be patched by a politician unusually artful at commanding trust. Pericles comes to mind, as do, closer to home, Andrew Jackson and Franklin Delano Roosevelt. As these very instances confirm, however, the royal road to popular trust commonly lies through playing on existing distrust, whether of politicians as a class or of other presumed enemies of the people ("economic royalists," for instance). As for especially fervent bonds between peoples and leaders, these draw more often than not on the special fervor of some popular resentment.

Not that the differences between ancient and modern, participatory and representative democracy, should be minimized. It is just that the prevalence of distrust happens to be one of the similarities. Such distrust is in no sense peculiar to modern representative systems. In fact these latter constitute a response to the problems posed by popular distrust, one that concedes the malaise while working to allay the symptoms.

Constitutional government represents an attempt at a nonpopulist democracy. It seeks to secure the loyalty of the leaders to the people, while sheltering them from merely temporary vicissitudes of popular opinion. The institutions that serve these ends—the whole machinery of representative democracy—foster a far greater distance between leaders and people than any known to direct democracy. To the leaders, they grant longish terms and thereby a longish leash; to the people, merely a longish wait. As for that large diverse society or "extended sphere" which is crucial to the success of modern republicanism (compare Madison's Federalist Ten), it works to disperse both leaders and led among a vast swirl of contending particular interests.

All these conditions can only deepen that popular "alienation" from politicians which would exist even without them. They also help, however, to keep it to a low simmer. Having elected representatives to govern us, we immerse ourselves in our private affairs. Our distrust we nurse until the next election, that terrible if bloodless day of popular wrath. Then we must decide for some years to come whether to renew or withdraw the trust that we bestowed on the incumbent some years ago. Thus do our institutions nudge us toward that responsible longer view of our leaders which Diodotus identifies as the one best hope for the success of democracy. The obstacle, as in his day, is populism. Under current conditions it expresses itself as a demand for shortcuts, by which the popular will of the moment can burst its institutional bounds. Even within those bounds, our leaders are prone to champion, as individuals, the distrust that we harbor against them collectively: the typical legislator, according to Richard F. Fenno, "runs for Congress by running against Congress." Distrust percolates, and life goes on.

All of which goes, of course, only for *successful* representative democracies. But then there has never been a successful direct democracy. It is worth considering why not. Many today yearn for community, political or otherwise, as something of which we enjoy much too little. They tend not to reflect on whether enough might not prove to be too much, and whether direct self-government might not aggravate some ills that we thoughtlessly ascribe to our lack of it. One such ill is the interplay of popular distrust and the willingness of demagogues to exploit it. This dynamic is intrinsic to democracy as such and stands to puncture every rosy dream of democratic community. You read it first in Thucydides.

PART III

VARIETIES AND REFINEMENTS
OF REALISM

5

FREEDOM AND EMPIRE: THE POLITICS

OF ATHENIAN IMPERIALISM

JACK RILEY

IMPERIALISM IS ONE OF THE main themes of Thucydides' *The War of the Peloponnesians and the Athenians*.[1] What interests Thucydides is the struggle between two imperial cities—Athens and Sparta—"at a height in all manner of preparation"[2] in the greatest "motion" (*kinēsis*) known to

---

1. A full review of the scholarship here is neither possible nor necessary. The conventionally accepted authority on this theme is Jacqueline de Romilly's *Thucydides and Athenian Imperialism*, trans. P. Thody (New York: Barnes & Noble, 1963). Other recent treatments of the subject are in Christopher Bruell, "Thucydides's View of Athenian Imperialism," *American Political Science Review* 68 (March 1974): 11–17; Steven Forde, "Thucydides on the Causes of Athenian Imperialism, *American Political Science Review* 80 (June 1986): 433–48; and Steven Forde, *The Ambition to Rule: Alcibiades and the Politics of Athenian Imperialism* (Ithaca: Cornell University Press, 1989).

2. *Thucydidis Historiae*, annotated with a critical apparatus by H. S. Jones (1902), corrected and enlarged (1942) by J. E. Powell (Oxford: Oxford University Press, 1974), book

him. Though we do get an occasional glimpse of internal politics, especially on the side of Athens, Thucydides' main focus is the external diplomatic and military interaction—what we would now call the international relations—between these imperial cities.

Though imperialism, particularly Athenian imperialism, is one of the main focuses of the work, how Thucydides understood imperialism is a matter of dispute. Thucydides' view of the matter is controversial because of his personal reticence. The greatest translator of *The War of the Peloponnesians and the Athenians*, Thomas Hobbes, noted that Thucydides was "the most politic historiographer that ever writ."[3] He meant by this that Thucydides was a cautiously prudent and effective teacher who adopted intentionally an "obscurity" of style.[4]

Thucydides' reticence has led to endless dispute over what the general teaching of his work is.[5] Thucydides' view of imperialism is no less controversial. There seem to be two categories of opinion here worth considering. Those of the first category hold that

---

1, chapter 1. Translations are my own. Unless otherwise indicated, all subsequent citations in this chapter are to this edition and are identified by conventional book and chapter.

3. Thomas Hobbes, "To the Readers," in *Hobbes's Thucydides*, ed. Richard Schlatter (New Brunswick, N.J.: Rutgers University Press, 1975), 7, 18.

4. For example, A. W. Gomme, *The Greek Attitude toward Poetry and History* (Berkeley: University of California Press, 1954), 307–308, and *More Essays in Greek History and Literature* (Oxford: Blackwell, 1962), 123–29; H. D. F. Kitto, *Poiesis* (London: Cambridge University Press, 1966), 307–308; Leo Strauss, *The City and Man* (Chicago: University of Chicago Press, 1977), 144–45; Thomas Engeman, "Homeric Honor and Thucydidean Necessity," *Interpretations* 3 (1974): 65–66. See also Marcellinus, "From the Comments on Thucydides and the Life of the Same Thucydides and the Form of His Speech," in *Thucydidis Historiae*, annotated with a critical apparatus by H. S. Jones (1902), corrected and enlarged (1942) by J. E. Powell (Oxford: Oxford University Press, 1974), 35.

5. Some have argued that Thucydides has no teaching. For example, see Sir Richard Jebb, "The Speeches from Thucydides," in *Essays and Addresses* (Cambridge: Cambridge University Press, 1907), 359–445, especially p. 409; and G. B. Grundy, *Thucydides and the History of His Age* (Oxford: Basil Blackwell, 1948), 2, 389–91. The opposing view had been argued by Paul Shorey, "The Implicit Ethics and Psychology of Thucydides," *Transactions of the American Philological Association* 24 (1893): 66–88.

Thucydides was a confirmed opponent of imperialism.[6] They argue that Thucydides may have begun as an enthusiastic supporter of Athenian imperialism, but changed his mind after its tyrannical character was revealed by the excesses of the Athenian democracy during such incidents as the Melian Dialogue and the Sicilian Expedition.[7] These commentators conclude that Thucydides' view of politics was pessimistic. Those of the second category contend that Thucydides understood the necessity of empire as a condition of Athens' freedom. But as the demands of empire require Athens to become more openly tyrannical, they conflict with her higher aspirations, such as those expressed in the Funeral Oration. As a result, the nobility of Athens' domestic life rapidly eroded. This view rests on the presumption that the universal aims of Athens, which become intertwined with her political life due to the eruption of philosophy in her midst, can never be reconciled with the necessities of empire.[8] Thus, Thucydides' view of political life is not merely that it is *apt* to fail, but that it is *doomed* to fail.

6. For example, T. J. Quinn, "Thucydides on the Unpopularity of the Athenian Empire," *Historia* 13 (1964): 257–66; and Donald W. Bradeen, "The Popularity of the Athenian Empire," *Historia* 9 (1960). G. E. M. de Ste. Croix, "The Character of the Athenian Empire," *Historia* 3 (1954): 1–41, agreed that Thucydides was opposed to Athenian imperialism, but thought that this position was wrong based on evidence in Thucydides' own account and from independent sources. This view was supported by H. W. Pleket, "Thasos and the Popularity of the Athenian Empire," *Historia* 12 (1963): 70–77. Also providing powerful support for de Ste. Croix was A. W. Gomme, *A Historical Commentary on Thucydides*, 5 vols., with vol. 5 edited by A. Andrewes and K. J. Dover (Oxford: Clarendon, 1981), 2:8.45, 3:47.2, 4:88.108, 5:110.

7. For example, Donald Kagan, *The Fall of the Athenian Empire* (Ithaca: Cornell University Press, 1987), 424–25, and Romilly, *Thucydides and Athenian Imperialism*, 362–70; Peter Pouncey, *The Necessities of War: A Study of Thucydidean Pessimism* (New York: Columbia University Press, 1981) and "Disorder and Defeat in Thucydides and Some Alternatives," *History of Political Thought* 7 (spring 1986): 1–14; Dennis Proctor, *The Experience of Thucydides* (Warminster: Ares and Philips, 1980); and Douglas Allanbrook, "The Inefficacy of the Good," *St. John's Review* (spring 1984): 2–14.

8. Harry Neumann, "Socrates and the Tragedy of Athens," *Social Research* 35 (1969):

Since Thucydides is regarded as a seminal thinker in the realm of political science, the potential consequences of either of these views are devastating for political science and politics. Thucydides' intention is to present the "deeds" (*erga*) of the greatest political motion known to him with "accuracy" (*akribeia*, 1.22). If this presentation of political life is accurate, then political science is pointless. The aim of political science, in whatever guise it has appeared, has not merely been theory-building for the purpose of explanation and prediction, but also for the moral improvement of political life by articulating the proper ends for politics and by educating statesmen. To admit that political life is futile is to concede that human affairs cannot be improved by philosophical statesmanship. Individuals and nations are, then, at the mercy of blind chance and necessity.

Both of these views on Thucydides assume that the higher aims of political life, including moderation, justice, and the common good, can never be reconciled with the demands of the conditions of a larger political order—empire, in the case of Athens. The requirements of empire, as manifested in the Athenian experiment, are conquest, tyrannical rule, and most importantly a "daring" (*tolma*) that always leads to a lawless excess. This excess is the internal contradiction within empire that must ordain, or at least make extremely likely, its downfall. The power politics doctrine of the Melian Dialogue, then, is the inevitable outcome of the Athenian defense of empire at Sparta; and the disaster in Sicily, the final consequence of Athens' power politics.

At first glance there seems to be compelling evidence to support both views. But a second look will reveal that they are fraught with difficulties. They presume that Thucydides speaks only through the Athenians and that his whole teaching centers on Athens' disaster. But there are other speakers in the work who are no less the voice of Thucydides. In addition, the inevitable

---

426–44; and Leo Strauss, "On Thucydides's War of the Peloponnesians and the Athenians," in *The City and Man* (Chicago: University of Chicago Press, 1977), 226–35.

failure of Athens—if indeed this is Thucydides' view—tells us no more than this: Athens failed. It does not tell us if Thucydides' final word on the matter is that empire, as the condition of political life, is incompatible with the requirements of healthy political life, moderation and justice. In fact, there is compelling evidence to support the notion that Thucydides did envision the possibility of their compatibility, as we shall attempt to show below.[9]

To read Thucydides carefully, then, one must avoid the excess of interpreting Thucydides' reticence as a failure to answer the issues raised in the work. Contrariwise, he must also avoid the deficiency of focusing on only part of what Thucydides says and mistaking it for his whole account. One must attempt to see his whole account, however conflicting and contradictory this appears at a first reading. It may be that the conflicts are resolvable and the contradictions intentional. This would apply no less to what Thucydides has to say about Athenian imperialism. In any case, to make a proper beginning, the reader must examine Thucydides' whole presentation of the theme, which means examining as much as possible all of the evidence exactly as the author understood it. But this is to do no more than imitate our author, who chastened "the many" for being "uncritical" (1.20) and "so very lazy in the search for truth that they turn more often to the views readily at hand" (1.21). Moreover, he vouches for the "accuracy" of his account because he wrote the facts, or "deeds," down "not even as they seemed" (1.22) to him, but rather as he could determine them from his impressions and from those of others.

THE ARCHAEOLOGY'S THESIS:
PROGRESS AND EMPIRE

Thucydides calls the war of the Peloponnesians and the Athenians the greatest and most noteworthy human "motion" (*kinēsis*)

---

9. Thucydides ends the work, as we have it, on an optimistic note. See John Wettergreen, "On the End of Thucydides' Narrative," *Interpretations* 9 (August 1980): 92–110.

known to him. He offers a defense of this view. This war brought to light something permanent about human affairs in the facts or "deeds" (*erga*) of the war itself (1.21). These facts Thucydides did not need to embellish in the fashion of the poets, who exaggerate "toward the greater" (1.21, 1.9, 1.10, and 1.11); on the contrary, he recorded them with scrupulous "accuracy" (*akribeia*, 1.22). As a result, he calls his work "an eternal possession" (1.22).

In order to prove his point, Thucydides must delve into what is known of the past to show that previous wars were insignificant. The competitors were the Persian War, recorded by Herodotus, and the Trojan War, recounted in the poetry of Homer. Thucydides concedes that little is known of the past (1.1). But however unreliable "the ancient things" might be, he is confident that "nothing great occurred either during the wars or in the other things" (1.1).

The reason for this "is clear" to Thucydides. At the origins, "present-day Greece" was not securely inhabited. Human beings wandered about without commerce, agriculture, or revenues. What little contact they did have with each other was with fear (1.2). The original condition of Greece was one of "factional strife" (*stasis*), which especially afflicted the Peloponnesus because of the richness of its soil. The result of this was that "they were strong neither in greatness of cities nor in any other preparation" (1.2) and "did not achieve a state of rest in order to increase in power" (1.12).[10] Greece was so enveloped by this strife that she could do nothing "in common" (1.3). In fact, there was no consciousness of Greek wholeness, but only of particular tribal affiliations. Even the consciousness of a barbaric otherness "in opposition" to Greekness occurred "at a much later time."

Not only was pre-Hellenic Greece enfeebled politically, economically, and culturally, but she was weak morally. The original

---

10. An excellent treatment of the relationship of rest, progress, and preparation (*paraskeuē*) is in June Allison, *Power and Preparedness in Thucydides* (Baltimore: Johns Hopkins University Press, 1989), especially in her analysis on 11–27.

inhabitants survived through robbery and piracy (1.4–8). This caused the inhabitants to adopt the habit of bearing arms like the barbarians (1.6). During these times, there was no moral disapproval of piracy. In fact, it was regarded as a positive good (1.5).

All of this "moving about" ends when Greece finally achieves peace or "rest" (*esukhia*, see 1.12, e.g.). And the condition of rest is empire. Crime ceases on the Hellenic Sea when Minos establishes his empire and "purges piracy, as is likely, for the better coming in to him of his revenues" (1.4). Only the rigid imposition of order by imperialists, acting for economic self-interest, ends crime. It is no accident that Thucydides follows the discussion of Minos and his empire, and piracy and its end (1.4–5), with the emergence of Greek culture in its two polar developments, the Athenian and Spartan characters (1.6).

Minos's naval empire not only benefited himself, but everyone else. It permitted human beings to devote themselves to gain and lead a more settled life (1.8). In turn, this allowed them to build walls around their settlements and establish regular commerce (1.7). As Greece progresses, the weaker give themselves over to the enslavement of the stronger, and the wealthier cities, having a surplus of money, bring the smaller cities into subjection, which leads to "a more settled way of life" (1.8). Thucydides deduces from this that Agamemnon's power rested not on the obligations created by the oaths of Tyndareus, but because he exceeded the rest in power. This could only mean that Agamemnon was the ruler of an empire and in possession of a powerful navy (1.9).

Though Thucydides indicates that the establishing of empire permitted considerable material progress, the accomplishments of early Greece—including the Trojan War—were still inconsiderable (1.3, 1.8, 1.10–12). Greece finally makes a decisive step forward and "becomes more powerful . . . when tyrannies are established in the cities" (1.13 and 1.17). Though the tyrants accomplished "no noteworthy deed," they do provide for much additional material progress. The Greeks begin to outfit more ships and involve themselves more with the sea, begin to produce more or less modern triremes—though still penteconters—and engage in even more commerce both by land and sea. Those who devoted themselves to commerce and navy "gained strength not least in income of money and empire over others." In fact, Greece is now, because of the progress in her material conditions, poised for greatness but is constrained by two conditions: first, she is still too divided and lacking in unity. "For they did not stand together under the great cities as subjects" (1.15). Second, they were constrained by another, greater empire, the Persian under Cyrus and Darius.

Greece finally achieves freedom from constraint, and so reaches the condition for greatness, when two things occur. First, the ending of tyrannies in the cities by the Spartans (1.18). Sparta establishes her own empire (1.19) and frees the Greek cities. The second event is the defeat of the Persians. With Sparta commanding the Greeks "because she was superior in power," the Athenians and the Spartans "in common" repelled the Persians. Greece becomes free of constraint when she repels the Persian empire, and this is only possible for her because of her own progress toward empire. After the defeat of the Persian, Greece divides itself into two imperial powers, that of Sparta and that of Athens, because "it was clear that these were greatest in power" (1.18). This permitted "their own private preparation to be greater" (1.19) than at any other time.

However much in tension their demands might be, Thucydides inextricably connects freedom, rest, and progress with a condition of imperial domination in the Archaeology.[11] The thesis of the Archaeology is this: empire is the condition of rest for material progress, and stability for political freedom. The greatness of the war of the Peloponnesians and the Athenians derives from the explosive growth of imperial Athens. For it is the fact that "Ath-

11. This point is made in A. G. Woodhead, *Thucydides on the Nature of Power* (Cambridge, Mass.: Harvard University Press, 1970), 12–13; see also in Virginia Hunter, "Thucydides and the Uses of the Past," *Klio* 62 (1980): 198–205.

ens became great and produced a fear in the Spartans that compelled them to proceed to war" (1.23)—the greatest and most noteworthy war (1.1). But how Thucydides understood this greatness, and whether or not he approved of it, is not clear from the Archaeology and remains to be investigated. The understanding of this greatness is the key to understanding the obscure teaching of this complex work, especially his teaching on imperialism.

The Defense of the Archaeology's Thesis: Compulsion and Empire in the Athenian Speech at Sparta and the Pentecontaetia

The war of the Peloponnesians and the Athenians grew out of the skirmishes in Corcyra-Epidamnus and Potidaea. These were the "charges" (*aitia*) and "complaints" (*diaphora*, 1.23–26) that each side had against each other. Though the "truest reason" (*alēthestatē prophasis*) for the war was Athenian greatness and Spartan fear, the charges and complaints did not yet amount to a genuine *casus belli*. At most, they represented a "confusion" of the treaty (1.146). In any case, for the Athenians' adversaries in Corinth, these events represented enough of a provocation to convene the Spartan allies at Sparta and attempt to move them all toward war with Athens (1.67).

The Corinthians, after making a disputable claim that the Athenians had done injustice, get to the core of their argument. Athens represents a mortal threat to Sparta and her allies and is already secretly plotting to depose Sparta from her hegemony over Greece (1.68–69). The purpose of Athens' empire is to make an eventual attempt on Sparta, which by degrees in fact has already occurred. The basis of Athens' empire, and her mortal threat to Sparta, derives from Athens' daring and the character differences that obtain between Athens and Sparta.

These character differences, though no doubt exaggerated for rhetorical purposes,[12] are outlined by the Corinthians (1.70). The Athenians are daring and innovative, always quick to act on whatever they conceive. The Spartans are timid, slow, and conservative, risking nothing in fear of losing what little they have. The Athenians are always hopeful and undaunted by a setback; the Spartans fearful and willing to do much less than her power will permit. In a word, the Athenians are in constant motion; the Spartans at rest. "Thus, if one should sum up their nature by saying that they neither have rest themselves nor permit it to other human beings, he would speak correctly" (1.70). The Corinthians urge the Spartans to innovate in order to meet this threat. For the Athenian character, which has already led to her empire and encroachments on Spartan power, must eventually lead to war.[13]

Several Athenian emissaries, in Sparta on other business for the city, answer the Corinthian accusations (1.72). They neither dispute the claims of the Spartan allies nor seek to justify themselves before Sparta (1.73).[14] Instead, they wish merely to display the power of their city, showing that they are "worthy of note," and that they hold their empire "not unfairly" (*oute apeikotos*, 1.73).[15]

The Athenians bluntly assert that they are worthy of empire. To support this, they present two important arguments. First, they claim that they were responsible for the victory in the Persian War. They sacrificed themselves by abandoning the city and

12. Mark Cogan, *The Human Thing: The Speeches and the Principles of Thucydides' History* (Chicago: University of Chicago Press, 1981), 22–33. Though embellished, these characterizations are substantially accurate, as Thucydides himself suggests (1.118, 4.55–56, and 8.96). See also W. Robert Connor, *Thucydides* (Princeton: Princeton University Press, 1984), 39–41, and Pouncey, *Necessity of War*, 57–63.

13. Forde, "Causes of Athenian Imperialism," 433–48.

14. The speech is analyzed by A. E. Raubitschek, "The Speech of the Athenians," in *The Speeches in Thucydides*, ed. Philip A. Stadter (Chapel Hill: University of North Carolina Press, 1973), 34–38.

15. It is worth noting that this is the only speech in the work preceded by a summary of its content, as discussed in Strauss, *City and Man*, 170–71.

acting for the common good of Greece. The Athenians also take full credit for the great victory at Salamis. Second, they claim that they were "compelled" (1.75) to take the empire. When Sparta was no longer willing to stand with the Athenians, she was forced to take it up. Further, when Sparta became suspicious of Athens without reason, Athens was forced to continue with the empire (1.75). The inexorable choice is either "to rule [the allies] forcibly or to be exposed to danger" (1.76). By embarking on empire, the Athenians are doing no more than following the necessities of human nature. "We have done nothing marvelous nor contrary to the way of the human thing, if we accepted an empire that was offered to us and did not give it up because we were con- quered by the three greatest motives: honor, fear, and profit. We were not the first to begin this, but it has always been established that the weaker should be constrained by the more powerful" (1.76).

Athens' argument here largely agrees with the thesis of the Archaeology. Empire is the condition for political freedom, mate- rial progress, and human greatness. Moreover, this defense of em- pire at Sparta is identical to the argument that underlies Pericles' two speeches in book 2. The city of Athens, as Pericles presents it in the Funeral Oration, seems to be free of any sort of compulsion internally or externally. What the Athenians at Sparta dwell on— the necessity of empire—is left almost unaddressed in the Funeral Oration. Pericles does take up the conditions of Athens' political freedom and good society in his second speech in book 2.[16] He urges the Athenians to understand that the good of each individ- ual citizen depends on the city, and the city depends on the exis- tence of the empire. "You should not believe that you are struggling only over the one evil of slavery instead of freedom.

---

16. The consistency of theme in the two speeches is analyzed in Lionel Pearson, "Three Notes on the Funeral Oration," *American Journal of Philology* 64 (1943): 399–407, and D. C. Pozzi, "Thucydides II.35–46: A Text of Power Ideology," *Classical Journal* 78 (1983): 221–31.

You are also struggling over the loss of empire and the danger of the hatred that you have incurred from your rule. From this empire it is no longer possible for you to stand away. . . . For you now hold the empire as a tyranny, which seems to be unjust to have taken, but is now dangerous to give up" (2.63).

Pericles makes it clear to the Athenians that the freedom and glory of the Athens of the Funeral Oration is dependent on Athens as an imperial city. Athens cannot resort to inactivity by playing the good man because inactivity is expedient only for a subject city. Though Pericles was loath to admit it before, in anticipation of Alcibiades he concedes that empire requires constant activity (2.63 and 1.144). This means constant consolidation and expansion. Athens is uniquely positioned for this because her total domination of the sea permits her also domination of land (2.62). In even bolder terms, Pericles restates the Athenian thesis from book 1 and Thucydides' thesis from the Archaeology.

In sum, both the Athenians at Sparta and Pericles support the thesis of the Archaeology. Human freedom, security, and progress derive from a condition of rest; and rest in turn derives from empire. Yet as we noted above, it may be too much to conclude here that the Athenian defense of empire is simply Thucydides' position. The Athenian defense needs to be examined against Thucydides' own treatment of the origins of Athenian imperialism in the Pentecontaetia (1.89–119). Up to the point of the speeches delivered at Sparta in book 1, only the "charges" and "complaints," which were evident in speech, were examined by Thucydides. The "truest reason" for the war—Athens' imperial greatness and Spartan fear—remained unexamined. The Pentecontaetia (the account of Athens' rise to power in the fifty years between the end of the Persian War and the beginning of the War of the Peloponnesians and the Athenians) is Thucydides' treatment of the *alēthestatē prophasis* of the war.[17] When he states

17. Lionel Pearson, "*Prophasis*: A Clarification," *Transactions of the American Philological*

the reason that he wrote the section, he refers not only to the need to correct Hellanicus's inaccurate chronology, but also because the section "at the same time displays in what way the Athenian empire arose" (1.97) and the "way that the Athenians were brought to those actions by which they increased their power" (1.89).[18]

The Pentecontaetia largely supports the Athenian claims, at least regarding the necessity of empire and the compulsion of fear and profit. After the Persians are driven from Greece, the Spartans develop an unprovoked hatred of the Athenians (1.92). Even though both sides are still on friendly terms, Thucydides notes that the Spartans and their allies, even before this, "were afraid of the Athenians' numerous fleet, which before did not exist, and of their daring, which arose during the Persian War" (1.90). This hatred and fear of Athens prompts Sparta to interfere with the rebuilding of Athens' walls. Themistocles, however, outwits the Spartans through diplomatic maneuvering.

Before Sparta can act further, problems arise with her general, Pausanias. His rule had become so severe and oppressive that the allies go to the Athenians "repeatedly" and "beg them to become their leaders" (1.95). When Pausanias is called home to answer the charges of tyranny, the allies went over to the side of the Athenians. In addition, the Spartans withdraw their command of the Greeks and "sent out no others" after Pausanias. They were tired of fighting the Persian War and thought Athens suitable to take over the leadership. Thucydides notes: "In this way the Athenians *inherited* (*paralabontes*, 1.9) the leadership from *willing* allies due to their hatred of Pausanias" (1.96, emphasis added).

Society 103 (1972): 381–94; Raphael Sealey, "The Causes of the Peloponnesian War," *Classical Philology* 70 (April 1975): 89–109.

18. Thucydides refers to this section as an *ekbolē*, which most readers take to mean a digression, a departure from the narrative. In fact, the word never has this sense in Thucydides. It is used in three other places: 4.1, where it means "blossoming" or "coming forth"; and 2.102 and 7.35, where it means "opening."

At first, the Athenians ruled over autonomous allies and deliberated in common councils (1.97).[19] But the allies become restive and begin leaving the Delian League, though the war was still being prosecuted (1.100). The reason for the revolts was that the Athenians were strict taskmasters "and were severe in applying necessity to men who were neither accustomed nor willing to do hard work" (1.99). But Thucydides points out that it was an easy matter for the Athenians to bring the allies back into the fold. For when given the choice of fighting at Athens' side or simply contributing ships or money, the allies opted for the latter. This had the effect of increasing Athens' fleet and sharpening her skills in naval warfare, leaving the allies unprepared and inexperienced for warfare (1.99). For this "the allies themselves were to blame" (1.99).

At this point the war against the Persians becomes insensibly intertwined with, and then replaced by, the campaign against the mutinous allies. This is clearly the case when the strategically important Thasos revolts, something the Thasians had been planning for a long time. The Athenians decisively defeat the Thasians and place them under siege (1.100). The Thasians, deeply angered over this, go to Sparta and extract a promise from the Spartans to invade Attica. The Spartans "promised in secret" and "were about to invade" (1.75), but are interrupted by the slave revolt at Ithome. Two things have clearly occurred by this time. First, Athens can no longer resist the temptations of rule and move from leader of the Delian League to commander of an empire. Second, Athens has secured the unprovoked enmity of Sparta, which further attaches her to the empire.

In spite of their secret enmity for Athens, the Spartans invite the Athenians to assist them in the siege of Ithome, where some of their revolted slaves had taken refuge. When the siege is prolonged beyond expectations, Sparta's suspicions of Athens erupt

19. N. G. L. Hammond, "The Origin and Nature of the Athenian Alliance, 478–7 B.C.," *Journal of Hellenic Studies* 87 (1967): 41–61.

again. "They feared the daring and innovating character of the Athenians, and moreover believed them to be alien to themselves." Suspecting groundlessly that the Athenians would come to the assistance of the besieged in Ithome, they sent the Athenians away, saying that they were no longer needed. The Athenians are insulted and storm away, "not deserving to suffer this from the Spartans." Thucydides points out that "from this principally open differences arose between the Spartans and the Athenians" (1.102).

Though it is true at this point that Athens is expanding the empire beyond, perhaps, the immediate strategic concerns with self-defense, she has represented no direct strategic threat to Sparta. Indeed, up to this point, Athens has harbored only good will toward Sparta. The Pentecontaetia certainly supports the Athenians' claim that she took the empire out of fear, an empire that she did not seize but was urged to take from willing allies. The hatred from Sparta explains why Athens cannot give up the empire. Moreover, Thucydides shows no direct violation of the Thirty Years Truce by Athens. The affairs involving Epidamnus-Corcyra and Potidaea represent only a "confusion" of the treaty. Though Athens has directly clashed with an important Spartan ally, Corinth, he only mentions that Corinth was still acting on her own and Athens' "power in fact had clearly risen and touched [Sparta's] alliance" (1.118). Sparta's suspicions had exploded into open hatred so that "they decided *by themselves* that the treaty had been broken and that the Athenians had done injustice" (1.118, emphasis added). Even the Spartans themselves conceded that they illegally started the war (7.18).

Freedom, Empire, and the Necessities of Human Nature: The Reconsideration of the Archaeology's Thesis

The Athenian defense of the empire at Sparta is supported by Thucydides' narrative in the Pentecontaetia. The Athenians also act in accord with the thesis of empire in the Archaeology. But the Athenian claim of necessity for their empire goes beyond external compulsions by a foreign threat. They claim that the impulse to rule is the "way of the human thing" (1.75 and 1.76). Not only fear and profit, but honor drives human beings to rule, they claim.[20] The Pentecontaetia seems to support the Athenian claim here also, since Athens' drive for empire continues long after the strategic threat of Persia is removed (see 1.109–110). However, Thucydides refrains from commenting on this additional expansion as he had done earlier on the initial acquisition of the empire. One is led to wonder about the relationship of ambitious expansion and the requirements of empire.

To grasp Thucydides' view of the matter, one must consult Diodotus's speech at Athens during the debate over the fate of Mytilene and the account of the Corcyraean sedition.

Early in the war, after Athens is smitten by the plague, the city of Mytilene revolts from the Athenian empire (3.2–5). The action was encouraged by Sparta. This revolt is distressing to the Athenians because Mytilene was a wealthy city, with a strong navy, and had been among the very few of the cities that fought at Athens' side. Because of this, Mytilene, along with Chios, remained autonomous and enjoyed equality with Athens. In their explanation at Sparta, the Mytilenaean envoys speciously claim that they feared eventual slavery at the hands of Athens because it had happened to all of the other cities (3.9–14). (One might assume that Chios, the other city left free and with a navy, remained autonomous until late in the war.)

After placing the city of Mytilene under siege, the Athenians decide the city's fate. Instigated by Cleon, the leader of the Athenian *dēmos* and the "most violent man" (3.36) of his time, the Athenians decide to kill the male population and sell the

20. The concept of necessity is discussed in Martin Ostwald, *Ananke in Thucydides* (Atlanta: Scholars Press, 1988), and Gabriella Slomp, "Hobbes, Thucydides, and the Three Greatest Things," *History of Political Thought* 11 (1990): 565–86.

women and children into slavery. The Athenians then dispatch their admiral, Paches, to carry out the order. But after an over-night mind change, the Athenians realize that their decision was "savage," and decide to reconsider the matter.[21] Cleon speaks again (3.37–40) and makes the case for severe punishment, ar-guing that the whole city of Mytilene is guilty for either complic-ity or negligence. According to Cleon the just course of action, since it is expedient and useful, is to make an example of Myti-lene. He urges the Athenians to act on their initial anger as swiftly as possible because this indicates the most reliable course of ac-tion. Indeed, he regards this as so clear that anyone speaking against it could be motivated only by self-interested treason.

After Cleon's tirade, the mysterious Diodotus rises to speak against Cleon. One must note that this is his only appearance in the work, and that there is no independent corroboration of Diodotus's existence.[22] Whatever the character's historical status, there is agreement that Diodotus comes closer to expressing Thu-cydides' views than any other character in the work.[23]

Diodotus counters Cleon by advocating a more humane pol-icy. He argues that reason, and not anger, ought to be the city's guide. He strongly upbraids Cleon for suggesting that all speakers are to be suspected of self-interested motives, even though their advice may be good. Rather he asks the Athenians simply to con-sider whether or not his counsel is beneficial without regard to his motives (3.42–43). Diodotus then meets Cleon on his own ground in the argument: that of expediency. He raises the ques-tion of what course of action is truly useful for Athens (3.44,

21. Clifford Orwin, "The Just and the Advantageous in Thucydides: The Case of the Mytilenaean Debate," *American Political Science Review* 78 (1984): 485–94.

22. Martin Ostwald, "Diodotus, Son of Eucrates," *Greek, Roman, and Byzantine Stud-ies* 20 (spring 1979): 5–13; Ostwald has no doubt that Diodotus is real, in spite of the lack of historical evidence.

23. David Bolotin, "Thucydides," in *The History of Political Philosophy*, ed. Leo Strauss and Joseph Cropsey (Chicago: University of Chicago Press, 1987), 28; Strauss, *City and Man*, 231; and Orwin, "Just and Advantageous," 485–94.

3.46–48). But more importantly, he raises the question of whether or not, in view of human nature, capital punishment is truly a deterrent to revolt. Human beings, he observes, are driven by powerful impulses of passion. "And even though they are invisible, they are stronger than the terrors that are seen. . . . This is not less the case for cities inasmuch as they venture for the greatest objects: *freedom and empire over others*. . . . Simply stated, it is impossible and very simpleminded for anyone to think, once human nature sets in motion zealously to do something, that he can divert it either by the strength of laws or by any other terror" (3.45, emphasis added).

Diodotus's argument partly supports the Athenian thesis from the speech at Sparta. Human nature is driven by powerful impulses of passion and spiritedness. When human beings act for the greatest objects—freedom and empire—the influences of these impulses is too great. But Diodotus also partly undermines the Athenian argument. The tendency of these powerful passions, whenever released, is to drive human beings to excessive destruction. This dimension of the argument, added here by Diodotus, seems to indicate this: by acting in accord with the impulses of human nature, Athens too will be bound for the same destructive excess as Mytilene. Thucydides views seem to be in transition from being a defender of Athenian imperialism to a virulent detractor of Athenian imperialism.[24]

Thucydides supports the latter view in his analysis of the Corcyraean Sedition. During that insurrection all forms of order gave way, words changed their meaning, and human beings reverted to the worst in them (3.82, 3.83).[25] Thucydides notes:

24. Romilly, *Thucydides and Athenian Imperialism*, 3–10; and K. J. Dover, "Strata of Composition," in *A Historical Commentary on Thucydides*, by A. W. Gomme, with vol. 5 edited by A. Andrewes and K. J. Dover (Oxford: Clarendon Press, 1981), 5:384–444.

25. Clifford Orwin, "Stasis and Plague: Thucydides on the Dissolution of Society," *Journal of Politics* 50 (1988), 831–47; and Felix Wasserman, "Thucydides and the Disintegration of the Polis," *Transactions of the American Philological Association* 85 (1954): 46–54.

The causes of this was the desire to rule on account of greed and love of honor, from which they were put into a state of a zealous love of victory. . . . As they were struggling by every means to gain an advantage over each other, they dared to do the most terrible things and executed still greater acts of vengeance. For they did not propose anything up to the limit of what was expedient for the city, but defined the limits by what was pleasing to either faction at any instant. . . . Thus, life in the city was thrown into confusion at this critical time. Once human nature prevailed over the laws by becoming accustomed to do injustice against the laws, it manifested delight in being unrestrained passion, stronger than justice and an enemy to its superior. (3.83, 3.84)

Once above the law, human nature in Corcyra was unrestrained daring with no regard at all for piety (3.82). Thucydides presents piety and daring here as unalterably opposed, as are daring and moderation (3.84). Thucydides supports the Athenian argument at Sparta that Athens was driven to acquire the empire not only by external necessity, but by the necessities of human nature. There is, though, this important difference: the Athenians, most significantly Pericles, approve of this; Thucydides here does not.[26] The reader is then forced to reflect on the Athenian defense of empire, and Thucydides' thesis on empire and progress from the Archaeology, in light of his remarks on the Corcyraean Sedition. While it may be that external compulsion initially compels human beings to establish empire as a condition of rest for material progress, human nature impels human beings to still greater ambitions for rule. Since it is inevitable that this overreaching will occur again due to the constancy of human nature (3.82), political history seems unalterably doomed.

Thucydides' early treatment of Sparta and Athens seems to bear this out. Though Sparta suffered from the primal *stasis* longer

---

26. The general differences between Pericles' view of things and Thucydides' view of things are discussed in Christopher Bruell, "Thucydides and Perikles," *St. John's Review* (summer 1991): 24–29.

than other Greek cities (1.18 and 1.2), she also had "good laws" (1.18). However subdued, only Sparta is praised without qualification for having good laws.[27] This goodness derives from the constancy of her regime—"for surely it was a little more than four hundred years up to the end of this war that Sparta made use of the same regime"—and its rootedness in the ancestral, as Archidamus makes clear in his Spartan praise of Sparta (1.80–85, especially 1.84–85). Though Sparta never reaches the heights achieved by Athens, her moderation prevents her from falling so low. At this point the impression is that Spartan moderation is superior to Athenian daring. One cannot forget this: Sparta wins the war.

This impression is heightened by reflecting on the causes of Athenian greatness. Athens' greatness derives from the daring that arose in her during the Persian War (1.90). Athens' daring derives from her abandoning of the ancestral traditions. She committed the extraordinary act of leaving her ancestral households and became "nautical men" (1.18 and 1.89). This leads to an unparalleled burst of energy portrayed graphically in the Pentecontaetia, especially in the description of the Athenian wall-building (1.93). How untraditional Athens had become is shown by the fact that in constructing her walls, she used stones from the households and "columns from tombs"—something that would be unthinkable in Sparta.[28] It is telling to note this in Thucydides: "daring" (*tolma*) and its various cognates are used with the greatest frequency in five places. In an optimistic sense in the Pentecontaetia (see especially 1.91 and 1.93) and Pericles' speeches (see especially

27. The praise of the Athenian mixed regime by Thucydides in book 8 is qualified. "And not least, indeed, for the first time in my lifetime at least, the Athenians appeared to have ordered their regime well. For it was a measured mix of the few and the many" (8.97). Note that this was Athens' best regime in Thucydides' lifetime. Whether the regime was simply good remains an open question.

28. The theological significance of the household and the attachment to the traditions is discussed by Fustel de Coulange, *The Ancient City* (Gloucester, Mass.: Peter Smith, 1979), 34–112, and in Leo Strauss, *City and Man*, 240–41.

2.40–41, 2.62), in particular the Funeral Oration; in a pessimistic sense in the Plague Scene (2.49–54), the account of the Corcyraean Sedition (3.82–84), and the Athenian tyrannicide (6.54–59). While daring is the source of Athenian greatness, it also produces a lawlessness in human beings which makes excess inevitable. Thus Athens' downfall and the failure of the Sicilian Expedition seem to be fated. Upon reconsideration of the original thesis, imperial expansion may be a necessary condition for rest and progress, but it is fated to overreach itself fueled by the ambitious love of honor and daring.

Thucydides suggests that the human desire to rule can only be restrained by devotion to the ancestral. Sparta seems to prove this. But even at this, one wonders if this is Thucydides' last word on the matter. For beyond the explicit praise of good laws and political stability, Sparta (along with Chios) also receives a praise from Thucydides for having maintained moderation amidst prosperity (8.24). No major Athenian character is praised for his moderation (*sōphrosyne*). Nevertheless, though Sparta and Chios did maintain moderation amidst prosperity, they also had more slaves than any other city (8.40). The need to police the large Helot slave population prevented Sparta from going on foreign expeditions, even with grave threats impending (e.g., 1.101, 1.103, 1.118, 1.128).

Thucydides invites us to wonder whether Sparta is moderate and restrained in her imperial ambitions because of her voluntary submission to the precepts of piety or whether it is the accidental or self-imposed necessity of her slave population that limits her. This wonder is heightened by observing two things. Thucydides is critical of Sparta's slowness right up to the end of his account (8.96). Moreover, that Sparta's moderation signifies an improvement of her character is further called into question by Thucydides' treatment of Pausanias. Far from being of a good nature, the Spartan soul revealed is nothing but a tyrant's (1.94–95 and 1.130). Pausanias demonstrates ambition equal to that of any Athenian in the work. One wonders, then, if even the Spartans are strictly speaking moderate.

Thucydides' reconsideration of the Archaeology's thesis seems to reveal that though empire is required as the basis for human stability and progress, the very things that empire requires—rule, ambition, profit, and honor—provide the causes of its demise. For once the immediate concerns of necessity are removed, human beings seem to overreach limits. Only necessity, perhaps in the guise of piety, seems to restrain human beings. Thus the demands of progress—empire to free human beings from necessity—seem to be incompatible with the requirements for maintenance of empire, namely, moderation and justice. The conditions of political life seem always to conflict with the highest aims of political life, creating an unalterably tragic situation for human beings. Human beings always require the limits of the ancestral for decent stable life, but they are compelled always to transgress these limits due to the compulsions of rule and human nature. Injustice is a transgression of divine law which human beings cannot help, and so they are consigned always to suffer divine retribution.[29]

THE RECONSIDERATION OF THE RECONSIDERATION: AMBITION AND EMPIRE, AND THE DISASTER IN SICILY

In view of the above, we would expect Thucydides' to teach us a lesson regarding Athenians sins, such as the immoderation of the Funeral Oration and Melian Dialogue, and especially for the insolence of the Sicilian Expedition. This expectation is plausible, since the Plague Scene follows quickly on the Funeral Oration; the disaster in Sicily, the Melian Dialogue. Vigilant angry gods, one would expect Thucydides to say, watch over human affairs and punish men for transgressions of divine law. We would expect Thucydides to come forward as a champion of piety with,

29. Clifford Orwin, "Piety, Justice, and the Necessities of War: Thucydides 4.97–101," *American Political Science Review* 83 (1989): 383–88.

for example, Alcibiades as the villain of the drama. But in fact he does not. In almost every case, Thucydides ridicules those overly concerned with the gods and oracles (e.g., 1.126, 2.54, 5.26). To grasp Thucydides' view of the matter, one must look at what he explicitly says. For however little it may be, it is surprisingly enlightening.

During the eulogy of Pericles in book 2, Thucydides criticizes those who came after Pericles for abandoning his policy of imperial restraint during the war (2.65). He notes that those who succeeded Pericles did the opposite,[30] motivated by the same impulses that drove the factions during the Corcyraean Sedition. They governed themselves and the allies badly "because of the private love of honor [*philotimias*] and gain." Pericles was able to forestall this because of his extraordinary political virtues. The lesser men who followed him, consumed by factional conflicts, committed blunders in ruling the city, among which was miscalculating the logistics for the Sicilian Expedition. But it is interesting to note that Thucydides does not censure the expedition as an example of Athens' and Alcibiades' overweening ambition.[31] "It was not so much an error of judgment, with respect to those whom they went against, as it was an error of those who sent them out, because they did not understand what additional provisions were required by those who had gone there. But on the basis of private slanders over the factional leadership of the *dēmos*, they acted very slowly to provide what was necessary in the encampment" (2.65).

Thucydides even goes further to point out that the disaster did not end Athens' empire, but she held out for ten more years and recovered almost completely from her losses in Sicily. In the end, it was her factional squabbling that destroyed her (2.65). Thucydides does not connect Athens' imperialism and ambition with her

30. A. B. West, "Pericles' Political Heirs. I," *Classical Philology* 19 (April 1924): 124–146.

31. Wesley E. Thompson, "Thucydides 2.65.11," *Historia* 20 (1971): 141–51.

factional squabbling. He seems to raise the surprising possibility that Athens' imperial ambitions and her political stability might have been compatible, and it may be that he shows the way to accomplish this.[32]

Thucydides commences his account of the Sicilian Expedition in book 6 with the Sicilian Archaeology (6.2–5). Among other things, this of course calls to mind the proem to the work (1.1–23) and its thesis of empire. After the Peace of Nicias, which was not really peace at all (5.26), the Athenians decide to act on their longing for conquest of Sicily (1.44) when the opportunity is presented by the Egesteans (6.8).[33] The Athenians assemble to consider the matter, which includes an exchange between Nicias and Alcibiades.[34] Nicias advises against the expedition, warning them that it is too big an enterprise to undertake while at war with Sparta. For Sparta will seize the opportunity to act against them (6.9–11). He also cautions the Athenians not to be swayed by Alcibiades, because he has only personal ambition at heart (6.12–13). He ends by calling on the older, hopefully wiser men to vote against the proposal.

Alcibiades responds by asking the Athenians to judge whether or not he had managed the affairs of the city badly. He claims to have brought Argos into the Athenian alliance, gained honor for the city at the Olympic Games, and nearly defeated Sparta and her allies at Mantinaea (6.16). Then, Alcibiades boldly defends his private ambitions. For private individuals with huge ambitions,

32. Michael Palmer, "Love of Glory and the Common Good," *American Political Science Review* 76 (1982): 825–36.

33. H. D. Westlake, "Athenian Aims in Sicily, 427–424 B.C.," *Historia* 9 (1960): 385–402, and I. Moxon, "Sicily and Italy in the Peloponnesian War: A Note on Thucydides II.9," *Mnemosyne* 33 (1980): 288–98.

34. How the style of the speeches reflects the different characters of the interlocutors is discussed in Wesley E. Thompson, "Stylistic Characterization in Thucydides: Nicias and Alcibiades," *Yale Classical Studies* 22 (1972): 181–214. As we shall show below, Alcibiades acts as if he and Nicias complement each other, in spite of their differences.

like Alcibiades, profit their cities as well as themselves (6.6).[35] Though this ambition may produce a temporary present resentment from lesser men, it leaves an everlasting testimony of honor (6.16), which is Alcibiades' ultimate reward. He continues by suggesting, based on unreliable information, that the Sicilians are a barbaric rabble who will easily be conquered. He advises that they appoint both Nicias and him as co-commanders to take advantage of his "mindlessness" (*anoia*) and Nicias's luck. He ends by pointing out that imperial expansion is necessary, reminding us of the dilemma of rule that is at the heart of Thucydides' work.[36] "Anyone who is in a position of superiority not only defends himself against an attack, but also seizes the initiative first lest others attack him. It is not possible for us to control the limits of how far we wish to extend our empire, but it is necessary, since we are in this particular situation, to plot against some and not to surrender to others because we would endanger ourselves from being ruled by others if we should not rule over others" (6.18).

Alcibiades' remarks, as we noted above, remind us of Pericles' policy of activity in his second speech of book 2, but they possess a greater consistency than what Pericles says. An active city would destroy itself by inactivity (6.18). The speech closes with a warning against factionalizing the city along generational lines, as Nicias attempted to do, and by reminding the Athenians of the need to continue their active life (6.6–7).

Seeing the Athenians "much more moved for the expedition than before" (6.19), Nicias responds. He exaggerates the requirements for the expedition so that the Athenians might be discouraged by the sheer magnitude of the undertaking (6.21–23). This strategy backfires altogether. Because of his reputation for sobriety, the Athenians thought that he had given them good advice:

35. Nathan M. Pusey, "Alcibiades and the *To Philopoli*," *Harvard Studies in Classical Philology* 51 (1940): 215–31.

36. Malcolm F. McGregor, "The Genius of Alcibiades," *Phoenix* 19 (1965): 27–46.

"they set in motion for it much more" (6.24). As a result, an "*erōs* fell on all alike" to sail to see far-off sights, for gain, and for security (6.24).

Thucydides' comments, inserted between Nicias's first speech and Alcibiades' speech, are surprising. One would expect here a criticism of both Alcibiades' and Athens' ambition. He does indicate clearly that Alcibiades had ambitious designs for conquering Sicily and Carthage, and indulged huge personal desires, which were a tremendous financial burden to the city. But the cause of Alcibiades', and so Athens', downfall was not ambition, passion, or expenses, but the suspicion aroused in the *dēmos* over his unconventional way of life. "Later, this very thing not least caused the downfall of the city. For the many, who were afraid of the magnitude of his unconventional way of life regarding his own body and of the magnitude of the plans that he effected on every occasion in whatever situation that he was involved, became his enemies on the belief that he desired to establish a tyranny" (6.15).

Thucydides further points out that Alcibiades conducted the public affairs of the city "best," but repeats that because of his unconventional private habits the *dēmos* turned to others for leadership. "After no long time, this caused the city to blunder" (6.15). It is important to appreciate Thucydides' point here, which is injected just before Alcibiades' speech: Alcibiades conducted the affairs of the city well, which would include the proposal to sail to Sicily. The errors referred to in 2.65 apply not to Alcibiades, but to his opponents.[37]

Where he had a perfect opportunity to establish a moral lesson on the errors of Alcibiades' ambition and the excess of the Sicilian Expedition, Thucydides does not. The reader then must reconsider Thucydides' reconsideration of the Archaeology's thesis and the Athenian defense of empire. Where Thucydides suggested in the first reconsideration that ambition is incompatible with

---

37. Clifford Orwin, "Democracy and Distrust," *American Scholar* 53 (1984): 313–25.

decent political life and contains the causes of its own destruction, he refuses to do so here. Here he acts as if Alcibiades' ambition and the expansion of the empire is sustainable. Thus there is no necessity to the demise of Athens and her empire. Alcibiades failed not because of his policy but because, unlike Pericles, he did not present a public image of virtue, and because of the irrational fear that this inspired in the *dēmos*. The problem of Athens may lie on a deeper level. It is not the abandoning of piety, but in this case at least the retention of piety that caused the suspicion of Alcibiades, his removal from the command, and the downfall of the city.

This irrational fear caused the *dēmos* to remove Alcibiades from the command at the first possible moment. During the preparation to sail, the Hermae were defaced, a sacrilege in the minds of the Athenian *dēmos* (6.27–28). Alcibiades, due to unconventional personal habits, was blamed for this offense. He asked for a trial immediately. If he was found to be unjust, he demanded that the Athenians should put him to death. His mortal enemies were too afraid of a trial with the army still in the city because of its favorable disposition toward Alcibiades. Accordingly, they decide, and Alcibiades agrees, to permit him to sail with the army and to deal with the charges later (6.29).

After the intervention of an exchange of speeches between Hermocrates and the Syracusan demagogue Athenagoras, Thucydides takes up again the account of Alcibiades and the accusations against him. He then includes a strange digression wherein he tells the story of Harmodius and Aristogeiton, and their involvement in the famous Athenian tyrannicide.[38] One would expect here that Thucydides would use this story to accuse Alcibiades of tyranny, and denounce him, and criticize Athens' erotic imperial designs. But he does not.[39] To get a sense of Thucydides'

---

38. Mabel Lang, "The Murder of Hipparchus," *Historia* 3 (1975): 395–407.

39. Robin Seager, "Alcibiades and the Charges of Aiming at Tyranny," *Historia* 16 (1967): 6–18; D. J. Stewart, "Thucydides, Pausanias, and Alcibiades," *Classical Journal* 61 (October 1965).

purpose, one must recall the context within which the story first appears. He begins it in the Archaeology while criticizing the "many" for their lazy search for truth (1.20). In fact, they are so undiscerning that they misunderstand the most famous event in their own history, the Athenian tyrannicide. It was not at all the tyrant, Hippias, but his brother, Hipparchus, who was killed.

This is understandable given Thucydides' own view of the *dēmos*'s nature. Though no doubt some of the Athenians for a time fit their description in the Funeral Oration, not all of them always were, nor did all who were so remain, daring men of action freed from their attachment to the ancestral traditions. At the start of the war, when Pericles orders the second removal from the countryside, Thucydides observes this: "They were distressed and bore it with great difficulty to leave their households and temples that, according to the ancient regime, had always been the places of their ancestral worship and to change, as they were just about to do, their way of life. For each of them it was doing nothing less than leaving his own city" (2.16).

For the most part, the *dēmos* of Athens was made up of traditional, pious Greeks. Thus, Alcibiades' inability to make his virtue apparent to the many causes distress and suspicion of tyranny. This prompts an extreme piety to reemerge precisely at the wrong time for Athens. The problem with "active" Athens here is not so much her imperial ambitions as a contradiction within the city that does not permit her to act properly on them.[40]

Thucydides explores this problem in his treatment of the tyrannicide. Far from denouncing tyranny, Thucydides is quick to point out that the Peisistratid tyrants "in the very greatest degree used virtue and intelligence in their practices" (6.54).[41] The attempted tyrannicide emerged from the misplaced *erōs* of a sordid

---

40. C. A. Powell, "Religion and the Sicilian Expedition," *Historia* 28 (1979): 15–31.

41. Based on this praise, and on the eulogy of Pericles, Hobbes notes ("Life and History," 13–14) that while Thucydides preferred the mixed regime of Theramenes to pure democracy, "he best approved of the regal government."

homosexual lovers' quarrel (6.54–57). Rather, Thucydides criticizes Harmodius and Aristogeiton. He notes that the plot was hatched "because of erotic pain and the irrational daring that occurred to Harmodius and Aristogeiton due to momentary fear" (6.59). The distorted memory of the tyrannicide, Thucydides points out, caused the Athenians to suspect tyrannical conspiracies where they did not exist (6.60). This caused the Athenian *dēmos*, in Alcibiades' case, to believe a fabricated story regarding the mutilation of the Hermae.[42] In an outburst of frenzied piety, they begin arresting and executing anyone implicated by the informants whether or not they had actually done injustice (6.60).

This irrational fear of nonexistent tyranny caused the Athenian *dēmos* always to suspect its best men. Pericles was constantly under suspicion, and moved in and out of office willy-nilly (2.65). It led them to force their best man, Themistocles, into exile based on a flimsy Spartan accusation. One should note that Themistocles is the only character in the whole work praised for his nature, and is perhaps the character the work praises most highly overall (1.138).

What this means in principle is that Athenian ambition did not set in motion some inexorable necessity for Athenian downfall. It may mean that the requirements for decent politics—justice and moderation (or if not moderation, at least a public continence)—are not incompatible with the demands of the conditions of politics, namely empire and ambition to rule. Thucydides seems to be qualifying his reconsideration of the Archaeology's thesis.

CONCLUSION: THE SYNTHESIS OF ATHENIAN DARING AND SPARTAN MODERATION

To shed some light on this final reconsideration, we may begin by returning to Diodotus's speech. While it is true that Diodotus

---

42. Michael Palmer, "Alcibiades and the Question of Tyranny in Thucydides," *Canadian Journal of Political Science* 15 (1982): 103–124.

refuses to appeal to justice and wishes to meet Cleon on the grounds of profit and expediency, one must note several things about this speech. In fact it differs widely from Cleon's argument. In anticipation of Machiavelli, Cleon reduces considerations of justice to those of necessity and expediency (see 3.40–41). Diodotus keeps the justice and expediency separate. Questions of justice and necessity are of different orders, and the Mytilenaean affair is one involving expediency only (3.44). This was the original position of the Athenians at Sparta (1.73) and is consistently maintained by the Athenians at Melos (5.89–90). In the strict sense Athenian imperial politics is never guided by a "might makes right" thesis.

On a deeper level, though, Diodotus returns to justice in the speech. Near the beginning, he contests Cleon's criticism of the Athenian love of speech and deliberation. Cleon counsels that reason should not be the guiding principle of action, but rather anger (3.37–38). Diodotus argues that reason and speech are the only reliable guides for actions (3.42). For him, reason and not passion ought to be the ruling principle in the soul. This is a view of the arrangement of the soul that resembles much more Socrates' view in the *Republic* or Aristotle's in the *Politics* and *Nicomachean Ethics*, wherein rightly arranged soul is the model for justice. Of all the Athenian speakers, Diodotus alone makes a successful case for reason and moderation (3.44).

Diodotus also attacks Cleon's notion that all counselors are driven only by gain (3.42). This causes all speakers to be suspected, and so the common good of the city is undermined (3.43). Diodotus's criticism here amounts to an assault on the idea that considerations of interest and expediency alone are sufficient for the common good of the city and maintenance of the empire. This calls into question his appeal to mere profit and self-interest later. Diodotus is aware of this because he says that any speaker who wishes to do the city good must deceive it (3.43). But Diodotus intends to argue for what "appears to be good for the city" (3.44) and "noble for the future" (3.44). The appeal to interest and expediency is then a deception masking his real intent, an appeal to justice.[43]

Diodotus's speech causes the Athenians to take a more just course of action, in spite of his affectations to the contrary (2.48). In fact, the effect of the speech undermines the appeal to expediency. Diodotus, in creating a common sympathy between the Athenians and Mytilenaeans, points out that human nature is driven by powerful passions which, when set in motion, often cannot be limited. The most powerful of these are the desire for freedom and empire (3.45). The outcome of Diodotus's speech demonstrates that these passions can be contained by reason. Thucydides points out that because of the revolt, the Athenians made up their minds to kill the Mytilenaeans "under the influence of anger" and "were seized by not the least impulse of passion" (3.36). Nevertheless, Diodotus turns the Athenians away from an ill-considered and angry act of violence.

However infrequently they may appear, Thucydides does portray instances of human beings being guided by statesmanship, moderation, justice, and considerations of the common good. One of the most salient of these, though commentators tend generally to ignore him, is Hermocrates.[44]

Immediately after the Athenian victory at Pylus and a dazzling string of successes, Thucydides inserts Hermocrates' speech.[45] The context is the Congress at Gela, where the Sicilians attempt to come to terms with the factional strife engulfing Sicily (4.61). Hermocrates succeeds, in the only example of its kind in the work, to end a *stasis* by appeals to the common good (4.59, 4.61,

43. Among commentators, Clifford Orwin stands alone in recognizing the significance of this point, in "The Just and the Advantageous in Thucydides," 485–94.

44. H. D. Westlake, *Individuals in Thucydides* (Cambridge, Eng.: Cambridge University Press, 1968).

45. An excellent treatment of this speech is in N. G. L. Hammond, "The Particular and the Universal in the Speeches of Thucydides: With Special Reference to That of Hermocrates at Gela," in *The Speeches in Thucydides*, ed. Philip A. Stadter (Chapel Hill: University of North Carolina Press, 1973), 49–59.

4.65) and moderation (4.60, 4.61, 4.64). To be sure, Hermocrates appeals also to the common threat presented by the Athenians, who were present on the island with a small force. But the Athenian threat is still far off: up to the instant that the Athenians sailed into the harbor of Syracuse, important elements in the city doubted the threat from Athens (6.32, 6.35, 6.36–40). In addition to this, Hermocrates ends factional strife within the city of Syracuse by making appeals—without Diodotean deception—to moderation and the common good (6.33–34). Hermocrates also sets the Syracusans in motion from their "habitual rest" by an appeal to "daring" to counter Athenian power and daring. Hermocrates is one of the two figures in the whole work who makes a successful appeal to both daring and moderation, and who manages to combine them in his character.

The other is the brilliant Spartan Brasidas. He is another character who is very important but generally ignored by commentators. He is the only Spartan to be praised for his daring (2.25, 5.7, and 5.10), and the first to receive singular honors. Like Hermocrates, he is the only other character who combines daring and love of honor with restraint and traditional Spartan virtues in his character. He is almost the only Spartan to make a successful appeal to daring (2.87, 5.9). Thucydides never portrays Brasidas's daring in a bad light.

The figures of Brasidas, Hermocrates, and Diodotus, as well as the success of their statesmanship, points to the possibility of a synthesis of the Spartan virtue of restraint, which is the source of her stability, and Athenian daring, the source of her greatness and empire. Though there is no doubt that the daring of empire and moderation of a just city are often in tension, Thucydides does not present them as irrevocably opposed. Thus, Thucydides holds out the possibility that political life is not futile.[46] The problem

---

46. Jacqueline de Romilly, "Fairness and Kindness in Thucydides," *Phoenix* 28 (1974): 95–100, and "L'optimisme de Thucydide," *Revue des Etudes Grecques* 78 (1965): 557–75.

for statesmanship—and Thucydides does not hide the fact that it is a problem—is to reconcile the tension between daring and moderate restraint, between empire and freedom. For however much they are in tension with each other, they cannot exist without each other.

As we noted, Thucydides does not criticize the daring and ambition of either Athens or Alcibiades to undertake the Sicilian Expedition. He makes it clear that if Alcibiades had not been removed, the expedition would have succeeded. It was Alcibiades' enemies who were responsible for the logistical miscalculation that led to disaster. The ambition to rule and daring, which are unavoidably a part of human nature, are dangerous only when they become lawless excess, as in the Corcyraean Sedition. The solution is found in directing and curbing daring and ambition.

The Spartans, along with characters such as Diodotus, Hermocrates, and Brasidas, provide a road map to a solution. As we saw above in the case of Sparta, Spartan restraint may not be strictly speaking moderation. In fact, Thucydides may not believe that moderation in Aristotle's sense is possible at all, if by moderation one means the completely voluntary submission of the passions to rational control.[47] At most, for Thucydides rare and extraordinary individuals can achieve *sōphrosyne*, but regimes certainly cannot. Thucydides shows this by his treatment of the "most distinct" Spartan, Pausanias. Spartan law, or any law for that matter, produces no qualitative improvement in human nature. But Sparta indicates that a kind of public continence is possible. Sparta's slave system, a constitutional invention of prudence by Lycurgus,[48] restrains her from acting on her ambition.

Diodotus's deceptive appeal to interest restrains Athens and results to a humane decision on the fate of Mytilene. Athens'

---

47. Aristotle, *Nicomachean Ethics*, 1099^a 12–30, 1099^b 27–34, 1102^b 13–34, and the whole discussion of the distinction between moderation and continence in book 7.

48. Plutarch, "The Life of Lycurgus," in *The Lives of Noble Grecians and Romans*, trans. John Dryden, revised by Arthur Hugh Clough (New York: Modern Library, 1992), 28.

decision unintentionally amounts to an act of justice. Hermocrates at Gela, slyly appealing to interest and fear, ends *stasis* and produces concord in both Syracuse and Sicily.[49] Human reason and statesmanship, though perhaps not always on the basis of the noblest appeals, can direct political life. What then accounts for Athens' failure? A full answer may never be possible, but let it suffice to observe this much. Thucydides never praises Athens for her good laws as he does Sparta. While Pericles may praise Athens for her good democratic laws and law-abidingness, this is not Thucydides' praise. It was "rule by the first man" (2.65) that accounted for Periclean Athens' greatness and not the democracy. Pericles did not give Athens good laws. When inevitably he was replaced by lesser men, Athens destroyed herself. There was no necessity to this destruction.

The recognition of this tension between justice and restraint, on the one hand, and daring and empire, on the other, is in its own way a sort of solution. But Thucydides goes further and points toward a fuller resolution. As rare as it may be, he never fails to present the high when he can; and by the power of his expression, he never fails to endorse the high. At the same time, he never fails to present the low as base, and so with disapproval. Herein he differs from Machiavelli, who presents the high, with scorn, as derivative from the low, and never fails to endorse the base.[50] Thucydides understands that the endorsement of the high is no guarantee of its permanent political efficacy, but the failure to endorse the high guarantees tragedy. Even amidst the account of "the violent teacher," war, he retains his gentle humanity (7.30). For that, we must be always grateful to Thucydides for his "eternal possession."

49. Clifford Orwin, "Hope, Fear, and the Power of Reason: The Speech of Hermocrates at Gela (Thucydides IV.58–65)," a paper presented at the Midwestern Political Science Association Meeting, April 10, 1992.

50. The differences between Thucydides and Machiavelli are analyzed in Steven Forde, "Varieties of Realism: Thucydides and Machiavelli," *Journal of Politics* 54 (1992): 372–93.

6

POWER AND MORALITY
IN THUCYDIDES

S T E V E N   F O R D E

D ESPITE THE OBVIOUS IM-
portance of the issue, interpreters of Thucydides have never been
able to achieve consensus on what the historian's view of the
moral aspects of politics and war might be. Thucydides is clearly
a "realist" of some kind, meaning that he is to some degree skeptical about the applicability of morality to the political world,
especially the world of international politics. It is the extent of his
realism that is in doubt. Some have maintained that Thucydides'
realism is thoroughgoing, that his only purpose in treating moral
issues is to show how illusory morality is.[1] The more common
interpretation though is that moral excellence, while tenuous, is

---

1. See for example Paul Shorey, "On the Implicit Ethics and Psychology of Thucydides," *Transactions of the American Philological Association* 24 (1893): 66–88.

admired by Thucydides, and that when it is overturned, which is especially likely during war, he regards the loss as deplorable. In this view, which I share, the tension between Thucydides' realism and his admiration for morality gives his work a tragic cast. Morality represents an important human achievement, but one that proves sadly vulnerable to the realist pressures of politics and war.

MORALITY AND THE ORIGINAL CONDITION

The opening section of Thucydides' work, the so-called Archaeology, introduces this theme. Thucydides' portrait of archaic times in Greece shows us a world dominated by insecurity, plunder, and rapine. Nomadic peoples displaced one another without apparently the slightest thought of justice or injustice, even where they were the ones being despoiled.[2] These peoples were weak, due to their primitive and unsettled life, yet their relations among themselves seem to be based only on relative power. Even within the early communities individuals apparently ordered themselves only on the basis of domination and servitude (1.8).

Progress out of this early condition was necessarily slow, but eventually it did take place. Thucydides chronicles two distinct types of progress in the Archaeology. The first, and most conspicuous, is progress in wealth and physical security. The second is progress toward the development of the *polis* as an advanced, and morally superior, form of community. This is ethical or moral progress, while the other is purely material. In the Archaeology, these two types of progress are intertwined in a way that foreshadows the complex relations of realism and morality in the remainder of Thucydides' work. The appearance of the *polis* as Thucydides knows it, a political unit based not on domination and self-interest but on shared ethical community, came rather

2. Thucydides, *The Peloponnesian War*, trans. Charles Forster Smith, Loeb Classical Library, 4 vols. (Cambridge, Mass.: Harvard University Press, 1980), book 1, chapters 2, 5. All subsequent references in this chapter are to this edition and are identified by conventional book and chapter.

late on the account of the Archaeology. The Athenians and the Spartans each contribute to this development, which represents the advent of civilization in the true sense of the word.[3] It is a qualitative rather than simply a quantitative advance over the earlier condition: it is civilization as opposed to barbarism. But it is fatefully dependent on the other type of progress, the quantitative advance in power, stability, and wealth experienced by the Greeks. The material forms of progress are preconditions for the ethical achievement of civilization, but Thucydides' account of their rise emphasizes how amoral the motives were that brought them into being. Minos for example was the first to rid the sea of pirates—but only in order to make his own imperial dominance more secure (1.4). Likewise, Agamemnon brought the cities together in the grand undertaking of the Trojan War. But it was his preeminence in power, Thucydides insists, not the moral commitments alleged by Homer, that allowed Agamemnon to induce the others to follow him (1.9).

The Greeks of Thucydides' day are at a peak of power, and a peak of civilization. But not only is the latter dependent on the former as a precondition, but the Archaeology suggests that power, while making civilization possible, has laws of its own that are at odds with ethical or moral achievement. The laws of power point to a world like early Greece, where power relations are the only currency among men. Thus the self-interestedness of Minos, thus the fact that many early communities were brought together only to plunder others more effectively (1.8). The laws of power point forward as well, to the realist thesis that imperial Athens develops in Thucydides' day, a thesis proclaiming that might always overcomes justice. The tension between the achievement of power and the achievement of civilization, implicit in the Archaeology, makes itself felt throughout the remainder of Thucyd-

3. For this interpretation I rely largely on 1.6, a pregnant passage in which Thucydides describes in very elliptical fashion the features that distinguish Greek civilization from the surrounding barbarism, as well as from its own barbaric past.

ides' book. One of the key themes of this book is the tension between the laws of power, which are realist in nature, and the ethical moral attainments of civilization. One of the tragedies of the Peloponnesian War was its tendency over time to unravel civilization, to plunge the Greeks into a new barbarism of their own making.

VIRTUE UNDER DURESS—PLAGUE AND CIVIL WAR

The ideal of civilized community adumbrated in the Archaeology seems to form the moral compass by which Thucydides judges politics. His moral thinking seems to come closest to what is today called "virtue ethics," rather than morality based on individual rights for example, or divine revelation.[4] The notion is that civilized community, based on moral commitments rather than mere self-interest, is a humanly superior mode of existence, and this is what gives it its normative character. An ethic with this as its foundation provides us with standards for moral behavior, but these standards are necessarily more vague than commands issuing from rights theories or from divine command. Thucydides believes a kind of communal decency is a high human achievement, but the outlines of that decency, and of its contrary, emerge only gradually in his work. The two passages that are generally regarded as most important in this regard are his accounts of the plague in Athens and the civil war in Corcyra. In both instances, civil community was seen to collapse under more or less extreme outside pressures. Thucydides uses these episodes to explore the vulnerabilities of moral community, and to show us by contrast what traits make such a community admirable while it persists.

In the case of the plague, the terror of a death which struck the good and the bad alike proved "beyond human capacity" to endure (2.50). Under the pressure of this disease, men lost sight

---

4. Discussion of moral theory centered on virtue was revived for this generation by Alisdair MacIntyre. See his *After Virtue: A Study in Moral Theory* (Notre Dame, Ind.: University of Notre Dame Press, 1984).

of any goal beyond the individual good of the moment. "What is called honor" was submerged in favor of momentary pleasure (2.53). This hedonism was restrained by neither human nor divine law, when their rewards and punishments lost their allure or their terror. A general lawlessness was the result, foreshadowing the failure of moral community that was later the cause of Athens losing the war (2.53, 2.65). Lawlessness was also the result of the civil strife in Corcyra. Here it was not individual misery but fanatical factionalism that destroyed civil relations among men. A "war of all against all" would probably have been less horrifying than the war of factions that was actually seen at Corcyra. Thucydides emphasizes the way that words of moral valuation were turned completely on their heads in the course of the strife, as men came to hold victory over their enemies, by hook or by crook, to be the only good (3.82). In fact, triumph by savage or duplicitous means actually came to be preferred over "honorable" combat. Accordingly, savagery and duplicity took on the names of the now-despised traditional virtues.

This corruption of language is emphasized by Thucydides as an important part of the horror of the civil war. It signals a form of barbarism that was in fact worse than anything existing in primitive times. The peoples of the Archaeology took piracy and spoliation to be simply another way of life, one they did not even think to condemn (cf. 1.2, 1.5). This demonstrates their barbarism as much as any other fact about them. But the civil war at Corcyra reveals that civilization paradoxically opens up the possibility of a kind of barbarism more virulent than anything seen before it.[5] In the first place, the very existence of civil community provides a platform for factional strife that would not exist without it. But more importantly, it seems that the moral valuations created by civilization make that strife more savage than anything seen

5. Compare Diodotus's assertion at 3.45 that punishments have actually become more severe with the advance of time. The early ages may have been gentler because justice, with its punishments and its reprisals, was less known or less felt.

among early peoples. When it became a point of "honor" to exact the most bloodthirsty revenges, even the desire for self-preservation was powerless to moderate the carnage (3.82). The simple, one might almost say naive, selfishness of a Minos or an Agamemnon could never have been this brutal.

The combined spectacle of plague and civil war casts the darkest of shadows over civil life. Of course the pressures of war and disease are extraordinary hardships, but if they are capable of destroying civilized life or turning it into its opposite, what faith can we have that civilization is more than an illusion or a pretense? It does not help that Thucydides treats these deformations unambiguously as expressions of human nature. The horrors seen at Corcyra, he insists, will be seen again and again so long as human nature is the same (3.82). Greed, love of power, and ambition drove events at Corcyra, and these are ineradicable. On the other hand, the very inversion that the civilized qualities suffer in these circumstances reminds us that it is their nature to be otherwise. Thucydides' description of their denaturing seems intended to inspire horror, making his very account of the barbarism a statement of sorts as to what these moral categories should look like when undisturbed.[6] Near the conclusion of his account of the civil war, Thucydides describes the general outlook most characteristic of nobility. The noble turn of mind, he says, involves a simple, ingenuous, or even naive outlook (τὸ εὖηθες, 3.83; cf. 3.82). Nobility takes a straightforward and somehow artless attitude toward society, an attitude innocent of at least the kinds of "sophistication" seen in the civil wars.

Thucydides' remark reminds us of the criticism leveled against the Spartans before the war, when the Corinthians told them that

---

6. Lowell Edmunds takes this approach, exploring in some detail the moral orientation implied by Thucydides' blame of civil war: see "Thucydides' Ethics as Reflected in the Description of Stasis (3.82–83)," *Harvard Studies in Classical Philology* 79 (1975): 73–92. An excellent discussion of this part of Thucydides' presentation may be found in Clifford Orwin, *The Humanity of Thucydides* (Princeton: Princeton University Press, 1994), 172–82.

their attitude of trust toward one another made them too unwilling to believe that others might be less worthy of trust (1.68).[7] In the Corinthian view, this trust is responsible for the fundamental decency of the Spartan regime internally but puts the city at a distinct disadvantage in the realist environment of international politics. The same point seems to be echoed by Thucydides' brief eulogy of Nicias, that he of all the Greeks least deserved his miserable end, since he had devoted his whole life to the cultivation of law-bred virtue (7.86). The qualifier "law-bred" (or even "conventional": νενομισμένην) casts an unmistakable shadow over this eulogy, but perhaps the unsophistication it points to is inseparable from nobility as practiced in politics. Unfortunately, the failure of Nicias to gain the end his virtue promised him, the incompetence of the Spartans in international affairs, and the destruction of simple nobility in the civil wars, all point to the great vulnerability of basic decency in the face of the realist aspects of the human condition. In the Corcyraean civil war, it was enough apparently that noble simplicity become an object of general derision for it to disappear without a trace (καταγελασθὲν ἠφανίσθη, 3.83). This kind of nobility is very sensitive to social context, and very vulnerable to certain kinds of pressures. These pressures, sadly, are all too common in the human condition, and they unleash parts of human nature that are capable of destroying civilization, it seems, utterly. Thucydides' accounts of the destruction of civilized decency in these circumstances show that he finds the truth of the realist view undeniable. But it is not for him the whole truth.

HUMANITY AND POWER IN WARTIME

We can pull back from the brink of barbarism as seen in the plague and civil war to find a more sanguine view of human

---

7. Edmunds ("Thucydides' Ethics") argues that Thucydides' catalog of civil war vices points to a fundamentally Spartan moral outlook.

affairs in Thucydides. This view is not blind to the realist truths seen most vividly in those darker moments, but finds room for civilization or decency in other kinds of circumstances.

Most readers of Thucydides are aware that one of the ways he conveys his lessons is by juxtaposing historical episodes. Thus Pericles' Funeral Oration and the plague are set jarringly close together (2.35–46, 2.47–54), as are the affairs of Thasos and Ithome in book 1 (1.101, 1.102), and many others. In book 3 Thucydides makes his account of the fall of Plataea to the Spartans and the fall of Mytilene to Athens such a diptych (and the account of the Corcyraean civil war follows them immediately). There are two debates, one at which Athens decides the fate of Mytilene (3.36–50), and a second at which Spartan judges decide the fate of Plataea (3.52–68). The story of the second can be told briefly. The Spartans ask the defeated Plataeans whether they have aided the Spartans and their allies in any way during this war (3.52), planning to kill any who say they have not. Since this is nothing less than a death sentence for them all, the Plataeans beg leave to speak at length. They do so, and attempt desperately to persuade the Spartans of their virtue. The Thebans then give a counter-speech. Finally, the Spartan judges proceed with their original question, and put all the Plataeans to death. Thucydides tells us that their primary motive in doing so was to placate the Thebans, traditional enemies of Plataea (3.68). Despite all the moral argumentation delivered in the debate, the Spartans decide the matter on the basis of power politics and self-interest. Thebes' importance to the Spartan alliance outweighs all else.

The Mytilenean Debate at Athens is an episode that has received much more attention from interpreters, for good reason. It pits Cleon and Diodotus in a far-ranging discussion of political and ethical issues, centered around the question of whether the Mytileneans, revolted subjects of Athens, should all be punished—all the men killed and the women and children sold into slavery. Though the Athenians had decided to take this step the previous day, they feel remorseful about decreeing punishment for innocent and guilty alike, and a second debate takes place on the issue (3.36).

Cleon, a "violent" and influential demagogue (3.36), favors the original decision, disfavors any reconsideration, and comes close to disfavoring all democratic debate. He makes the same reproach to the Athenians that the Corinthians had made to the Spartans, that their trusting ways render them incompetent to run a viable foreign policy, at least an imperial foreign policy (3.37). He cites the very remorse they are now feeling over Mytilene. In Cleon's view, political realities have put Athens in a situation where mercy and compassion are luxuries that the city cannot afford. From this he generates the sweeping principle that pity, love of eloquence in debate, and "decency" (ἐπιεικείᾳ) are all incompatible with rule, pure and simple (3.40). The Athenians can practice virtue or philanthropy (ἀνδραγαθίζεσθαι, 3.40) if they like, but not if they wish also to rule over an empire. The two cannot go together.

The last point reflects Cleon's brutality to be sure, but we must also recognize that his argument is not groundless—or unprecedented. Pericles, whose rhetoric Cleon apes in so many ways, made virtually the same point in his final speech in Thucydides (2.60–64). That speech, delivered in the midst of the plague, reflected a much more sober or chastened outlook than the Funeral Oration delivered before it. Pericles admitted there for the first time that the empire was at least "like" a tyranny (2.63; Cleon removes all nuance by simply declaring the empire a tyranny, 3.37). But he still maintained that it was something splendid to hold on to. He roundly chastised any who would give up this empire in order to give up its burdens, saying the politically apathetic and those who would play the virtuous man (ἀνδραγαθίζεσθαι) would destroy the empire if they got the upper hand. His conclusion was even more sweeping than Cleon's: such men would endanger the security of any city they inhabited, not only an imperial city, unless that city was already a subject state (2.63). The "virtue" Pericles criticizes, the type of virtue that creates second thoughts about empire, is in his view an enemy to all security, all freedom, indeed all political action. His argument seems to anticipate the view of writers like Hans Morgenthau and Reinhold Niebuhr in the twentieth century, that political action as such involves one in evil.[8] Cleon claims to be simply applying this insight to the case of the Mytileneans.

When Diodotus rises to speak in opposition, therefore, his task is not an easy one. The way he goes about it moreover reflects more agreement with Cleon than meets the eye. This agreement is seen not so much in Diodotus's realist premise that justice should be disregarded in the deliberations over Mytilene (3.44), since he violates that premise in his speech. He has been forced by Cleon to proclaim the realist premise, but toward the end of his speech, after the groundwork has been properly laid, Diodotus appeals forthrightly to the Athenians' sense of justice: they will be punishing the innocent along with the guilty if they kill all the men and sell into slavery the women and children (3.47). This is exactly the sentiment that led the Athenians to reconsider the Mytilenean case a second day (3.36), and Diodotus plays upon it deftly. But the body of his speech raises questions of its own about the place of justice in politics, especially international politics.

The Athenians' remorse over their initial condemnation of Mytilene is perhaps the most striking manifestation of a moral sentiment having actual political impact in Thucydides.[9] It is rein-

8. Hans J. Morgenthau, *Scientific Man vs. Power Politics* (Chicago: University of Chicago Press, 1974), and *Politics among Nations*, 5th ed. (New York: Alfred A. Knopf, 1978), 6–15; Reinhold Niebuhr, *Moral Man and Immoral Society* (New York: Charles Scribner's Sons, 1960).

9. Many moral sentiments are expressed by speakers in Thucydides, but their effect, as with the speech of the Plataeans, is ambiguous at best. There are some moral sentiments that have a negative effect, such as the sanctimoniousness of the Spartans at Plataea or of Cleon on this occasion. These moralisms only confirm the respective decisions to carry out a slaughter. For a fine discussion of the Diodotus's speech, bringing out the interplay of justice and realism in it, see Orwin, *Humanity of Thucydides*, ch. 7.

forced by the touching spectacle of the Athenian ship sent out to remand the slaughter, making haste while the first ship dallied owing to its horrid mission (3.49). Yet it is striking that Diodotus, who is fully aware of this change of heart in Athens, evidently believes he can appeal to it only surreptitiously. Why does he not proclaim openly from the beginning of his speech that the Athenians should follow justice and spare most of the Mytileneans? Part of the answer is that Cleon has framed the terms of the debate, but why should Cleon have been able to submerge the natural impulse to pity so completely? A fuller answer is found in the key middle section of Diodotus's speech itself. Here, he maintains that the death penalty has always been powerless to stop wrongdoing, for men and cities both are by nature prone to transgress (3.45). No law, no punishment, no power of restraint has ever been found effective against this tendency. The reason, Diodotus says, is that human nature is prey to lawless impulses that cannot be brooked. These he identifies as hope (ἐλπίς) and desire (ἔρως). Desire—erotic desire—leads the way, and hope promises success. The fickle nature of fortune serves only to inflame prodigal hope.

Thus, Diodotus tells the Athenians, subjects will inevitably rebel as the Mytileneans rebelled, whenever hope seems to promise them success. Attributing the Mytileneans' action to compulsion lays the groundwork for Diodotus's later appeal to justice, for it shows that they are guiltless. There are two other consequences of this argument though. First, it shows that the Athenians in their imperialism are as guiltless as the Mytileneans in their revolt; second, it shows that all the Mytileneans are guiltless, the ringleaders as well as the followers—perhaps more than the followers—though Diodotus only advocates saving the followers (3.48). These two are not unrelated. Diodotus explicitly says that cities are most prey to the compulsions he speaks of because they contend for the greatest things, freedom for themselves or empire over others (3.45). If the first exonerates the Mytileneans, the second exonerates the Athenians. Diodotus does not emphasize the latter—he wants to get the Athenians to indulge the Mytileneans, not themselves—but the fact remains that he shows Athenian imperial policy to be itself a product of compulsion. This explains why Diodotus does not even attempt to argue the Athenians out of their imperialism pure and simple. The most that can be hoped for is a somewhat gentler Athenian approach to empire, which is what Diodotus advocates (3.46). Pity, and concern for justice, can carry the day in this instance, but it would be too much to expect their consistent application to policy, given the compulsion to dominate that Athens, and all powerful cities, feel. Even in this instance, Diodotus is obliged to sacrifice the "more guilty" of the guiltless Mytileneans to Athenian imperial self-interest. This is where he comes closest to Cleon in fact, though his motive and his understanding are entirely different.

The Athenians have maintained since before the war that their imperialism is guiltless because the product of certain human compulsions (1.75, 1.76). Diodotus corroborates this argument, but casts it in a much darker light. The Athenians, in the beginning at least, believed honor to be one of their compulsions, and hence believed the empire to be an honorable and glorious enterprise. Diodotus focuses instead on the irrational and self-destructive character of the compulsions that rule men and cities. Hope and desire, he says, lead men irresistibly into dangerous and destructive courses (3.45). When they assert themselves, they overcome even prudent or rational self-interest. Then, even reason in the mouth of a Diodotean statesman will not be enough to overcome them. It is thus natural that Diodotus should appear at this moment, on a successful mission of mercy, but never again. The political circumstances surrounding the Mytilenean debate, including Athenian remorse, create a window of opportunity for his action. But he cannot parlay this remorse into a permanent or fundamental change of Athenian policy, and the other circumstances are evanescent. Neither Diodotus apparently, nor anyone else, could prevail upon the Athenians to show mercy on a famous, later occasion when they voted to slaughter the Melians.

The Mytilenean episode represents a peak of humanity in the midst of war, a peak of which the Athenians alone would seem to be capable, since it depends upon their sophisticated understanding of human compulsions, as well as their moral sense. Yet it may be an isolated incident. They show themselves perfectly capable of acting barbarically on other occasions, under the influence of self-interest and other compulsions. The Spartan behavior at Plataea is repugnant next to the Athenian clemency toward Mytilene, juxtaposed by Thucydides; but it, rather than clemency, would seem to be the ordinary thing in war. Thucydides' account of the Plataean episode is clearly orchestrated to make us sympathetic toward the Plataeans, and arouse repugnance for the Spartans. But there is only one passage where Thucydides overtly laments the destruction of a place (7.30), and Plataea is not it. As tragic as the fate of Plataea is, it is also simply the way of the world. Plataea's fate was sealed the moment war broke out. Gentleness of the sort the Athenians display toward Mytilene is admirable, but can rarely be expected.

AMBITION AND HONOR

The Greek word for ambition, φιλοτιμία, literally means "love of honor." And indeed, ambition is supposed to be wedded to virtue, virtue being the only means of gaining true honor. As all observers of human events have noticed, however, this link can easily fail. We recall that ambition was one of the key motives that triggered the horrors of civil war in Corcyra and elsewhere (3.82). In Thucydides, the problem of ambition and honor can be explored at two levels, the level of individual statesmen and the level of cities. Athens is a city with definite ambitions, and those ambitions, according to the Athenians at least, are driven in part by thirst for honor. The Athenian argument at Sparta before the war is that the city was driven by fear, honor, and self-interest to take up its empire (1.75, 1.76). Thucydides' presentation of Athenian imperialism, at least at the beginning of the war, seems to support the notion that there is a genuine love of honor in it. When Pericles exhorts the Athenians in his Funeral Oration to support the city out of love of glory, he is describing a genuine experience that the Athenians seem to have had about the politics of their city (2.42, 2.43).[10]

The element of honor in Athenian imperial ambition is an important theme in Thucydides. Thucydides is interested especially in the question whether honor and empire are compatible. The two are combined at the outset, but if that combination is untenable, it will deteriorate over time, under the pressure of the reality of imperial rule. This is precisely what happens over the course of the war. In Pericles' Funeral Oration itself, which has to be regarded as a peak of the synthesis of honor and empire, there are discordant notes. Pericles rarely speaks of "honor" (τιμή) per se in the speech, though he speaks a great deal of nobility and ignobility (καλόν, αἰσχρόν). Yet when speaking of the tie that should bind the Athenians most of all to their city, that should make them willing to die for it, he exhorts them to contemplate the *power* of the city, and fall in love with it (2.43). At this climactic moment, he appeals not to nobility or virtue, but to erotic desire inspired by power. The amoral thrust of this is only compounded when he adduces as proof of the city's power the magnitude of evil as well as of good that it has done: in a remarkable boast, he proclaims that Athens has left "immortal monuments of evil and good, everywhere."[11] Yet he insists that the service of this city is noble.

The tension between these things is too great to be sustained for long. In Pericles' final speech, under the chastening influence of the plague, the soaring vision of Athens seen in the Funeral Oration is deflated in almost every respect. Pericles' bid to com-

10. See also Leo Strauss, *The City and Man* (Chicago: University of Chicago Press, 1977), 210; cf. 225–26.

11. Most translators, incredulous at the brazen character of this remark, gloss it as "good done to friends and evil to enemies." The original however is as stated.

bine nobility and imperialism seems to suffer disproportionately. This is where he concedes that the Athenian empire is at least like a tyranny (2.63). Accordingly, he, like Cleon, emphasizes the danger involved in giving it up. He continues to insist that maintaining it is also a glorious thing (2.63, 2.64); this glory however is now even further removed from moral worth. It now seems more natural to speak of the city's "splendor" or its "greatness" rather than its moral worth, as Pericles begins to do here (though without completely abandoning the language of honor and nobility). And what makes the city great is its toughness, its resolution, its willingness to sacrifice for the sake of expanding and maintaining its (quasi-tyrannical) empire. It is in this spirit that Pericles claims that citizens who insist on playing the virtuous man (ἀνδραγαθίζεσθαι) are destructive of all political greatness (2.63).

The transition between these two speeches of Pericles is illuminating because it indicates how the tension between honor and imperial ambition must assert itself ever more insistently with time. Pericles strives to keep the two together, but the pressure of events drives them increasingly apart. It seems that he is the last Athenian who even attempts to do so. We have seen how Cleon disdains the very attempt: the empire is a tyranny *tout court*, which must be maintained without regard to justice (3.40). The Athenian generals at Melos bring this understanding of empire to its culmination by explicitly renouncing all claims of worthiness for their rule, even the tenuous sorts of worth that earlier Athenian apologists of empire alleged (5.89). For them, empire is based on nothing but fear and self-interest, compulsions under which gods as well as human beings labor (5.105). The one gesture they make in the direction of an argument from honor is to suggest that it is foolish for a weak city like Melos to seek honor (5.111). This might imply that great cities like Athens can contend for honor with equals, but this is like limiting justice to equals (5.89). Under these conditions justice, and honor, become mere pawns of brute force.

STEVEN FORDE

What makes the Athenians' position on Melos notorious is not that they say anything wholly new about their empire; it is rather that they have abandoned the pretense of honor, or of any kind of moral worthiness, as part of their title to rule. Where they proclaimed their dedication to honor in the beginning, the Athenians now make no attempt to do so. They could easily have proclaimed this motivation as part of their rationale for adding Melos to the empire. Instead, they are openly tyrannical, claiming to rule by force alone, and saying they attack Melos only out of fear for their own security (5.91, 5.95, 5.97, 5.99). The Athenians have here made considerable progress, to say the least, in the direction of barbarism. Yet in retrospect, this progress demonstrates that Athenian imperialism degenerated because it had to degenerate. The Athenians were genuinely motivated by honor in the beginning, and their self-understanding struggled valiantly for two generations perhaps to keep honor and imperialism together. But the effort was doomed, for the simple fact is that imperialism is not honorable. It is not honorable because it is inescapably a form of tyranny, and will eventually reveal itself as such. Rule based on mere force necessarily becomes ever more brutal with time and with the resistance of one's subjects, and such rule eventually takes a toll on the rulers themselves. Athenian imperialism threatens to turn Athens from a supremely civilized community into an outpost of barbarism. It is a tragedy of human ambition that it may begin as love of honor, but turn to barbarism in the very act of grasping for its prize. Yet this misguided love of honor comes all too naturally to men.

The incipient "barbarization" of Athens can be seen not only in the development of its imperial policy. The moral basis of Athenian community was also undermined from within. Thucydides tells us as early as his eulogy of Pericles (2.65) that Athens lost the Peloponnesian War only because she defeated herself. Over time, he says, individual ambition at Athens divorced itself from the public good. This degeneration can doubtless be attributed to many causes, but among them has to be the imperialism of the city as a whole. From the beginning, imperial policy was based frankly on the proposition that the strong rule the weak, by virtue of their strength alone. The attempt to conjoin this with honor, or with some elevated sort of "worthiness," failed in the end. And all the while, Athenian imperialism was having a corrosive effect on the moral community of the city itself. The principle that the strong rule the weak regardless of justice, proclaimed as the official basis of the city's foreign policy for a generation and more, eventually began to assert itself in the domestic arena as well. For why should not the strongest, the cleverest, the most ambitious individuals within the city then conclude that they may rule over their fellows on the basis of strength alone? At a minimum, they will conclude that they may be excused for pursuing their individual self-interest, just as the city excused its own pursuit of empire, on the grounds of "compulsion." The resulting failure of public morality was unfortunate in two ways. It not only led to Athens' defeat in the war, but represented a loosening of the communal bond that was the key characteristic of civilized life as it emerged out of barbarism. The Archaeology showed that civilization was predicated on a discovery of, and moral dedication to, the common good. Athenian realism ultimately threatened the demise of that achievement within the city.

The demise of Athens thus understood makes a fine morality tale. But as always with Thucydides, the story is somewhat more complicated. To begin with, there is the fact that Thucydides acknowledges the truth that lies in the realist Athenian argument about power and rule. That this truth is corrosive to civilization is unfortunate, but does not detract from its truth. It may not apply to domestic politics, or not in the same way, but it is clear that for Thucydides, the simply moral or patriotic understanding of political leadership is not adequate either. Pericles is the benchmark for the ordinary patriotic understanding, as the leader who selflessly dedicated himself to the welfare of the community, submerging his own interest when it conflicted with the public good. In his final speech, Pericles outlines the criteria for good leadership, as he believes he has fulfilled them: the leader must be able to determine the correct policy, and to explain his determination; he is a lover of the city, and superior to the influence of money (2.60). A good leader, he explains, needs all four qualities; the lack of any single one will vitiate his title and his ability to lead.

The qualities Pericles identifies are in fact the key to his own success in Athens. Indeed, these four virtues were so conspicuous in him that the Athenians trusted him implicitly. It is essential in a democracy precisely that these virtues be conspicuous, and Pericles made a superhuman effort to leave no doubt as to his possession of them. Plutarch says that, during the decades of his political career, Pericles essentially had no private life, by design. He virtually renounced friendship, in an effort to avoid even the slightest appearance of favoritism. Thus did he attain unchallenged preeminence. Yet it seems unreasonable to expect such self-abnegation of leaders, and unjustified to hope that many would be willing to practice it. It would be understandable on these grounds alone why none of Pericles' successors attained to the position he did. From this point of view, we would have to say that the Periclean period in Athens was the exception, that what came after him is the rather more typical situation, in democracies at least. This message is conveyed in a muted but distinct way in Thucydides' eulogy of Pericles, where the failure of Pericles' successors is decried (2.65). It is indicated there that the failure of leadership after Pericles was not only due to a moral decay in Athens, but in part was a reversion to the norm.

Thus, one of the problems with the would-be leaders after Pericles is that they were more equal among themselves, so that none could rise above the political fray the way Pericles did.[12] They had to compete for position, which led them to cater to popular appetites—hardly an unusual situation in democratic pol-

---

12. Of course, even Pericles was able to do this only in the latter parts of his career, a fact that Thucydides does not point out.

itics. Other problems with Pericles' understanding of leadership become visible if we look at examples of superior leaders in Athens, both before and after him. Themistocles was a towering political talent, whose genius was instrumental to the Greek defeat of the Persians. It was also he who first set Athens on the course to power and preeminence. In a eulogy devoted to him, Thucydides praises Themistocles more highly than he does anyone else in the work for native talents and ability (1.138). As far as natural endowments go, it appears that Themistocles was superior to Pericles. Yet, with regard to the four qualities of leadership that Pericles recited, Thucydides says only that Themistocles was superior at determining the best course of action, and at expounding it to others. These are the two qualities most related to natural talent. The other two named by Pericles were primarily moral in character, involving dedication to the public over the private good, and Thucydides is conspicuously silent about these in his eulogy of Themistocles. Themistocles was not a wicked leader, and he did not turn against Athens, if he ever did turn against the city, until he was attacked without justification (1.135). Still, he did finish his career in the court of the Persian king, whom he apparently promised to help against the Greeks (1.138; cf. Plutarch's *Lives*). At a minimum, the case of Themistocles shows that natural talent—the ability to foresee events, the ability to devise policies to meet them, and the ability to persuade others to undertake these courses of action—is not naturally paired with the patriotic virtues that Pericles added to them.

Alcibiades is an even clearer case of the divorce of natural talent from selfless or patriotic virtue. Thucydides indicates that Alcibiades' natural strategic talent was very great, and that only Alcibiades could have brought the audacious Sicilian Expedition to a successful conclusion. Thucydides even suggests that Alcibiades' departure was responsible for the overall demise of Athens (6.15). Yet not only does Alcibiades fail to reassure the Athenians concerning the moral qualities Pericles put at the center of leadership, he consciously and conspicuously refuses to do so. Alcibiades would have been perfectly happy to remain in Athens, expand the Athenian empire, and occupy a position like that which Pericles had occupied. But he refused to make the sacrifices Pericles did in order to attain that position, and in fact flaunted his private extravagances and his sense of his own superiority. The Athenians accordingly suspected him of aspiring to tyranny, and ultimately exiled him and condemned him to death (6.61). Once in exile however, Alcibiades shows in more spectacular fashion than anyone else how far natural talent can divorce itself from patriotic attachments—and how successful it can be in the process. Alcibiades serves the Spartans, the Persians, and the Athenians again before Thucydides' work draws to a close, and it seems that whatever side he moves to begins to prosper. At Sparta, he claims paradoxically that he remains all the while an Athenian patriot; but his patriotism, he claims, is conditional on being treated with sufficient respect by the city (6.92).

This is not what is ordinarily understood by patriotism, to put it mildly. It reflects a resolute refusal to subordinate private to public interest, precisely the kind of failing that Thucydides identified as the cause of Athens' eventual defeat. Yet to repeat, Thucydides suggests that Alcibiades was Athens' only hope, not her destruction. Alcibiades' case, particularly in tandem with Themistocles', raises interesting questions. In neither case is justice exclusively on the city's side. The Athenians prove eager to condemn both before they have heard any evidence (6.53, 6.61; cf. 1.135). In the case of Alcibiades, we know that his behavior arouses suspicion and animosity, but the Athenians condemn him without making any serious effort to confirm the allegations against him. Indeed, Thucydides' account of the events suggests more a witch-hunt in Athens than anything else (cf. 6.27, 6.60). In light of these facts, Alcibiades' opponents seem to fit more into the pattern of degeneracy foreseen in the eulogy of Pericles than does Alcibiades himself (cf. 6.28, 6.29).

The difference between Alcibiades and his opponents is simply that his talents, his ambitions, and his conception, are expansive enough that he can literally embrace the city's interest within his own—so long as the city cooperates. But his type of leadership inevitably provokes backlash. Ultimately, it is not compatible with the Athenian political community, or perhaps any political community, and is doomed to failure. In its context, Alcibiades' failure seems to put the leadership of his archrival Nicias in a better light. Nicias, we recall, was the man of law-bred or conventional virtue, a type of virtue that is the direct opposite of Alcibiades' unrestrained talent. We also recall that this kind of virtue was vulnerable and naive—but that it was somehow indispensable to the continuance of political nobility. It was most unfortunate for the Athenians that they had gotten themselves into a situation by the time of the Sicilian Expedition in which the conventional leadership of a Nicias was no longer adequate. Yet this is precisely what happened. Conventional leadership and its type of nobility seem to thrive only within a limited range, where their exposure to realist pressures like international conflict or civil war is contained. The human condition does anything but guarantee this limited exposure. It would certainly be possible, however, to insulate society from these pressures better than the daring and expansive Athenians have done. In quasi-Machiavellian fashion, they have reveled in the realism of international politics, they have conformed themselves to it and it has proved their undoing.[13] Political moderation, of a type the Athenians forsook, would seem to be the only solution to this problem. But what, according to Thucydides, are the prospects of attaining it?

CONCLUSION: PRUDENCE AND POLICY

What gives Thucydides' outlook its tragic cast is precisely the conflict between simple nobility, which is a key part of the ethical basis on which civilization distinguishes itself from barbarism, and

13. The similarities and differences between Thucydides and Machiavelli are a very interesting subject in themselves. My interpretation of them is developed more fully in "Varieties of Realism: Thucydides and Machiavelli," *Journal of Politics* 54 (1992): 372–93.

the harsh, realist truths of the political world. For Thucydides, the civilized achievement is worth preserving simply because it is a superior way of life for human beings. It is a more fully human or humane existence, but it also seems to be a rare achievement. The Greeks developed such a way of life only over the course of centuries. Then they engaged in a war that threatened this achievement, and indeed submerged it completely in some times and places. One aspect of this tragedy is that it reveals that the two strains of progress experienced by the Greeks over those centuries—progress in power and progress in civilization—are interdependent, yet at odds with one another. Civilization, as we learn from the Archaeology, is dependent on accumulated wealth, stability, and communal power. Yet power, both in its accumulation and in its exercise, has laws of its own. And these are realist in character.

For Thucydides, there is no perfect or permanent way to resolve this tension. We might wish for a combination of Spartan restraint and Athenian realism; but the first step toward Athenian realism, which is so effective in mastering the world of international politics, seems to be a repudiation of that restraint. We might then turn toward the Spartan solution pure and simple; but the Spartans are both dangerously vulnerable in foreign affairs, and hypocritical when forced to act in realist fashion despite their moral pretensions. Their behavior at Plataea is a case in point. Athens, particularly during the Periclean period, represented precisely an attempt to square this circle, and the enduring appeal of the Periclean period is that it held together empire and honor, power and at least a measure of nobility. But the subsequent history of Athens reveals that those things were incompatible over the long term.

What then should a statesman do who has been persuaded by the Thucydidean analysis of human events? He will first of all have a sense of the fragility of his community, of how it is threatened in particular by the realist exercise of power. In Athens' case, perhaps it was necessary to become powerful, given the circumstances after the Persian Wars, but a Thucydidean statesman would be extremely apprehensive about this development. Once the city became powerful, he would certainly be guided more by the insights of Diodotus than of Pericles. Pericles was a great supporter of the empire who tried to follow a relatively measured policy. But he did not understand the tension between those two things. A more prudent statesman would know the dangers of power and make a more concerted effort to forestall them. Things like traditional virtue and piety are among the most important restraints on the excesses of state behavior, and as such they would be very important to any Thucydidean prescription regarding politics. However, in their full-blown form virtue and piety lead simply to the Spartan solution, with the shortcomings just mentioned. And once a city like Athens has forsaken them they are extremely difficult, if not impossible, to reconstruct. Even when in place, they are not entirely reliable as restraints. A statesman informed by Diodotus's vision would know that the temptations of power cannot always be resisted, if the temptations are strong enough, that neither virtue nor piety nor even the long-term rational interest of the city will be of avail. He will be guided by the knowledge that the excesses of power are barbarizing as well as self-destructive, but he will also be conscious that the laws of power and the power of irrationality is great enough in politics that disasters of the type that struck the Greeks cannot always be avoided.

7

THUCYDIDES AND PLURALISM

LOWELL S. GUSTAFSON

ONE OF THE ATTRIBUTES
which Thucydides considers necessary for sustained greatness is
the acceptance of pluralism. Thucydides is not a realist who advocates unchecked self-interest and the struggle for domination. He
is not prescribing politics as an arena in which self-interested
actors struggle for domination. To the contrary, Thucydides is
observing that when politics does become characterized by unchecked self-interest and the struggle for unlimited power, behavior and thought deteriorate. To maintain or restore a polity,
he contends that pluralism must be valued.

Why should individuals check their desire to impose unity
under their own control? It may be that Thucydides does not
believe that the human desire to rule can be restrained by devotion to the ancestral or by piety.[1] It may be that individuals' desire

---

1. [Jack Riley addresses this issue in chapter 5. *Ed.*]

to rule and their acceptance of pluralism may result from the accurate calculation of their own and others' power. Pluralism, not domination, is the logical end of power politics, since power is always distributed to some degree.

Pluralism is the acceptance by political actors of the need for freedom of individuals, various groups in society, cities, and nations. Actors are most rational when they desire their own freedom and accept that of others because they have accurately calculated distributed power. Excessive love of personal power, feelings of vengeance, greed, excessive ambition, wishful thinking, a loss of a sense of limits, or other factors often cause irrational estimates of relative power in one's own favor. Irrational thought or inaccurate calculation lead to overreaching one's capacity, which can cause one's own destruction as well as that of an entire political system.

Rational calculations of power are not precise and certain, but reasonably accurate, based as they are on wisdom and prudence. In this vein, judgment is crucially important for Thucydides.[2] This is so because not everything can be calculated. Chance and fortune place limits on rational calculation. Not everything can be known and factored into calculations; hence, not everything can be predicted and controlled. We cannot have unchecked intellectual or political power.

Morality and religion serve society well when they are based on a sense of limits. Religion comes in part from the sense that there are forces beyond humanity's control which influence our destiny and conditions. Morality comes from a concern for how persons or groups treat each other. Ultimately, this concern comes from the enforceable demand by others that they be treated in a way that does not harm them. When morality is based on a denial of the realities of power, it can be as destructive as an unbridled power lust. When religion becomes the attempt to

2. [Laurie M. Johnson Bagby discusses the role of judgment in Thucydides in chapter 2. *Ed.*]

know the unknowable, to predict chance and fortune, it too leads to irrational and destructive behavior.

THUCYDIDES AS A REALIST

Thucydides has often been said to be the founder of realism.[3] Hans Morgenthau, in *Politics among Nations*, argues that "realism assumes that its key concept of interest defined as power is an objective category which is universally valid." To develop this view, he quotes Thucydides' observation that "identity of interests is the surest bonds whether between states or individuals." Power, Morgenthau writes, "may comprise anything that establishes and maintains the control of man over man."[4] Morgenthau also quotes the Athenian argument made in the Melian Dialogue that "of the gods we know and of men we believe, that it is a necessary law of their nature that they rule wherever they can."[5] The accurate quote from Thucydides (5.105) and common views hold that of gods we believe and of people we know rather than the interesting and misquoted reverse made by Morgenthau. Nevertheless, Morgenthau's purpose here is to help demonstrate that "the tendency to dominate, in particular, is an element of all human associations, from the family through fraternal and profes-

3. For example, see David A. Baldwin, ed., *Neorealism and Neoliberalism: The Contemporary Debate* (New York: Columbia University Press, 1993), 11; Barry B. Hughes, *Continuity and Change in World Politics: The Clash of Perspectives* (Englewood Cliffs, N.J.: Prentice Hall, 1991), 56; Richard W. Mansbach and John A. Vasquez, *In Search of Theory: A New Paradigm for Global Politics* (New York: Columbia University Press, 1981), xiii; Joel H. Rosenthal, *Righteous Realists: Political Realism, Responsible Power, and American Culture in the Nuclear Age* (Baton Rouge: Louisiana State University Press, 1991), 1.

4. Hans J. Morgenthau, *Politics among Nations: The Struggle for Power and Peace*, 5th ed., revised (New York: Alfred A. Knopf, 1978), 8, 9.

5. Thucydides, *History of the Peloponnesian War*, trans. Rex Warner (New York: Penguin Books, 1972), book 5, chapter 105. All subsequent references in this chapter are to this edition and are by conventional book and chapter. The passage cited here is also quoted in Morgenthau, *Politics among Nations*, 38.

sional associations and local political organizations, to the state."[6] Morgenthau, the proponent of realism, the national interest, and domination, claims Thucydides as one of his own.

Morgenthau was not the first to argue that Thucydides was primarily concerned with power. Werner Jaeger wrote in 1939 that "Thucydides . . . thinks only of power." Many since Morgenthau have also discussed his view of Thucydides and realism. Robert Keohane accepts Morgenthau's interpretation of Thucydides. Thucydides and Morgenthau "both assume that states will act to protect their power positions, perhaps even to the point of seeking to maximize their power." Another author writes that "Thucydides' History as a whole corroborates the Athenian argument concerning justice and power in international politics. The Athenians' assertion that the strong universally dominate the weak is supported by examples from the most ancient period (1:1–18) to contemporary communities such as Syracuse (4:61, 64; 6:33) and even the Spartans themselves." Mansbach and Vazquez write that "weak states that stand in the path of the strong tend to be swept aside or confronted with demands for capitulation, such as those made to the island of Melos by the Athenians as recorded by Thucydides." In the section on realism in his collected-readings book about international relations, Vazquez includes only the Melian Dialogue from *The Peloponnesian War*, presumably because the Athenian position expressed in that dialogue is the essence of Thucydides' teaching. Baldwin notes that "E. H. Carr, another realist, . . . echoes Thucydides' Melian dialogue: 'The majority rules because it is stronger, the minority submits because it is weaker.' " When Mansbach and Ferguson refer to Thucydides, they mention only the Melian Dialogue. Donelan does the same. When Mansbach and Vazquez mention something other than the Melian Dialogue, it is about Cleon,

---

6. Hans J. Morgenthau and Kenneth W. Thompson, *Politics among Nations: The Struggle for Power and Peace*, 6th ed. (New York: Alfred E. Knopf, 1985), 37.

who wanted all the rebel Mytilenians put to death. In all of this, Thucydides is often said to argue for the amoral nature of interstate relations, the quest for power by each state, each state's primary focus on security, interstate relations as anarchy out of which order can be established only through domination, human behavior as rational, the motivations in interstate relations as constant across time, culture and place, and the city-state or largest political unit as the basic unit of analysis and action. As Gregory Crane argues, "The compulsive and unbounded quest for power and profit that Solon had described at the opening of the sixth century and of Athenian recorded history becomes in Thucydides, almost two centuries later, a unifying force that drives the weak and the mighty alike." A critic of realism assumes that it is "the eternal return of the ghost of Thucydides."[7]

This often repeated reading of Thucydides comes from equating Thucydides' own position with that expressed by the Athenians throughout much of the book, but most famously in the Melian Dialogue. It is in that dialogue where the Athenians make their famous claim that the strong do what they have the power to do and the weak accept what they must (5.89). Some distin-

---

7. Werner Jaeger, *Paideia: The Ideals of Greek Culture,* trans. Gilbert Highet (New York: Oxford University Press, 1939), 383; Robert O. Keohane, ed., *Neorealism and World Politics* (New York: Columbia University Press, 1986), 7, 164; Steven Forde, "Classical Realism," in *Traditions of International Ethics,* ed. Terry Nardin and David R. Mapel (Cambridge: Cambridge Studies in International Relations, 1992), 72; Mansbach and Vazquez, *In Search of Theory,* 318; John A. Vasquez, ed., *Classics of International Relations,* 2nd ed. (Englewood Cliffs, N.J.: Prentice Hall, 1990), 16–20; David A. Baldwin, ed., *Neorealism and Neoliberalism: The Contemporary Debate* (New York: Columbia University Press, 1993), 159; Richard W. Mansbach and Yale H. Ferguson, "Values and Paradigm Change: The Elusive Quest for International Relations Theory," in *Persistent Patterns and Emergent Structures in a Waning Century,* ed. Margaret P. Karnes (New York: Praeger Special Studies, 1986), 14; Michael Donelan, *Elements of International Political Theory* (Oxford: Clarendon Press, 1990), 27; Mansbach and Vazquez, *In Search of Theory,* 111; Gregory Crane, *Thucydides and the Ancient Simplicity: The Limits of Political Realism* (Berkeley: University of California Press, 1998), 297; James Der Derian, "A Reinterpretation of Realism," in *International Theory,* ed. J. D. Derian (New York: Macmillan, 1995), 382.

guished scholars have contended that Thucydides uses the Athenian spokemen as his own mouthpiece. For example, Jaeger wrote that an "Athenian ambassador's speech on the historical necessity which compelled Athens to develop her power is a justification of that power, on the grand scale of which Thucydides alone is capable. They are Thucydides' own ideas."[8]

A PROCESS OF DIALOGUE AND EVENTS

The Athenians are not Thucydides' mouthpiece, with everyone else acting as foils. No one city's representatives are mouthpieces for Thucydides. The process of dialogue, debate, negotiations, alternating between speech and action, and even fighting reveals Thucydides' advocacy of pluralism. Thucydides' history is an account of the debates between groups within cities and representatives from different cities, of the allied congress at Sparta, the Mytilenian Debate, negotiations with Argos, the Melian Dialogue, the debate at Syracuse, the debate at Camarina, and so on. IIis focus on debate and negotiations shows his view of human condition as one of frequent and ongoing communication. Political reality is plural, not single, Thucydides observes, and to be rational, anyone must be aware of this. When this communication is successful, it brings about the accurate calculation of power and interests. Because of various factors, discussed later, it is very often unsuccessful, which has tragic consequences.

There are debates throughout the book, but there is also a constant interplay between speech and action. The book is not a monologue by Athenians, nor is it merely a parliamentary or diplomatic record. After sections of speeches and debates, there are sections of minutely described battles and military campaigns, revolts, and a plague. It is the dialogue between people on the one hand, and the interaction between communication and action on the other, that fascinates Thucydides.

8. Jaeger, *Paideia*, 393.

There is constant communication between people and constant interplay between communication and action. Reason is not reified; rationality is not external to history. He is a historian, not a philosopher. He seeks to report events factually and impartially. However, to do so, he has made it a "principle not to write down the first story that comes my way" (1.22). A principle is necessary for an accurate understanding of events. The father of history is no passive describer of facts. If communication between people is to be successful, it must rationally arrive at an understanding of the logic between speech and action. Negotiations and debates must incorporate the results of the battles. At the same time, there is war or peace as a result of certain debates and speeches. And finally, a historian must comment, discuss, and analyze as well as describe.

It is the description and commentary of the process of communication and the interplay between speech and action, not any one speaker or event, that expresses the views of Thucydides. This is a book of over six hundred pages, not the eight or so that are so often reprinted in various anthologies. Because of this, one cannot read only a couple of debates, or only one set of speakers, and claim Thucydides is advocating that position. Instead, it is necessary to consider the entire book. When this is done, Thucydides can be read as advocating pluralism.

PLURALISM AND FREEDOM

The father of political history observes that pluralism has characterized Peloponnesian politics at many levels: ethnic, party, city, and national. Thucydides begins his account of the Peloponnese with an observation of ethnic pluralism in the Archaeology. In ancient times, there had been a series of tribal migrations (1.2). Attica was unique in that it was inhabited by only one race of people (1.3). In most of Hellas, there usually was tribal or racial pluralism. There were also many cities in the peninsula, many of which were racially pluralist.

The first joint action of these cities appears to have been the expedition against Troy. Thucydides, ever the non-romantic, says this joint action was not organized because Helen's pursuers were bound by oath, but because of Agamemnon, the most powerful ruler of Hellas in his time. Many cities of the time were fortified bases for seafaring pirates, who found no dishonor in their profession. The distinction between commerce and plunder was not always clear. Still, while Agamemnon was powerful enough to organize an expedition against Troy, he did not rule a Hellenic empire. There were no alliances of small states under the leadership of great cities. There were many independent and semi-independent tribes and cities in Hellas, which often fought among themselves in local wars. Even if one concedes the point that Greece made material progress only after Sparta and Athens began to build their empires, there was even then at the least more than one empire and no total unity.

The first threat to the independence of the Hellenic cities as a group came from King Cyrus and the Persians. The Persians came with a vast armada to conquer Hellas. "It was by a common effort that the foreign invasion was repelled" (1.18). The discussion about the Persians shows that Hellas is but one country in a world of many countries.

Thucydides then discusses the unrest in Epidamnus caused by the struggles between the established people and foreign inhabitants of the city, as well as between the democratic and oligarchic parties. The presence of these two parties in many cities in Hellas is frequently noted by Thucydides. Epidamnus is but the first city which is said to begin with tribal and political pluralism, but then suffer when one party attempts to exclude the other from sharing power. The immediate cause of the Peloponnesian War is found in the democratic party driving out the oligarchic one in Epidamnus. This action led to the creation of political unity where pluralism had been the status quo. The excluded party goes to other cities asking for their support. This initiates a complex series of events, due to the increasingly tense relations among Hellenic cities. The bid for unity in Epidamnus was so serious because it took place after Athens had been increasing its power, leading Sparta and other cities to fear that Athens planned to bring unity to Hellas. In this and other stories of the rudimentary two-party system of his time, Thucydides shows that he "prefers a mixture of oligarchy and democracy to either of the pure forms."[9]

There is pluralism at different levels. There are many tribes and often two political parties within the cities of Hellas. There are many cities within Hellas. Some are completely independent; some are semi-independent; some are dependent. Hellas is but one political entity, sharing a common language and culture, within a world of other larger entities, such as Persia, which could loosely be called nations. Pluralism is the status quo. A city at rest de facto accepts this status quo. It would be only an ambitious, innovative, restless city seeking empire that would be trying to replace pluralism with unity under its direction.

The principal value of pluralism is freedom. The freedom of individuals, tribes, parties, cities, and nations is the primary value in Thucydides' writing. By definition, pluralism can be maintained only if each entity maintains its freedom and that no one entity gains complete power over all of the others. As Pericles says in the Funeral Oration, "happiness depends on being free" (2.43). With freedom, there can be unfettered debate and discussion in which the greatest possible number of individuals realize rationality and community.

A principal fear is the fear of losing freedom and of becoming a slave. Feeling this fear, it is necessary to be courageous enough to fight to maintain one's own freedom and that of others. Fear of losing their freedom to Persia was the Athenians' chief motive for fighting that foreign state fifty years before the Peloponnesian War (1.75). At this point, Athens is acting honorably and rationally. After that war, which united Hellenic cities against losing their freedom to Persia, Athens changed from leading a fight

9. Leo Strauss, *The City and Man* (Chicago: Rand McNally, 1964), 238.

against foreign domination to building its own empire and becoming a threat to the freedom of other Hellenic cities. The fear of losing Hellas's freedom to Persian domination changes to fears within Hellas about Athenian domination.

The cause of the Peloponnesian War is found in the basic change of purpose, in the corruption, of Athens in the period just after the war against Persia. The Corinthians warn the Spartans that "Athens has deprived some states of their freedom and is scheming to do the same thing for others, especially among our allies, and that she herself has for a long time been preparing for the eventuality of war" (1.68). The Mytilenians said that "so long as the Athenians in their leadership respected our independence, we followed them with enthusiasm. But when we saw that they were becoming less and less antagonistic to Persia and more and more interested in enslaving their own allies, then we became frightened" (3.10). Pagondas, one of the two Boeotian commanders from Thebes, told his fellow Boeotians that "in all relations with one's neighbors, freedom is the result of being able to hold one's own, and as for these neighbors, who, not content with those close to them, are trying to spread their domination far and wide, with them we must simply fight it out to the last." He continues that "the Athenians are the most dangerous of all people to have living next door to one." He concludes that "we make it a point of honor always to fight for the freedom of our country and never unjustly to enslave the country of others, and from us they will not get away without having to fight for it" (4.91, 4.92). Thucydides' own analysis was that "what made war inevitable was the growth of Athenian power and the fear which this caused in Sparta" (1.23). Athens had been a leader of Hellenic states when they all feared that Persia's power would enslave Hellas; now the growth of Athenian power caused fear in much of Hellas's cities that their freedom was threatened.

UNLIMITED POWER

The use of power for the sake of maintaining one's own freedom and, if possible, that of others is laudable and rational. The use of power in the unlimited search for domination over others ultimately leads to self-destruction because the goal is unattainable. Too many others, all of whom have at least some power, value their freedom enough to resist enslavement. The search for unlimited domination caused fear in Hellas and the destruction of Athens. After one Athenian victory, Sparta thought Athens would be willing to make peace. "The Athenians, however, aimed at winning still more" (4.21). This was the crux of the problem with Athens; the Athenians always aimed at winning still more. Even the Athenian who told the Spartans that Athens had not gained its empire by force also said that considerations of right and wrong had "never yet turned people aside from the opportunities of aggrandizement offered by superior strength. . . . It has always been a rule that the weak should be subject to the strong" (1.76).

The loss of a sense of limits is related to a love of unlimited power for its own sake. An example of this is the civil war in Corcyra, during which politics became wholly perverted. Some Corcyraeans accused others of conspiring to overthrow democracy, when their real motive in killing the others was personal hatred or unpaid debt. "There was death in every shape and form. And, as usually happens in such situations, people went to every extreme and beyond it" (3.81). The process became "savage"; what had been called aggression was now called courage. "Any idea of moderation was just an attempt to disguise one's unmanly character. . . . Revenge became more important than self-preservation. . . . Love of power, operating through greed and through personal ambition, was the cause of all these evils" (3.82). Unlimited love of power and greed, the unlimited love of wealth, had caused Corcyraeans to devalue the most basic of needs: self-preservation.

The classic statement of the love of power unlimited by morality is made by the Athenians in the Melian Dialogue. The Melians ask what the Athenians' subjects believe to be fair play. In a case of what may be projection, the Athenians respond that, "So far as right and wrong are concerned they think that there is no difference between the two" (5.97). The Melians place great emphasis on justice. When they lose the fight, the Athenians "put to death all the men of military age whom they took, and sold the women and children as slaves. Melos itself they took over for themselves" (5.116).

CALCULATING POWER

Careful and accurate calculation is essential in order to maintain freedom in a world where power is so important. The failure to calculate relative power carefully can occur because of excessive love of power, anger, wishful thinking, unrealistic hope, haste, hatred, overconfidence, or other reasons. It is exemplified by both the Melians and the Athenians, leading to the destruction of them both. The Melians hardly take relative power into account at all. They see fairness as an independent and superior category, not as intimately related to calculating relative power. The Athenians are no less guilty; while they love power, they do not carefully calculate their relative power. They demonstrate this both in the chapter before and after the Melian Dialogue. In book 4, Thucydides notes of their allies what might also have been said of the Athenians: their "judgement was based more on wishful thinking than on a sound calculation of probabilities; for the usual thing among men is that when they want something they will, without any reflection, leave that to hope, while they will employ the full use of reason in rejecting what they find unpalatable" (4.108). The "pleasurable excitement of the moment" made them "undertake all kinds of risks."

It is often thought that because the Melians are utterly destroyed, Thucydides is saying that their concern for justice in international affairs is shown to be a dangerous chimera and that the Athenians' single-minded concern for power is vindicated. Reading the very next section on launching the Sicilian Expedition shows something quite different. In the paragraph immediately after the Melian Dialogue, Thucydides writes that in the same winter that they defeated Melos, the Athenians decided to sail against Sicily to conquer it. "They were for the most part ignorant of the size of the island and of the numbers of its inhabitants, both Hellenic and native, and they did not realize that they were taking on a war of almost the same magnitude as their war against the Peloponnesians." The Athenians unlimited love of power, fueled by their victory over Melos, led them to violate the crucially important rule of carefully calculating their own relative power.

One of the Athenian generals, Nicias, argues that the goal of conquering all of Sicily was a mistake. He says that the decision is being made hastily, that the undertaking will be very difficult, and that a second war is being initiated when many enemies are still being left behind. He says that "this is no time for running risks or for grasping at a new empire before we have secured the one we have already" (6.10). He continues that even if the many Sicilians could be conquered, they could not be controlled. He reminds his fellow Athenians that "success comes from foresight and not much is ever gained simply by wishing for it" (6.13).

Nicias is ignored; the Athenians prefer the advice of Alcibiades, who, Thucydides chooses to tell us, hoped to command the forces in Sicily and Carthage. This would bring him wealth and honor, Alcibiades hoped. Thucydides tells us that Alcibiades showed "enthusiasm for horse-breeding and other extravagances [that] went beyond what his fortune could supply. This, in fact, later on had much to do with the downfall of the city of Athens" (6.15). His private life, spirit, and habits showed "lawlessness." Alcibiades makes no analysis of Athens' power relative to that of Sicily. He tells the Athenians that he is worthy to lead the expedition against Sicily because he entered seven chariots at the Olympic Games and took first, second, and fourth place. One can almost see Thucydides throwing up his hands in despair when this seems to persuade the Athenians.[10]

---

10. [As Jack Riley argues in chapter 5, it was not Alcibiades' ambition, nor even the cities' imperial expansion, that made inevitable the disaster, but the failure to calculate what was needed for the campaign. *Ed.*]

Nicias again warns his fellow Athenians about the Sicilians' numbers of hoplites, javelin throwers, triremes, and horses, and about their economic and agricultural resources, too. Hoping to dissuade them from deciding to do so, he says that if Athens chooses to go to war against Sicily, they will have to make extensive preparations. They miss Nicias's point and get excited about the preparations: "The Athenians, however, far from losing their appetite for the voyage because of the difficulties in preparing for it, became more enthusiastic about it than ever, and just the opposite of what Nicias had imagined took place. His advice was regarded as excellent, and it was now thought that the expedition was an absolutely safe thing. There was a passion for the enterprise which affected everyone alike" (6.24). The expedition Athens sent out was the "most costly and the finest-looking force of Hellenic troops that up to that time had ever come from a single city." Athenians were "full of hope" and "thinking of the conquests that might be made" (6.30, 6.31). Although Nicias had opposed the expedition, once his city decided to conduct it, he loyally served his city as well as he could. The invasion started off well, but ultimately failed. Nicias was killed. Thucydides says that "of all the Hellenes in my time, [he] least deserved to come to so miserable an end, since the whole of his life had been devoted to the study and the practice of virtue" (7.86). Thucydides concludes that "this was the greatest Hellenic action that took place during this war, and, in my opinion, the greatest action that we know of in Hellenic history—to the victors the most brilliant of successes, to the vanquished the most calamitous of defeats; for they were utterly and entirely defeated; their sufferings were on an enormous scale; their losses were, as they say, total; army, navy, everything was destroyed, and, out of many, only a few returned. So ended the events in Sicily" (7.87). The Melian Dialogue leads to the events in Sicily. The Melian Dialogue finds its culmination not in the Athenian destruction of Melos, but in the Sicilian destruction of the Athenian forces. The love of power unchecked by careful calculation led to the most calamitous defeat of the greatest of expeditions.

PRUDENT CALCULATIONS

Thucydides' call for careful calculations is not one for calculations that are necessarily precise or certain. Thucydides is calling for grounded wisdom rather than mathematically derived prediction of political events. After the Mytilenians' unsuccessful revolt against Athens, the mother city decided to react harshly. Diodotus supports a second debate to reconsider Athenian policy. He disagrees with Cleon, who, Thucydides tells us, had a violent character. Cleon said it was a bad thing to have frequent discussions on matters of importance. Diodotus responds that "haste and anger are, to my mind, the two greatest obstacles to wise counsel—haste, that usually goes with folly, anger, that is the mark of primitive and narrow minds" (3.42). Athens is still virtuous enough to reconsider its decision and follow Diodotus's more considered advice.

The Melians argue not only for fair play in their debate with the Athenians. They also make the point that arguments that fall short of mathematical accuracy should be accepted (5.90). This is a sensible position. The problem is that the Athenians consider only power and the Melians only fairness. Neither wisely considers all the major factors necessary to consider—and both pay a high price for their failure to do so.

FORTUNE

Careful and prudent calculation is necessary for a free people to remain so. However, there is no comprehensive and perfect calculation that accounts for everything. There is always an element of the unknown and unknowable that bedevils the best calculation. To believe that one can account for everything is as foolish as believing that one can have unlimited power in any respect. Careful calculation is guided by wisdom, which checks a love of knowledge with an appreciation of chance and fortune. Early in the book, in the Spartan debate about whether to aid Corinth in its fight against Athens, the Athenian representative wisely states, "Take time, then, over your decision, which is an important one. . . . Think, too, of the great part that is played by the unpredictable in war; think of it now, before you are actually committee to war. The longer a war lasts, the more things tend to depend on accidents. Neither you nor we can see into them: we have to abide their outcome in the dark" (1.78).

The Athenian representative was right. Brasidas, a Spartan general, in book 4 explained to the Acanthians why Sparta had come late to that city: "It is because the war at home has taken an unexpected course" (4.85). The Athenian representative was wrong only in that he directed his comment to the Spartans rather than to his own countrymen. Athens too suffered because of the unpredictable. When it invaded Syracuse, the campaign started off well enough for Athens. However, events changed when Syracuse enjoyed "an unexpected piece of good fortune" (7.46). These and other examples show Thucydides' emphasis on chance, fortune, and the unpredictable in the development of events in the Peloponnesian War.

FREEDOM AND WAR

To prevent falling under the complete power of others, or to maintain freedom, it is necessary to calculate one's power relative to that of others, and consider the role of fortune in future events. If others are acting or speaking in a way that may lead them to enslave one, it may be necessary to fight. In book 1, the Corinthians tell the Spartans that

> they should not shrink from the prospect of choosing war instead of peace. Wise men certainly choose a quiet life, so long as they are not being attacked; but brave men, when an attack is made on them, will reject peace and go to war, though they will be perfectly ready to come to terms in the course of the war. In fact

they will neither become over-confident because of their successes in war, nor, because of the charms and blessings of peace,
will they put up with acts of aggression. He who thinks of his
own pleasure and shrinks from fighting is very likely, because of
his own irresolution, to lose those very delights which caused his
hesitation; while he who goes too far because of a success in war
fails to realize that the confidence in which he goes forward is a
hollow thing. (1.120)

In the hierarchy of goods, freedom trumps peace.

Similarly, Pericles says in book 2 that, "If one has a free choice
and can live undisturbed, it is sheer folly to go to war. But suppose the choice was forced upon one—submission and immediate slavery or danger with the hope of survival; then I prefer the
man who stands up to danger rather than one who runs away
from it" (2.61). The decision to go to war is made correctly only
when it is forced by the threats of others, because, as a Sicilian
speaker said, "war is an evil . . . , and it would be pointless to go
on cataloguing all the disadvantages involved in it" (4.59). We
have already noted the many harmful effects that prolonged war
had on Corcyra. In spite of the danger that war itself can harm a
polity, it is considered necessary by Thucydides to fight if freedom and pluralism are endangered by a drive to power by an
imperial city. However, war for the sake of gaining unlimited
power leads to utter destruction.

COLLAPSE AND PLURALIST REDEMPTION?

Following the destruction of the Athenian forces in Sicily, Athens' fortunes first turn from bad to worse. Athens had once
helped lead the Peloponnesus to defend its freedom against Persia.
It then had built an empire. It then sought to control the entire
Peloponnesus and beyond. Each step parallels the deterioration of
Athens' polity. A democratic city in a pluralist city-state system
had sought first to establish an integrated, centralized system. It
then became a centralized city itself. In its domestic and inter-

city relations, it rejected pluralism. This led to its utter defeat in Sicily. It then led to instability in its own government.

Following the Sicilian defeat, "the whole of Hellas . . . turned against Athens" (8.2). All of its subjects were ready to revolt. The Persians again prepared to intervene in Hellenic affairs. Alcibiades, who had betrayed Athens and fled to Sparta, conspired with the most powerful class of Athenians, who had lost the most in the war, to carry out an oligarchic coup in Athens. Democracy was destroyed and oligarchy emplaced over Athens' remaining subjects. Few dared to oppose this, and for anyone who did, "some appropriate way was found for having him killed. . . . The people kept quiet, and were in such a state of terror that they thought themselves lucky enough to be left unmolested even if they had said nothing at all" (8.66). However, democrats from the Athenian subject city of Samos conspired to restore democracy in Athens. A period of confusion and panic ensued.

> To make matters worse, Athenian forces then lost a battle in Euboea.
>
> When the news of what had happened in Euboea came to Athens, it caused the very greatest panic that had ever been known there. Not the disaster in Sicily, though it had seemed great enough at the time, nor any other had ever had so terrifying an effect. And indeed there was every reason for despondency: the army at Samos was in revolt; they had no more ships, and no more crews for ships; there was civil disturbance among themselves, and no one could tell when it might come to actual fighting. (8.96)

Athenian fortunes had never been so low. The great imperial city had virtually no armed forces left. Its domestic polity was in shambles. It had been dealt the full blow of its bid for unchecked power.

There was no place to go but up. The Five Thousand democrats deposed the Four Hundred oligarchs. A constitution was drawn up and "the Athenians appear to have had a better government than ever before, at least in my time. There was a reasonable and moderate blending of the few and the many, and it was this, in the first place, that made it possible for the city to recover from the bad state into which her affairs had fallen" (8.97). This is a crucially important point. Athens had restored a pluralist government at home, with a role for both the few and the many. The event which immediately led to the Peloponnesian War was the civil war in Epidamnus, in which one party excluded the other from sharing power. The event at the end of the book is the restoration of plural government in Athens. Immediately after this, there is an account of the Athenian victory at Cynossema. This success is in stark contrast to the failure immediately following the Melian Dialogue. The book ends at this point.

MORALITY AND RELIGION

Leo Strauss argues that Thucydides may be making a silent teaching about natural or divine law. That the plague follows Pericles' speech, which mentions nothing about the gods, and that the Sicilian disaster follows the Melian Dialogue, to Strauss showed that there are heavy costs in violating the divine law. Jaeger, on the other hand, wrote that "it is absolutely wrong to imagine that he thought the Sicilian disaster was God's punishment for Athenian aggrandisement, for he was very far from believing that power is a bad thing in itself."[11]

Strauss also discusses the role of the good in Thucydides. Strauss notes that Thucydides speaks of three causes of the war: the Spartans' fear of growing Athenian power, the breach of the treaty, and the pollution contracted at the time of Cylon. Thucydides, Strauss continues, "does not speak there with equal emphasis of a fourth cause or justification which would seem to be the most noble: the liberation of the Greek cities from Athens' tyranny. This cause is based on the premise that, as of right, every

11. Strauss, *The City and Man*, 153; Jaeger, *Paideia*, 401.

city is independent or is an equal member of the whole compris-
ing all Greek cities, regardless of whether it is large or small,
strong or weak, rich or poor. Accordingly there is a good common to all Greek cities which should limit the ambitions of
each."[12]

Strauss is right: Thucydides does not speak of a common good
that should limit ambition. Thucydides does not start by asking
cities to be good; he begins by asking them to use their intelligence to calculate as accurately as possible the relative power of
all cities, and not to overreach their own power. The large,
strong, and rich cities need to remember that even the partially
free small, weak, and poor cities have some power and the desire
to maintain what freedom they possess.

However, Thucydides also shows respect for virtue, justice,
and religion; not when they are used to ignore or dominate reality, but when they indicate a sense that the self is limited by things
beyond itself. Could Thucydides be like Diodotus, who argues
in terms of interest that his (corrupted) audience can understand
so that he can encourage the practice of virtue?[13]

CONCLUSION

The point of *The Peloponnesian War* is not that the strong do what
they will and the weak suffer what they must. It is not merely
a description about power politics and self-interest. While the
Athenians say and do much to this effect, they are not Thucydides' mouthpieces. Thucydides uses the constant dialogue and debate among many individuals and groups, and the interplay
between discussion and events, as a technique that furthers his
substantive point: power is always limited. Because power is always limited and because others always have a degree of power,
pluralism is the natural condition.

12. Strauss, *The City and Man*, 238–39.

13. [Craig Waggaman and Nick Pappas analyze Thucydides' views of virtue in part
IV. *Ed.*]

Wise people in a city accept this limitation in their ideas and actions. They accept that fortune and religion is beyond their control, and hence knowledge is always imperfect. They know they cannot control all people. They value their own preservation and freedom, calculate their own relative power, and fight if necessary to prevent enslavement. If they fail to realize this limitation and search for domination and centralization of power under their leadership, they are doomed to failure. If they restore their original appreciation of limitation, they can regain their balance and reestablish a pluralist polity, in accordance with an accurate understanding of power politics and perhaps even virtue.

PART IV

ETHICS OF INTERNATIONAL RELATIONS

8

THE PROBLEM OF PERICLES

CRAIG WAGGAMAN

THE QUESTION OF WHAT defines national greatness is central to the study of international relations. The relationship between the goodness of a regime and the sorts of human beings that are produced by it is a central concern of political philosophy. Unfortunately, too often these two questions are considered in isolation from one another, with the result that ideas about goodness rarely enter into discussions about greatness. For many theorists and ordinary citizens, the necessities of power in an anarchical international system dictate a foreign policy that concerns itself with power rather than justice. The city surely has a right to survival, and relatively good cities especially have the right to protect and defend themselves in the sometimes hostile environment of international relations. What is often ignored, however, is the impact that the pursuit of wealth and power in foreign affairs has on the character of the regime itself. This ignorance should not be surprising among those who already believe that all politics is nothing but the struggle for power and wealth. But many thoughtful people who think the study of the regime is about much more than that appear too easily to accept the realists' view of foreign affairs.

We are all familiar with the contention that Thucydides is a teacher of political realism.[1] What political realism exactly consists of is the subject of yet another debate. Critics of political realism point to its Hobbesian qualities—the elevation of the passions (or one master passion) and the reduction of reason to passion's servant. This crude realism worships power, assumes that politics is about domination, and either advocates an aggressive, imperialist foreign policy or steps back and cynically predicts that history will always repeat itself.

A more refined version of realism focuses on the benefits of a political science that understands the role of passion and uses that understanding to create and sustain order and prosperity. This refined realism can be found in Machiavelli and in one of the founding fathers of modern realism, Hans Morgenthau.[2] The defenders of this second version of realism point to the need to be "realistic" in recognizing the role that power plays in political life and call on statesmen to prudently use power to create a stable and prosperous political order. Some writers focus on the need to do this primarily at the level of the national political community, leaving international politics to the mercy of anarchy and the balance of power. Others, including Morgenthau himself, suggest that realism points to some sort of world order which brings the benefits of the "modern project"[3] to as many people as possible.

1. [I discuss this point in chapter 7. *Ed.*]

2. See especially Hans J. Morgenthau, *Politics among Nations: The Struggle for Power and Peace*, 5th ed., revised (New York: Alfred E. Knopf, 1978). Morgenthau is often associated with a post-war realism that emphasizes national power and national interests. Yet Morgenthau concludes in this major work that only a world government founded on a world-wide culture will be able to solve the dangers posed by a nuclear world.

3. The modern project (a term borrowed from Leo Strauss) describes a political science, beginning with Machiavelli and including the philosophers of modern liberalism,

Interestingly, much of both the left and the right falls into this same category of refined realism. The right argues the need for U.S. leadership to build and sustain a New World Order, while the left prefers a broader vision of world order that moves more power and responsibility into the hands of such public international organizations as the United Nations. Realists on the moderate right trust the United States and existing economic and political elites to sustain the modern project, while the moderate left wants more emphasis put on bringing the benefits of modernity to the have-nots.

It is the contention of this essay that the refined realists have dominated the debate about foreign policy, differing only in the variations of the modern project that they propose. The willingness of the neoconservatives to embrace the "world order" politics of the Persian Gulf War and the Mexican bailout reflects an embrace of the idea that politics is about peace and prosperity simply. Neoconservatives tend to look out for the stability of a "core" world economy and are willing to wait for the rest of the world to catch up with us, provided they don't threaten that core in the meantime. In an article called "Defining Our National Interest," Irving Kristol sounded the theme of post–Cold War neoconservatives: a strange mixture of sadness at the decline of Western civilization coupled with an aggressive willingness to use American power to realize the "national interest."[4] But it seems that the national interest now is intimately tied to an "international interest" that emphasizes stability and prosperity, and that the power of the United States (the only remaining superpower)

which attempts to solve the problem of order by the creation of regimes which provide freedom to the majority to satisfy as many of their appetites as possible. For a more detailed discussion of this "enlightenment project" and the Socratic response to it, see Allan Bloom's interpretive essay in Plato, *The Republic*, trans. Allan Bloom (New York: Basic Books, 1968), 368–69.

4. Irving Kristol, "Defining Our National Interest," *National Interest* 21 (fall 1990): 16–25. Also see Charles Krauthammer's argument in his essay "Universal Dominion: Towards a Unipolar World," *National Interest* 21 (winter 1989–90).

needs to be put at the service of this less than grand task—the only one left to us now that the noble struggle of the Cold War is ended. If Irving Kristol were merely another realist, his words would not be worth noting. Yet he concludes his essay by admitting that he fears that America increasingly has "nothing higher" to offer the world and he is saddened by a popular culture which is "so recklessly subversive of the traditional ethos on which this democracy was founded and for so long sustained." What Kristol refuses to consider is the possibility that it is the very definition of an expansive national interest that reflects and fuels our cultural decline. Does he really believe that we will be saved by our power and our wealth once we have lost our virtue?

Some intellectuals within the neoconservative movement have frequently used classical political philosophy to remind us of the flaws of modern liberal states. On the other hand, many of these writers have also been the fiercest defenders of the American regime. During the Cold War, this defense made a lot of sense. To criticize liberal democracies at the very moment when they were threatened by gnostic totalitarian movements would have been extremely irresponsible. Now that the Cold War has ended, however, this defense of the American empire rings hollow. I can understand it when my freshman students come in with no other definition of the greatness of a nation than its wealth and power. But when Irving Kristol joins with them in arguing that being anything other than "Number One" is unacceptable to Americans, one cannot but wonder if the neoconservatives have become anything but cheerleaders for the modern project and the empire required to sustain it.

Machiavelli argues that a prudent prince must always take people as he finds them. Alcibiades echoes this sentiment, saying that "the safest rule of life is to take one's character and institutions for better and for worse, and to live up to them as closely as one can."[5]

5. Thucydides, *The Peloponnesian War*, trans. Richard Crawley, revised and updated by T. E. Wick (New York: Modern Library, 1982). All subsequent references in this chapter are to this edition and are by conventional book and chapter.

The question is whether a democracy which tries to satisfy the passions of its citizens ultimately will corrupt itself and bring to the fore leaders who take the corrupted state as a normal one and "live up to" it as closely as they can. Under these conditions, wealth and power are no longer by-products of national greatness, they are its only measure. As Irving Kristol said, Americans will not be satisfied with anything but being number one. Pericles might have said the same thing about his fellow Athenians. But where did this logic lead the Athenians? To their cynical justification of the massacre at Melos by recourse to the most vulgar political realism. As the material fate of the United States becomes more and more connected with that of the rest of the world, we might ask ourselves a question as we reflect on *The Peloponnesian War*. What would we be willing to do to maintain our wealth and power and what sort of language would we use to justify our actions?

THUCYDIDES AND PERICLES

The Peloponnesian War remains a wonderful text from which to learn international relations precisely because it is so enigmatic. The usual interpretations of Thucydidean "teaching" about politics lie somewhere between the loose categories of vulgar and refined realism outlined earlier in this essay. More recently there has been a movement away from viewing Thucydides as a vulgar realist, someone who believed that a constant human nature formed the foundation of politics as merely a struggle for power, the historical debris of which can be seen in the rise and fall of cities, nations, and empires. Instead, Thucydides is portrayed as someone who understood that political life exists in a space delimited by necessity and justice, *anankē* and *dikē*. While this "space" may not be very large at times, it is at least large enough to turn around in, and this makes the question of leadership and the choices that political communities make regarding ends and means much more interesting and important.

The existence of choices makes the quality of leadership a

much more important variable in studying the politics of any age. For the refined realists, Pericles was a great statesman because he understood the relationship between means and ends, how to persuade the *dēmos* to make difficult choices, and he always put the public interest ahead of his or others' private interests. He was, to use a word particularly popular these days, a prudent man, who seems to embody all that is right about statesmanship.[6] Thucydides' own praise of Pericles reflects this judgment of him. If the policies of Pericles had been continued by those who followed him, a better outcome of the war could have been expected. What is not clear, at least to this reader, is whether a "better outcome" means that Pericles would have made peace with the Spartans before Athens was ruined by the war or whether Pericles would have led Athens to victory over the Spartans and increased the size of the Athenian empire.

Realists stress Pericles' understanding of the requirements of politics and the central role of power. Those who think politics is about more than power admire his public-spiritedness and his praise of Athenian democracy. And to cinch it, Thucydides himself distinguishes Pericles from the lesser men who led the Athenians after Pericles' death. "In short, what was nominally a democracy became in his hands government by the first citizen. With his successors it was different. More on a level with one another, and each grasping at supremacy, they ended by committing even the conduct of the state affairs to the whims of the multitude" (2.65). If Thucydides is primarily a defender of Athenian imperialism, then his praise for Pericles would appear unmixed. Pericles' moderation and public-spiritedness, if continued by subsequent leaders, would have probably improved Athens' chances in the war. But this argument is not really as clear as it seems. As we shall see, Thucydides was not entirely happy with the results and requirements of Athenian imperialism. If Pericles

---

6. Recently, both William Bennett in his popular *The Book of Virtues* and Garry Wills in *Certain Trumpets: The Call of Leaders* extol the virtues of Periclean leadership.

was an architect of that imperial policy, his differences with the leaders which followed him may be less striking than is often assumed.

Beyond Pericles' praise for Athenian culture and Athenian democracy, few deny that he was an ardent imperialist. Thucydides noted that he "opposed the Lacedaemonians in everything" and "ever-urged the Athenians onto war" (1.127). Pericles' speeches make it clear that for him Athenian greatness is linked to Athenian wealth and power. But Alcibiades suggests that greatness lies more in the acts of acquiring these things than in the things themselves and so sees the process as an endless one. The city that isn't in "motion" is a city that is dying. The connection between Pericles, Cleon, and Alcibiades on this issue is only confused by the argument that Cleon and Alcibiades are more self-interested than Pericles. This is no doubt true, but it does not answer the question of whether Alcibiades' arguments about politics are natural extensions of those of Pericles. Does Pericles' praise of Athens in the Funeral Oration set limits to her size or wealth? One is hard-pressed to find any sorts of limits in Pericles except temporary ones imposed by necessity.

If Pericles is superior in public-spiritedness and public and private virtue to such successors as Cleon and Alcibiades, why do his core beliefs sound so similar to theirs? The excessive praise of Athenian democracy in the Funeral Oration asks the citizens to form an erotic attachment to the city in order to carry out its imperial designs. It asks citizens to fall in love with its wealth and its beauty and especially its power. The value of self-sacrifice and public-spirited attachment to the regime ultimately rests with the character of the regime to which one is attaching oneself. The hollowness of Athenian virtue is shown quickly as the plague strikes the city. "Perseverance in what men call honor was popular with none" (2.53). Perhaps circumstances by necessity "bring most men's characters to a level with their fortunes," but it is also true that virtue isn't worth much if it can't stand up to adversity.

Pericles' plague speech reminds the now disgruntled Athenians of the harsh political realities that lay beneath the beautiful surface of the Funeral Oration. Pericles begins by reminding his listeners of the connection between public power and private advantage. Like Machiavelli, patriotism for Pericles means love and loyalty for the city, whose success is the precondition for citizens obtaining those things that they desire. Communities built on the satisfaction of democratic desires always run the risk of falling apart as private interests try to substitute themselves for the public interest. This is a particular danger in times of adversity, when inattention to justice and character shows itself most clearly. If Pericles' strength as a leader was his ability to rally the people in these difficult times in the name of the public interest, one might ask whether a "political system was doomed if it could maintain itself in existence only by the miracle of a succession of Periclean personalities."[7]

When the Athenians spoke at the first Spartan Congress, they suggested that their empire was justified by their actions against the Persians. They also said that although they had acquired it by "no violent means," it was no longer safe to give it up, and that it was natural that "the weaker should be subject to the stronger" (1.76). The necessity of power is often used as power's excuse. But the question always remains whether the changes in a regime and in the character of its citizens that come about as a result of a public commitment to the pursuit of power and wealth as the primary ends of political life are good or bad. If they are bad, one ought to look for ways to minimize the pull of necessity, to decrease the need for power. One might also ask what could or should be done to maintain or improve the character of citizens in order to protect the regime from itself.

Does Pericles address these problems? Quite the contrary. He says that the Athenians "cannot decline the burdens of empire and still expect to share its honors" (2.63). "For what you hold,

---

7. Eric Voegelin, *The World of the Polis* (Baton Rouge: Louisiana State University Press, 1957), 363.

is to speak somewhat plainly, a tyranny; to take it perhaps was wrong, but to let it go is unsafe. And men of these retiring views, making converts of others, would quickly ruin a state. . . . such qualities are useless to an imperial city, though they may help a dependency to an unmolested servitude" (2.63).

If taking the empire was really wrong and Pericles was concerned with what was right, it would seem that at best he would be a reluctant supporter of empire. Yet there is no indication of this anywhere. Toward the end of the plague speech, Pericles talks about the "general law of decay," which reminds us that nothing lasts forever. Often, reminders of the mortality of individuals and of empires are used to redirect our souls toward that which is eternal and unchanging. But Pericles, who never mentions the gods at all in his Funeral Oration,[8] draws a different lesson. "Still it will be remembered that we held rule over more Hellenes than any other Hellenic state, that we sustained the greatest wars against their united or separate powers, and inhabited a city unrivaled by any other in resources or in magnitude. These glories may incur the censure of the slow and unambitious; but in the breast of energy they will awaken emulation" (2.64). The *hubris* of an Athens which needs neither a Homer nor the gods would appear as the ridiculous arrogance of a second-rate empire if her legacy was measured only in terms of the extent of her rule. Of course, Athens is really remembered not for the successes mentioned by Pericles, but for the immortal works of Homer and Plato.

Pericles' distaste for the *apragmōn*, the lovers of tranquillity, might appear at first to be merely concern for the current exigencies of protecting Athens against the Peloponnesians. If this were

---

8. In a pious city such as Athens, the implicit atheism of the Funeral Oration prepares the reader for the behavior of the Athenians during the plague. This aspect of the Funeral Oration is examined in Clifford Orwin, *The Humanity of Thucydides* (Princeton: Princeton University Press, 1994), 15–29. Paul Rahe also notes Pericles' lack of mention of the gods in the Funeral Oration in *Republics Ancient and Modern* (Chapel Hill: University of North Carolina Press, 1994), 1:185.

true, power would simply be the unfortunate but necessary guarantor of a private or peaceful life that represented the true end the political community. But in fact, one looks in vain for any evidence that Pericles believed this. Compare the excerpts from Pericles' speeches quoted above to the following taken from speeches by Cleon and Alcibiades, respectively:

> You entirely forget that your empire is a despotism and your subjects disaffected conspirators, whose obedience is insured not by your suicidal concessions, but by the superiority given you by your own strength and not their loyalty. . . . For if they were right in rebelling, you must be wrong in ruling. However, if right or wrong, you determine to rule, you must carry out your principle . . . , or else you must give up your empire and cultivate honesty without danger. (3.37–40).

> For if all were to keep quiet or to pick and choose whom they ought to assist, we should make but few new conquests, and should imperil those we have already won. Men do not rest content with parrying the attacks of a superior, but often strike the first blow to prevent the attack being made. And we cannot fix the exact point at which our empire shall stop; we have reached a position in which we must not be content with retaining but must scheme to extend it, for if we cease to rule others, we are in danger of being ruled ourselves. Nor can you look at inaction from the same point of view as others, unless you are prepared to change your habits and make them like theirs. . . . Understand, too, that by sinking into inaction, the city, like everything else, will wear itself out, and its skill in everything decay, while each fresh struggle will give it fresh experience, and make it more used to defend itself not in word but in deed. (6.18–19)

The premises underlying the speeches by Cleon, Alcibiades, and Pericles are all the same. Cities at rest are unambitious, dead places, doomed to be swallowed up by more active powers. As Hobbes viewed the individual, these men view the city as always in motion, subject to the "universal law of decay" that comes out of a dialectic between power and necessity. Those, like Nicias, who challenge the necessity of such motion are "men of retiring views" and should not be listened to. Eli Sagan, in his book *The Honey and the Hemlock*, notes the continual reference in Thucydides to a stark choice between empire and slavery that is echoed in the speeches of all three leaders quoted above. Sagan calls this attitude a form of paranoia, and argues that Thucydides suffers from it as well.[9]

In the often quoted passages where Thucydides uses the events of the Corcyraean revolution to reflect on the fact that "war is a rough master," realists find a recognition of the universality of human nature. "In peace and prosperity states and individuals have better sentiments, because they do not find themselves suddenly confronted with imperious necessities; but war takes away the easy supply of daily wants, and so proves a rough master that brings most men's characters down to a level with their fortunes" (3.82).

But the descriptions of the events of the time are not presented by Thucydides as a simple reflection of human nature. They are presented as a terrible breakdown of order, a breakdown which the flaws in human nature make a permanent possibility. If they were inevitable at any given time, there would be no real need to talk about justice at all. Thucydides wrote about what he considered to be the "greatest movement yet known in history." But he doesn't appear to agree with Alcibiades that there is no end to this motion or to the expansion of power. In fact, *The Peloponnesian War* chronicles the decline of a civilization and the sickness of the Athens of the sophists. He recognizes the demise of the "ancient simplicity," but he lacks the ability of a Plato to diagnose the illness that he describes. The more refined of the political realists would argue that the proper ends of politics are peace and prosperity, but would point out that these ends often require the use of force to establish and to preserve the city or the nation

9. Eli Sagan, *The Honey and the Hemlock* (New York: Basic Books, 1991), 362–75.

that would give these blessings to its people. But Thucydides, in describing the changes in the character of the Greeks, goes further than these realists. If virtue matters, and the pursuit of power (even in the name of peace and prosperity) undermines the virtue of a citizenry that once pursued quieter ends (honor and piety, for example), then war and empire ought to be avoided wherever possible. Thucydides saves his strongest praise for Nicias, not for Pericles. Nicias was the general whose mistakes may have caused the disaster in Sicily, but who wanted more than anyone to end the war and bring the Athenian soldiers home to their families.

Pericles' imperialism was more prudent and more conservative than that of Cleon or Alcibiades. Had the Athenians followed Pericles' advice, they might not have lost the war and they might have kept hold of their empire longer. But we should remember that it was the same Athenians whom Pericles asked to "realize the power of Athens, and feed your eyes upon her from day to day, till love of her fills your hearts" (2.43) that "fell in love with the enterprise" of the disastrous Sicilian Expedition (6.24). If Pericles fed the democratic passions for power and wealth that necessitated an imperial foreign policy, then he must bear at least some responsibility for the events and the leaders that that passion precipitated and encouraged.

Despite his obvious admiration for Pericles' leadership and tactical judgment, it would seem that Thucydides' final judgment of Pericles is a function of his judgment regarding imperial Athens herself. If Athens was suffering a sort of sickness that brought her away from a concern with honor, piety, and justice toward the sophistic pursuit and justification of the ends of power and wealth, then Pericles could be viewed as at least a victim of the disease. Even if Thucydides believed that there is a kind of tragic necessity about political life whose roots lie in human nature, then the glory of Pericles is dimmed by the sadness of all politics, where our sins appear to play themselves out in an inevitable fashion. Only if Thucydides is an unabashed realist who believes and celebrates that political greatness is about the pursuit of power and the glory that comes from wealth and empire can we read his praise of Pericles without a balancing skepticism. This skepticism is strengthened when we move from Thucydides to Plato.[10]

SOCRATES' CRITIQUE OF PERICLES

Those who praise Pericles as a great statesman and defender of the common good of Athens ought to look carefully at what Socrates thought of Pericles. In *Gorgias*, Socrates and Callicles are discussing the nature of good statesmanship. Socrates asks Callicles whether Pericles, Cimon, Miltiades, and Pericles were good citizens in the sense that it is the duty of a public man to make the citizens better instead of worse.

CALLICLES: I do.

SOCRATES: Then if they were good, obviously each of them made better citizens of those who were worse before. Did he do this or not?

CALLICLES: Yes.

SOCRATES: So when Pericles began to speak before the people, the Athenians were worse than when he spoke for the last time?

CALLICLES: Perhaps.

SOCRATES: There can be no "perhaps" about it, my good friend; it must be so from what we have admitted, if he was really a good citizen.

CALLICLES: Well, what then?

SOCRATES: Nothing, but tell me next whether the Athenians are said to have been improved by means of Pericles or, quite the contrary, to have been corrupted by him. For I am told that Pericles made the Athenians idle and cowardly and talkative and cov-

10. [For a much more complete comparison of Plato and Thucydides, see chapter 2 by Margaret Hrezo. *Ed.*]

etous, because he was the first to establish pay for service among
them.

CALLICLES: You hear this, Socrates, from the gentlemen with bat-
tered ears.

SOCRATES: Well, this at least is not a matter of hearsay, but you
know it as well as I do, that Pericles enjoyed a good reputation at
first and was never convicted on any disgraceful charge by the
Athenians, when they were worse. But when he had made good
and worthy citizens of them, at the end of his life, he was convicted of theft by them and narrowly escaped a death sentence,
obviously because they held him an evil man.[11]

To Socrates, Pericles enjoyed a good reputation with Athenians
only when he undertook actions which corrupted them. When
he tried to make them "good," however, they turned against
him.

If, as Socrates believed, happiness comes from possessing a
well-ordered soul, then statesmanship must be measured in terms
of its impact on the souls of citizens. This is Socrates' contention
in his conversation with Callicles. To call Pericles and other
Athenian heroes like Themistocles and Cimon expert leaders
who know what is good for their citizens is like calling a baker
or wine vendor the equivalent of a trainer or a doctor. Instead of
guiding citizens towards the good with reasoned speech, Pericles
has appealed to the basest parts of his fellow Athenians, even if he
has done so with lovely words.

> You talk to me of servants who cater to our desires but have
> no fine or sound views about them, men who, if it so chances,
> will gorge and fatten men's bodies and win their praises for it, but
> will finally rob them of what flesh they had before. And their
> victims in turn, in their ignorance, will not blame for their mala-

---

11. Plato, *Gorgias*, in *The Collected Dialogues of Plato*, ed. Edith Hamilton and Huntington Cairns, trans. Lane Cooper et al. (New York: Pantheon Books, 1961), 515d–516a.
All subsequent references to *Gorgias* in this chapter are to this edition.

dies and for the loss of their original flesh those who feasted them, but any who may happen at the time to be present and give them any advice when the surfeit of the past has some time later brought sickness upon them, because it disregarded the rules of health—these they will blame and abuse and injure, if they can, while they praise the others who were responsible for their troubles.

You are now doing much the same thing as this, Callicles. You praise those who have banqueted our citizens with all the dainties they desire. And men say it is these who have made our city great, never realizing that it is swollen and festering through these statesmen of old. For they have paid no heed to discipline and justice, but have filled our city with harbors and dockyards and walls and revenues and similar rubbish, and so, when the crisis of her infirmity comes, they will hold their present advisers responsible and will sing the praises of Themistocles and Cimon and Pericles, who caused their misfortunes. (*Gorgias* 518e–519d)

This "rubbish" is the politics of Pericles, Machiavelli, and the modern project. It is the politics that Socrates takes on in *The Republic*.

At the beginning of book 2 of *The Republic*, Glaucon and his brother Adeimantus elaborate a theory of politics that begins with the assumption that all men wish to be bad and are made good only by a system of rewards and punishments that effectively restrains their external behavior. Passions are filtered through reason to form interests. These interests can be understood and dealt with by prudent statesmen whose rhetoric and laws encourage men to act reasonably by developing their rational self-interestedness and tying it to the interests of the state. Here is the life work of Pericles. He seems to agree with Machiavelli that if men are rational and self-interested, they can be governed by princes who understand their human nature. The prince will earn the loyalty of his citizens if only he protects their property and their honor and "banquets them with all the dainties they desire."

Pericles was perhaps the first huckster for the modern project, telling his fellow Athenians that the greatness of the city represented their greatness and the success of the city was the essential precondition to their success. In the beginning of the dialogue *Menexenus,* Socrates parodies the Funeral Oration of Pericles:

> SOCRATES: O Menexenus! Death in battle is certainly in many respects a noble thing. The dead man gets a fine and costly funeral, although he may have been poor, and an elaborate speech is made over him by a wise man who has long ago prepared what he has to say, although he who is praised may not have been good for much. The speakers praise him for what he has done and for what he has not done—that is the beauty of them—and they steal away our souls with their embellished words. In every conceivable form they praise the city, and they praise those who died in war, and all our ancestors who went before us, and they praise ourselves also who are still alive, until I feel quite elevated by their laudations, and I stand listening to their words, Menexenus, and become enchanted by them, and all in a moment I imagine myself to have become a greater and nobler and finer man than I was before. And if, as often happens, there are any foreigners who accompany me to the speech, I become suddenly conscious of having a sort of triumph over them, and they seem to experience a corresponding feeling of admiration at me, and at the greatness of the city, which appears to them, when they are under the influence of the speaker, more wonderful than ever. This consciousness of dignity lasts me more than three days, and not until the fourth or fifth day do I come to my senses and know where I am—in the meantime I have been living in the Islands of the Blessed. Such is the art of our rhetoricians, and in such manner does the sound of their words keep ringing in my ears.[12]

Socrates well understood the power of linking in speech the individual citizen with the might of an imperial city, a rhetorical tactic that has been used by statesman in all kinds of regimes throughout

---

12. Plato, *Menexenus,* in *The Collected Dialogues of Plato,* ed. Edith Hamilton and Huntington Cairns, trans. Lane Cooper et al. (New York: Pantheon Books, 1961), 235c–235d.

history. But, for Socrates, this is a dream world that leads our sight and our loyalties away from the things which matter most.

Defenders of Pericles and of the modern project might argue that Socrates is being too harsh and is unrealistic in his definition of good government and in his sarcasm regarding the statesmanship of Pericles. Surely nations that are free and relatively prosperous afford the opportunity for those who choose to pursue virtue, piety, or any other notion of the good life. A democracy that is free and prosperous and strong would appear to be an ideal both noble and attainable. But Plato raises questions about the long-term viability and desirability of a regime which depends on interest alone, however enlightened, to sustain itself. *The Republic* challenges the political realism of Glaucon and Adeimantus, who reflect the character of Athens in the age of Pericles.

Few would argue that a primary purpose of foreign policy is to secure the lives and the property of citizens. But if power and wealth are merely conditions for living the good life, there are limits to the amount of time and energy that one ought to put into securing and increasing them. If the good life consists at least in part in a life lived in accordance with justice and piety, a foreign policy that leads citizens away from those goals cannot be justified with reference to the absolute desirability of wealth and power. The issue is further complicated by the fact that just as those who seek private advantage often try to make it look like the public advantage, so leaders who seek unlimited power or wealth often say that they are only seeking to secure what they already have. The terms national interest and national security thus ought to be looked on very skeptically by citizens who share a more modest (or more elevated) view of the good life.

The proper ends of government and foreign policy cannot be divorced from the question of the good life. For realists like Machiavelli and Hobbes, the ends of human life are easily found, and are given to us by an understanding of human passions. Prudence, then, can be defined as a kind of cleverness which allows us to choose means that will guarantee our success as an individual or as a nation. That success is defined as our ability to satisfy a multitude of desires without destroying ourselves in the process. Yet one can question, as Socrates does consistently, whether a life or a politics which begins with the primacy of appetites can ever be "rational," let alone good. Aristotle understood this when he defined the value of prudence (*phronesis*) with reference to the excellence of ends chosen. Practical wisdom should not be divorced from wisdom simply. To substitute the study of mass psychology or majoritarian politics for wisdom is to detach *phronesis* from that which gives it value.

If the body and its longings are all there is, some form of the realist argument is the right one. But if the soul or the spirit exists and has its own nature and its own longings, then to deny this nature or these longings or to try to subsume them under a narrower category is to be radically unrealistic and unempirical. This is the perspective from which Plato draws his critique of Pericles. Thucydides leaves us with a paradox. Athens is a good and a beautiful city that increasingly begins to act in ugly and unjust ways. A once-healthy city is now diseased in some way, and Thucydides appears unable to provide a definitive diagnosis, let alone a prescription for a cure. Plato gives us both, but the effort needed to do so is enormous.

The soul and the divine are under attack in the Athens of the sophists, where man is increasingly "the measure of all things." Plato's response to this is the vision of the soul and the divine articulated in *The Republic*. The decline of leadership so often pointed out from Pericles to Cleon to Alcibiades can be better understood by looking at the conversation that takes place in book 1. Socrates and his friends have made the trip down to the Piraeus, the seaport of Athens, and the home of Athens' imperial navy. In the home of the elderly Cephalus, Socrates listens to a series of definitions of justice that begin with Cephalus's argument that justice is telling the truth and paying one's debts and ends with Thrasymachus boldly announcing that justice is the advantage of the stronger. In-between is Cephalus's son, Polemarchus, who modifies his father's argument and says that justice is helping friends and harming enemies, a very political definition that imposes a Periclean moderation on Thrasymachus's more radical realism. Why does Thrasymachus come after Polemarchus? Perhaps because Plato sees the "prudence" of Polemarchus as the midwife to the rejection of justice entirely that is evident in Thrasymachus and expressed in grisly detail by Glaucon and Adeimantus at the beginning of book 2. Eric Voegelin describes the significance of the opening scenes of *The Republic* in this manner: "The older and middle generations, who have caused the disaster by their emptiness and weakness, are now followed by the younger generation, Glaucon and Adeimantus, the victims of the corrupt society. In their role as the victims they draw a general picture of the pressure which the surrounding society through its various agencies brings to bear on their souls with such intensity that they can barely resist. In the Thrasymachus scene the soul of the individual sophist becomes articulate; the following scene with Glaucon and Adeimantus introduces the sophistic society in the massive impact of its existence."[13]

Just as the corruption of Athenian youth is a product of the "emptiness and weakness" of previous generations, one must reasonably ask whether leaders such as Cleon ("the most violent man in Athens") and Alcibiades are not products of the regime fashioned by the elder statesmen of the empire, including Pericles. "The Athenians on Melos, in contradistinction to Callicles or Thrasymachus, limit themselves indeed to asserting the natural right of the stronger with regard to the cities; but are Callicles and Thrasymachus not more consistent than they? Can one encourage, as even Pericles and precisely Pericles does, the city's desire for 'having more' than other cities without in the long run encouraging the individual's desire for 'having more' than his fellow citizens? Pericles was indeed dedicated wholeheartedly to

13. Eric Voegelin, *Plato and Aristotle* (Baton Rouge: Louisiana State University Press, 1957), 72.

the common good of the city but to its common good unjustly understood."[14]

Some might argue that the common good "unjustly understood" as Strauss describes it is nevertheless inevitable and necessary. But either justice exists or it doesn't. If we are sometimes compelled to do injustice by the power of necessity in an imperfect world, aren't we particularly obligated to understand what justice and injustice consist of, and to admit and ask forgiveness when we are forced to do wrong? "Thucydides does not expect the Athenian masses to act against their interests, to surrender their profitable occupation and agreeable life. . . . they are 'compelled' to organize their empire. Nevertheless, the 'compulsion' to commit injustices and atrocities still is a moral breakdown; and never is it more evident than when the compulsion of interest is erected into the law of action which justifies transgressions of morals and justice."[15] Thucydides understood injustice when he saw it. As a product of an earlier time, he was both amazed by the accomplishments of his city and appalled by its present behavior. His understanding by habit and custom of right and wrong could not stand up to the brand of realism preached by the sophists of the day, just as the pious Cephalus must give way to Polemarchus and Thrasymachus before Socrates can attempt a restoration of the real meaning of justice.

Thucydides tells us that among the calamities of the war is a loss of piety. This is shown most clearly in the Melian Dialogue, when the Athenians extend their own thesis about the rule of the stronger to the gods themselves. "Of the gods we believe and of men we know that they rule where they can." Is it any wonder that the erotic love of the goods of an imperial city that Pericles promotes in the Funeral Oration takes place in a speech which is

14. Leo Strauss, *The City and Man* (Chicago: University of Chicago Press, 1964), 193–94.

15. Voegelin, *The World of the Polis*, 360.

silent with regard to the gods? Realists begin by insisting that all men are motivated by the same things and calling anyone who disagrees a naive fool. They end by having to murder the gods themselves in order to make their pathological thinking appear normal. In order to reconstitute the soul of the Athenians, Plato is forced to confront the realists of his own age and to reconstruct heaven itself.

If understanding and choosing the good where possible is the real condition for human happiness in this world and the next, as Socrates asserts, then the leaders of human communities really ought to try to leave their citizens better men and women than they found them, and the consideration of what justice consists of ought to be a public activity of the highest importance. Eric Voegelin notes that Thucydides considers the failure of leadership that may have lost the war for Athens accidental, "an unpredictable misfortune playing havoc with the co-ordination of means and ends in the order of necessity in the same manner in which the plague disturbed the well-laid plans of Pericles."[16]

Reflections of this kind show an unclearness in the mind of Thucydides concerning the connection between rationality and ethos. Apparently his sense was numbed, like that of his sophistic contemporaries, and he could not see that the sphere of power and pragmatic rationalism is not autonomous but part of human existence which as a whole includes the rationality of spiritual and moral order. If the controlling order of spirit and morality breaks down, the formation of ends in the pragmatic order will be controlled by the irrationality of passions; the co-ordination of means and ends may continue to be rational but action will nevertheless become irrational because the ends no longer make sense in terms of spiritual and moral order. When the corrosion of reason has reached a certain degree in depth and has befallen a sufficiently large proportion of the people, effective leadership in terms of

16. Ibid., 363.

reason becomes difficult and perhaps impossible, even if the man at the head under more favorable conditions could exert such leadership; in a further degree of corrosion a man of such qualities will, precisely because he possesses them, find it impossible to reach the position of leadership; and in a final degree the society by its corruption may prevent the formation of a man of such qualities even if by nature he should not be lacking in gifts. This connection between corruption of society and the impossibility of rational leadership Thucydides was unwilling to admit.[17]

Because the prudence of the realist statesman is based on the subordination of political life to dominant human passions, it can never make sense of the world from the standpoint of "spiritual and moral order." The realist is thus forced in the end to deny the existence of such an order, or at least to deny that it has any connection to life in the "real world."

CONCLUSION—THE PROBLEM OF PERICLES

The "problem of Pericles" is about much more than an interpretation of what Thucydides thought about the events he was describing. Thucydides seemed to recoil from the decline of behavior, character, and rhetoric that he witnessed during the war. Yet he doesn't go nearly as far as Socrates did in laying the blame for what he saw at the feet of the Athenian "heroes" who built "ships and walls and dockyards and many other such things," but left no room for virtue or moderation.

What makes Thucydides a "possession for all time"? Is it his political realism or his ability to create from actual events a story that shows realism's terrible consequences? Perhaps those consequences are inevitable. Perhaps at best we live in a world of "moral man and immoral society." But the inevitability of terrible things is no excuse to celebrate them. If we make the madness of empire the measure of goodness, how are we to avoid teaching

17. Ibid.

our children that justice is merely an invention of the weak to protect themselves from the strong? Such a society would see politics as simply a struggle among competing interest groups for advantage. It would bring forth a political science that called such a view of politics empirical. It would create citizens who would criticize and despise such a politics, but nevertheless adopt its methods in their own lives, calling such behavior appropriate to "real world." Such a culture would create institutions of higher education that cared nothing about the souls of their students, only about providing them with the requisite and measurable competencies that would ensure them and their city material success. Such a society would preach tolerance and equality while the hearts of its citizens became increasingly hardened from lack of contact with the good and the beautiful.

The United States emerged from its own Persian Wars of the twentieth century as a powerful and wealthy nation. It entered the Cold War arguing that it was distasteful but necessary to become a world power. It entered the game of power politics that it had once rejected as unworthy because it saw no choice when confronted with the Soviet empire. Now that that reason has been taken away, we find every reason to retain our position. We cannot give up being number one. Our identity and pride come from our wealth and our power. Some even suggest that we go further and rule the world in a sort of "ultraimperialist" alliance with the old corrupt states of Europe and the new economic juggernaut of Japan.

One can find many arguments regarding the teaching of Thucydides. Yet it is the questions raised by Thucydides' ambiguities and silences that are his most important possession. We could discover once and for all what the definitive teaching of Thucydides was, but we would still be left to answer the question of whether he was right. This essay has avoided that more difficult question by focusing on Pericles. Some would argue that a Socrates could not have existed without Pericles or those like him. That may be true, but if moral or spiritual progress is possible, either for individuals or for communities, it is important that we not ignore the argument between Pericles and Socrates about the character of the good life. Who was right—Pericles or Socrates? Those who claim to admire both cannot put off answering that question forever.

9

ATHENS AND AMERICA

NICK PAPPAS

INSTANCES OF REMEMBRANCE
(*anamnēsis*) can be very revealing. Sometimes they allow us to put
the pieces of our lives in order, exposing some hidden truth. My
understanding of reality and of American foreign policy is pro-
foundly affected by three such memories. In 1965, in the spring,
when kings make war, I went down into the harbor to board
the troop ship that would carry me and 1,400 other souls the
13,000 miles to our version of the Peloponnesian War. Amidst
the *imposing* warships and scowling (or bawling) battalions a shudder of unreality made the whole picture blur—just for an instant.
The shudder recurred when our C-130 Hercules banked to star-
board over the white beaches of the Republic of Vietnam and
the giant air base at Da Nang came into view. Overriding the
spectacle of America's warplanes painted for war, and even the
feeling that "This is kind of neat," was that same "This is not

real!" But how could such massive physical reality generate such a shudder?

The parallel or antithesis to the shudder was Lieutenant Doug O'Donnell, a friend of mine at the Basic School, Quantico, Virginia. Doug was killed in 1966 in an operation with the Force Recon people. What I remember was an Irish face with Irish eyes and a laugh that was likewise stereotypically Irish, but there the stereotype ended. Doug had the deltoids of a Celtic war god and scampered over the obstacle course like a giant fox squirrel. Married and a father, Doug radiated a kind of calm strength—or what I really mean is reality, the reality of a soul existing under God.

The paradoxical juxtaposition of the shudder of unreality finally was completed about a year later when I found myself looking down on my bleeding body and feeling content and even amused. The blast of high explosive had—for a second—removed the miasma that made thinking about reality so hard.

All three experiences point to the same questions. When is power real and when is it illusion? What is the connection, if any, between the lives of citizens and the life of their political community? Ought the same rules to apply to both individual and collective experience? Hesiod gives us two possible answers which highlight the tension between reality and illusion and between individual and collective political experience. Perhaps the reaction "this is not real" was only the fleeting misgivings of a mind that could not take in the vastness and inevitability of America's military might. Hesiod writes:

> And here's a fable for kings, who do not need it explained:
> It's what the hawk said high in the clouds
> As he carried off a speckle-throated nightingale
> Skewered on his talons. She complained something pitiful;
> And he made this high and mighty speech to her:
> "No sense in your crying. You're in the grip of real strength now,
> And you'll go where I take you, songbird or not.

I'll make a meal of you if I want, or I might let you go.
Only a fool struggles against his superiors.
He not only gets beat, but humiliated as well."
Thus spoke the hawk, the windlord, his long wings beating.[1]

Isn't it only the fool who struggles against the inevitable? What difference does it make if a cause is just, if its power is weak?

But what if there is more to power than might? Hesiod gives us a glimpse of this side as well. He follows his depiction of raw power with a passage which reads as if the schoolmaster had walked out on the playground and caught his students telling dirty jokes. "But for those who live for violence and vice, Zeus, Son of Kronos, broad-browed god, decrees a just penalty, and often a whole city suffers for one bad man and his damn fool schemes."[2] Does genuine power require more than predominance of force? What if justice demands the ordering of power to "right" ends in order to keep from "molting" its wings and "falling" to earth?

These questions form a minor theme in Hesiod. They take on major significance, however, in Thucydides' *The Peloponnesian War*. The conclusions Thucydides reaches offer important insights into American foreign policy since World War II. My trio of anamnestic experiences point to the same conclusions. What is it that the sense of unreality in the face of overwhelming physical evidence, the feeling of being touched by a truly beautiful soul, and the glimpse of the right relationship between the temporal and the eternal share? How do they transcend the years 1965–1967 and form contemporary examples of Thucydides' work "done to last forever"? Do my anamnestic experiences and Thucydides' powerful *syngraphē* share some common themes? I think they do. Dive deeply enough into the bottomless *aperion* and the message of both is the same.

---

1. Hesiod, *Works and Days*, trans. Stanley Lombardo (Indianapolis: Hackett Publishing, 1993), 30.
2. Ibid.

What is that message? The nature of man does not change. Human beings have the potential for both good and evil within them. Man lives in an in-between world; a position above the material world and below divine existence. Therefore, a part of human experience is the attempt to link the human and the divine. All men and all societies interpret existence and attempt to make such a linkage. Although some men and societies may have clearer conceptions of a right existence under God, there is no clear line of progress from "primitive" to "advanced" modes of existence. Material progress does not equal spiritual progress. As societies attempt to find their way towards transcendence, the possibilities for deformation are as great as the possibilities of grace and salvation. Human beings will as often confuse their own selfish desires for those of God or the Good as they will achieve a genuine understanding of the demands of transcendence.[3] This is as much a lesson for the twenty-first century A.D. as for the fifth B.C.

ATHENS

Like most things, the beginning of the Peloponnesian War is located somewhere in its middle. The beginning of a book is determined by its middle, which must exist in the mind of the writer in order to construct the series of events that rush toward and recede from that middle. All the work's energy streams toward it, all things rush away from it. In book 6, not long after the Melian Dialogue, we find the Athenians going down the Long Walls that connect Athens with its suburban seaport, the Piraeus. There in the harbor was the magnificent armament assembled for the ex-

3. Eric Voegelin, *Israel and Revelation* (Baton Rouge: Louisiana State University Press, 1956), 60. Stating that the nature of man is constant only refers to human mundane existence. It leaves out, for a moment, the discovery that life is a process of immortalizing towards imperishability. See Eric Voegelin, "Immortality," in *Published Essays,* vol. 12 of *The Collected Works of Eric Voegelin,* ed. Ellis Sandoz (Baton Rouge: Louisiana State University Press, 1990), 88.

pedition to Sicily and it "was a sight that could not but comfort them."[4] The armament represented the culminating moment in Athens' ascent to empire; it would be the subject of the greatest devastation in the story of the Athenian descent.

Plato's *Republic* begins with a similar downward movement as Socrates and Glaucon go down to the Piraeus to pray to the goddess and witness the new celebration.[5] Socrates and Glaucon are walking down the four and one-half miles that separate the Piraeus from Athens in space. They are also walking down the sixty-odd years that separate the Athens of Marathon from the Athens of imperial sea power and the nightmare of the Peloponnesian War.[6] The Piraeus also represented the kind of freedom that permeated the Athenian democracy. It was freedom without *aretē* (virtue) and so represented the kind of tyranny that results when the appetites and the *libido dominandi* are unrestrained by reason attuned to goodness. What happened to Athens in that interval?

For all the problems of its internal politics and foreign policy, the Athens of Marathon symbolized one of those translucent moments in history, when justice and power, righteousness and necessity met in a golden balance. The "Athenian Thesis" of the earlier years of the Persian Wars was "fear of the Mede, friendship for our fellow-citizens, and reverence for the dear gods."[7] Justice, as described by that rough combatant at Marathon, Aeschylus, was diving deep to find *dikē* (righteousness) amidst the pressures of dire *anankē* (necessity).[8]

---

4. Thucydides, *The Peloponnesian War*, trans. Richard Crawley (New York: Modern Library, 1982), book 6, chapter 30. All subsequent references in this chapter are to this edition and are by conventional book and chapter.

5. Plato, *The Republic*, in *The Dialogues of Plato*, vols. 1 and 2, trans. B. Jowett (New York: Random House, 1920).

6. Eric Voegelin, *Plato and Aristotle* (Baton Rouge: Louisiana State University Press, 1957), 52–53.

7. Plato, *The Laws*, in *The Dialogues of Plato*, vol. 2, trans. B. Jowett (New York: Random House, 1920), book 3:699.

8. Eric Voegelin, *The World of the Polis* (Baton Rouge: Louisiana State University Press, 1957), 247–53.

From this fleeting but lovely understanding of political life under God and the burden of sin, Athens began its own *katabasis*, or downward journey of the spirit. This downward journey can be symbolically reconstructed by briefly looking at a real succession of thinkers as they made themselves felt in the Hellenic world. In his soul Parmenides (c. 450 B.C.), the Eleatic philosopher, had found that he was part of something called Being that in some way was the world transcendent of a primordial community of god and man, world, and society. Anaxagoras (?500–428 B.C.) retained the language of the transcendent experience of Parmenides but drained it of its spiritual substance by announcing that *nous* is the sovereign part of being. Finally, the sophist Protagoras (c. 480–410 B.C.) completed the deformation of Parmenides' eruption out of the *metaxy* by declaring "man is the measure of all things." Now Anaxagoras and Protagoras were noble men. But when their teaching enters the soul of Pericles the nobility is transmuted by the luciferous personality of the statesman into the *erōs tyrannos* that emerges as public policy in the form of the *new* Athenian thesis: fear, ambition, and interest. Justice now is the submission of the weaker to the stronger.

At the end of the first year of the Peloponnesian War, the most powerful man in Athens, Pericles, son of Xanthippus, gave a beautiful funeral oration for the city's hoplites, sailors, and marines who had fallen in the year's campaign. The speech is a model paean to the virtue of courage and the worthiness of serving the common good. The speech gradually builds its power and momentum as it points to an overwhelming conclusion. Pericles begins with praise for the ancestors who made all this possible in the war with the Mede, moves on to praise the constitution and quality of life enjoyed by the Athenians, leaps to an unashamed exuberance about the Athenian pathos, and finally reaches a climax in which the greatness of the city and the sacrifice of its citizens form one majestic spiritual unity.

"So died these men as became Athenians," he begins, and you survivors must do the same, and must "feed your eyes upon her from day to day, till love of her fills your hearts; and then when all her greatness shall break upon you, you must reflect that it was by courage, sense of duty, and a keen feeling of honor in action that men were enabled to win all this." And so Athenians, Pericles concludes, "This take as your model and judging happiness to be the fruit of freedom and freedom of valor, never decline the danger of war" (2.36–43). The pathos has reached its peak. Beyond the formal structure of the rhetoric is the unarticulated but real sense of Athenian glory and grandeur. "For Athens alone of her contemporaries is found when tested to be greater than her reputation, and alone gives no occasions to blush at the antagonist by whom they have been worsted, or to her subjects to question her title to rule" (2.41). The language is perfectly suited to its audience, which is basking in the midday radiance of Athenian imperialism.

Yet there is an umbra slowly casting its darkness over the gorgeous public buildings and the fleet anchored in the Piraeus. What is the common good Pericles asks his fellow citizens to defend? What are the ends to which honor and valor should be directed? Pericles' answers to these questions fascinate the reader with a long slow horror as we realize the two most important implications of Pericles' words.

The first implication is the uneasy attempt to reconcile the imperatives of necessity and the requirements of righteousness. Pericles' argument betrays a certain nervousness and the need to justify the Athenian concupiscent expansion by the absurd claim that even its conquered subjects love its greatness! The thinness of the argument is betrayed by Pericles himself when he delivers a "morale builder" during the plague that struck Athens in the same year: "For what you hold is, to speak somewhat plainly, a tyranny; to take it perhaps was a wrong, but to let it go is unsafe" (2.63). Pericles' admission works its way out in the icy dialogue at Melos a few years later and finally swallows Athens in 404 when the allies vent their fury at the fate of the Melians by demanding the butchery of the Athenians. Only Spartan intervention stopped them.

The second implication immediately follows the assertion that necessity and righteousness are in balance: "Rather, the admiration of the present and succeeding ages will be ours since we have not left our power without witness, but have shown it by mighty proofs; and far from needing a Homer for our panegyrist, or other of his craft whose verses might charm for the moment only for the impression which they gave to melt at the touch of fact, we have forced every sea and land to be the highways of our daring, and everywhere, whether for evil or for good, have left imperishable monuments behind" (2.41). Here, Pericles has sounded the battle call for the assault on the gods themselves. "Whether for evil or for good" was not the rallying cry of the Athens of Marathon. Against the Persians, we are told, the Athenians were motivated by fear, friendship, and reverence.[9]

The Athens that met the Mede was still a kind of monarchy, not a democracy. The monarch's name was *nomos* and this ruler lived in the heart of each Athenian. *Nomos* means "law," and the Greek term gives us our word "numismatic" because, like small coins, it could be found everywhere. *Nomos* meant the constitution of a city or a man in harmony with the divine order, in this case with the order of Zeus, which attached the soul of each human to the divine by the spider strand of faith. To disobey *nomos* meant acting shamefully, and in the close-order, face-to-face battle, your neighbors could see any shameful action. *Nomos* meant that the Athenians would fight like tigers and typhoons to save their honor and their city's walls.[10]

However, after Marathon, the creative tension between *anankē* (necessity) and *dikē* (righteousness) began to become unhinged. A sign of this deformation was the emergence of a new kind of man, symbolized by Themistocles, creator of the master stratagem

9. Plato, *The Laws*, book 3:606.
10. Voegelin, *World of the Polis*, 301–308.

used by Athens at the Battle of Salamis. Themistocles was the first "modern" Athenian leader and became the *stratēgos autocratōr* of the people. He directed the Athenians toward empire by rebuilding the long walls that made the Piraeus impregnable and, thus, able to serve as the basis of Athenian expansion. Themistocles becomes the role model for Athenian leadership from his own time through that of Pericles and Alcibiades—the leadership that will be responsible for Athens' rise and fall.

By the time of Pericles, *nomos* has been deformed into "statute law," or more bluntly, "the advantage of the stronger." Likewise, the city's connection with the order of the gods is abandoned in favor of the order of power. Instead, the Athenians openly lay siege to the order of the gods by averring that they—*like everyone else*—are driven by fear, honor, and interest and that justice is subjection by the weak to the strong (1.76). This assault opens a breach in the spiritual fortifications of Athens, through which dark forces of disorder flow, but no one recognizes the source of the breach, in the forms of Cleon and Alcibiades, as the work of sappers within the walls. Pericles argues that Athens has no need of a Homer. The irony of Pericles' remark is lost on the audience, who remembers Homer only as the teller of bawdy stories about the gods rather than as a chronicler of the spiritual collapse of Mycenaean civilization and the conveyer of the tragic and perennial conflict between necessity and righteousness. By the time of the Melian Dialogue the order of Zeus as articulated through the poets (Homer, Hesiod) really has made its exit, leaving only a shudder and a horrified Thucydides. When *dikē* (righteousness) left Athens, the city's core—and therefore its real power—turned to illusion. Self-interest, it seems, no matter how enlightened, is a weak foundation for a lasting foreign policy. It has no heart for the spiritual deserts and painful awakenings that mark the growth of the soul into the realms of reality.

For the Athenians prudence has been immanentized from the extremely difficult art of making policy in accordance with the moral order of the cosmos to the art of balancing policy objectives with national power. When this happens rational policy making is no longer possible because reason has been reduced to mere calculation. This can be a fatal foreshortening, indeed, as nihilism replaces any notion of moral order.

This nihilism is the spiritual substance of an Athens that has lost faith in the ordering power of the mythical theology of Homer and Hesiod and has abandoned the order of Zeus for the order of power. The moment, in fact, is described succinctly by Thucydides in the Melian Dialogue. The moment of final separation is not quite as powerful as the description of Israel's exodus from the order of Yahweh described in Jeremiah 36, but it is brutal enough. The Melians aver that they shall trust in an alliance with the Spartans and the good fortunes of the gods. The Athenians respond with cold disdain:

> When you speak of the favor of the gods, we may as fairly hope for that as yourselves, neither our pretensions nor our conduct being in any way contrary to what men believe of the gods, or practice among themselves. Of the gods we believe, and of men we know, that by a necessary law of their nature they rule wherever they can. And it is not as if we were the first to make this law, or to act upon it when made: we found it existing before us, and shall leave it to exist forever after us; all we do is to make use of it, knowing that you and everybody else, having the same power as we have, would do the same as we do. (5.105)

In this remarkably compact statement the Athenians revealed that they have accomplished in life what the Sophists only discussed—perhaps in jest. They have projected their own libidinous egos out onto the rest of mankind and, not stopping there, onto the gods themselves. The murder of the gods completed, the Athenians are permitted everything.

This is the same Athens that serves as the background of the works of Plato, who must desperately articulate the new truth of the soul that could replace both the truth of the myth of Homer and Hesiod and the lie of the Athenian thesis. These works help us in our task of a spiritual archaeology to penetrate beneath the thin covering of strategic-diplomatic action and reveal a pneuma-pathological society.

In *The Republic* Plato shows us how truth is replaced by opinion as Glaucon and Adeimantus watch the procession of generations move farther and farther away from the first Athenian thesis to the sophistic formulation of Thrasymachus: justice is the will of the strongest. Socrates must hold them in the depth of the Piraeus—a depth of freedom without *aretēm* until they can form a tiny city within a city that will carry them out of the cave of illusion to the new truth of the soul under God. This eerie blindness to reality surfaces at the pragmatic level of power politics as an inability to relate means to ends, or even really to rationally formulate ends, as in the case of the Sicilian Expedition. To illustrate this inability to think rationally Plato has Socrates tell his "whopper," the Phoenician Myth, or the Myth of Metals, as a kind of false story. So unbrotherly are the Athenians that they have to hear the simple truth that all men are brothers told as a lie![11]

In *Menexenus* Socrates does a cruel parody of the Funeral Oration of Pericles. In the *Menexenus* version Athens is praised, foremost, as being dear to the gods, in sharp contrast to Pericles' boast that Athens needs no Homer to celebrate her fame and, in fact, his failure to mention the gods at all. Pericles' desperate effort to justify the Athenian pathos for existence and expansion is shattered by Socrates' remarks on those killed in battle. Pericles had held up the *Spartan* notion of *aretē* as being the ability to stand the bloody slaughter of battle and hold one's place in the phalanx. Socrates says, "O Menexenus! death in battle is in many respects a noble thing. The dead man gets a fine and costly funeral, although he may have been poor, and an elaborate speech is made over him by a wise man who has long prepared what he has to say, although he who is praised may not have been good for

11. Voegelin, *Plato and Aristotle*, 104–108.

much."[12] He continues with an encomium that is a masterpiece of damnation by ironic praise. The city's ancestors are praised, those still alive are praised, everything is praised so that the listener can "imagine myself to have become a greater and finer man than I was before" (*Menexenus* 234–235). By the end of the passage the listener finds out by indirection that the greatest evil of Pericles was that he told the Athenians that they were good when they were not. If the irony in *Menexenus* seems a bit harsh, the *Critias* make it sound felicitous indeed. *Critias* recounts the great war fought long, long ago between an incredibly just Athens and the superpower Atlantis. Athens is pictured as the leader of a pan-Hellenic alliance. Her qualification for leadership was her reputation for justice and piety. The Atlantians are portrayed as the offspring of the god Poseidon and a mortal woman. For the longest time they prospered on their island kingdom, generating vast wealth and massive public works. But at some point the divine portion in them began to fade away and they began to act in an unseemly fashion. For those with an eye to see it, the Atlantians were losing their fairest precious gifts, but "to those who had no eye to see the true happiness they appeared glorious and blessed at the very time they were full of avarice and power."[13] The dialogue ends with a convocation of the gods and Zeus and the intimation that Atlantis will have to be overthrown. Our knowledge of the Melian Dialogue reveals that Athens had by the alchemy of power transmuted itself into the perverted Atlantis of the story. The judgment of the gods would be carried out by the Athenians themselves at Aegospotami in 404.

In the dialogue that precedes *Critias, Timaeus*, we are given an account of the creation of the world, the animals, and men and women. In the story it is God who ultimately is the creator and

---

12. Plato, *Menexenus,* in *The Dialogues of Plato*, vols. 1 and 2, trans. B. Jowett (New York: Random House, 1920), 234–35. All subsequent references in this chapter are to this edition.

13. Plato, *Critias* in *The Dialogues of Plato,* vols. 1 and 2, trans. B. Jowett (New York: Random House, 1920), 120.

who gives man the sovereign part of the soul—the spark of divinity in each one of us. Since we are a plant not of earthly but of heavenly growth we are raised "from earth to our kindred in heaven."[14] Now in discussing the creation of the race of birds we are told by Timaeus that they emerged from "innocent lightminded men, who, although their minds were directed towards heaven—imagined in their simplicity, that the clearest demonstration of the things above was to be obtained by sight." Likewise, the race of wild pedestrian things came "from those who had no philosophy in any of their thoughts, and never considered at all about the nature of the heavens, because they had ceased to use the course of the head, but followed the guidance of the soul which are in the breast" (*Timaeus* 91). The not so oblique reference to the birds is, of course, a commentary on the Sophists who still believed in conventional morality after chopping away at its roots; the race of wild pedestrian things refers to the Sophists who thought that the second Athenian thesis was the height of, well, *sophistication.*

Thucydides was a Sophist of the noblest and finest sort. Sitting in exile in Thrace he could watch the events before him unfold with a certain detachment. Thucydides, like the Pseudo-Xenophon of *The Constitution of the Athenians,* saw the Athens of Marathon and Salamis turning into a bloated parody of itself as the same energy that powered her to greatness had a demonic side that expressed itself in imperial tyranny. Thucydides was appalled at the loss of conventional standards of morality, and in his icily controlled prose writes the last tragedy of Athens—last because the tension between righteousness and necessity is broken in favor of necessity.

On the other hand, Thucydides' method may have prevented him from fully dissecting the inner dynamics of the phenomenon he had in front of him. At some point he realized that the Archi-

---

14. Plato *Timaeus,* in *The Dialogues of Plato,* vols. 1 and 2, trans. B. Jowett (New York: Random House, 1920), 90. All subsequent references in this chapter are to this edition.

damean War and the Ionian War were parts of a single drama—a drama which he saw stretching back to the end of the Persian Wars and the rise of strategic autocrats like Themistocles. The whole period was the "greatest movement," or *kinēsis*. But how could Thucydides produce a work of analysis that would be a "possession for all time" and, by implication, outrank the works of Homer and Herodotus? Recall *Timaeus*'s description of the plight of those who thought of heaven but relied on their sight to find it.

In book I we are given a hint of Thucydides' method in his description of Homer's treatment of the causes of the Trojan War (1.9). Homer's less than scientific method, Thucydides implies, made him overlook the most obvious cause of the war, a change in power relations among Agamemnon, his federal associates, and Troy. Agamemnon's power was a more effective bond than the oaths to Tyndareus, and his increased naval power now made it possible to contemplate and launch the amphibious operation to Ilium. The irony here will soon be apparent. Thucydides' treatment of Homer neglects the fact that Homer (with Hesiod) has created a Hellenistic theology complete with mythical symbols of order (the order of Zeus and the gods). At the same time *Iliad* and *Odyssey* are powerful etiologies of the decline of a Mycenaean civilization—a decline that begins as a pathology of heroes and finally works its way into the ordinary folks of Ithaca.

Establishing his credentials as someone who respects Homer but exceeds the poet in scientific precision, Thucydides unfolds his method further. He also rejects, as too unscientific, the Herodotean hypothesis of a cycle in history that shows that success must be attained at a price: "There is a wheel of human affairs which, turning, does not suffer the same men to prosper always."[15] Thucydides turned to the newly developed Ionian science of medicine. The Hippocratic science examined the various symptoms of diseases to come up with the *idea* of a disease, which

15. Voegelin, *The World of the Polis*, 337.

would be used to recognize the phenomenon when it appeared again, and even to predict its outbreak under certain circumstances. Thucydides uses the method in chapters 47 through 51 of book 2 to describe the symptoms of a malady, to give it a name (the plague), and to note its widespread nature. He hopes that the method will prove useful for understanding if it ever occurs again.

Applying the method to the events in the Hellenic world floating by him, Thucydides detects the symptoms of something—civil wars, protracted conflict, words changing their meaning, and the like. He then gives the great movement, or *kinēsis,* a name—the Peloponnesian War—and hopes that his method will prove to be useful in understanding things in the future. By a macabre twist of irony, Thucydides' method has itself become a part of the *kinēsis!* To double the irony, the Hippocratic method may have been the empirical basis for Plato's study of the soul and its relationship to eternity surfacing in his work as the *ideas.* Thucydides' use of the method becomes part of the general deformation of sophistic Athens; the Platonic formulation becomes the springboard which allows us the kind of transcendent (from the Latin *transcendere,* literally, "to climb over or beyond") perspective that culminates in a study of the soul which penetrates the surface of the *kinēsis* and explores its existential core in the minds of Pericles, Cleon, the Athenian populace, and the Hellenic world itself.

This is not to slight the nobility and sense of moral outrage that makes the tightly restrained prose of Thucydides so useful in studying relations between political units. It even makes the study of Thucydides the perfect complement for the study of Plato. Plato offers us a study of the sources of order in the soul and the city; Thucydides provides us with a study of the lethal diseases of order. *The Peloponnesian War* is a wonderful field manual for national suicide.[16] However, for all his personal virtue Thucydides the analyst has become a bird.

16. Ibid., 357.

AMERICA

What moral has the story of Athens for the conduct of American foreign policy? Political philosophy is sometimes thought of in terms of the dialectic between the moderns and the ancients. The ancients, we say, taught that virtue was the result of the internal orientation of the soul towards the Good, a process that could only occur as a result of patient persuasion. The moderns are said to teach that virtue is attained by arranging the external order of things in a way that makes passion check passion, ambition check ambition, and power check power. To extend the modern argument, if the best minds of a nation wisely direct the passions of both rulers and the ruled, the result will be a large powerful political unit that protects the lives of the citizens and satisfies the appetites of the many by war or commerce. This, in short, is the modern project, or what Thomas Hobbes called *Leviathan*.

Yet perhaps there is no sharp dichotomy between "classic" Athens and "modern" America. Instead, Periclean Athens may be a microcosm of the modern project: a powerful city-state that satisfied the appetites of its citizens by war and commerce. Athens, like America today, was a political unit running on passions. Similarly, Athenian political science was reduced to a calculation of power relations, and virtue (*aretē*) was looked upon as a human artifice.

If the theme of the modern project can be seen in a smaller form in fifth-century Athens, perhaps the parallel theme of a society falling into spiritual disorder can be found in contemporary America. That is, perhaps we can find the same process at work that "solves" the dialectic between power and justice by equating them, reduces man to an organism in a closed and earth-bound environment, and wraps the whole thing up in the attractive package of promotion of self-interest. Does America ever argue that promotion of its self-interest makes it the "friend" of countries in need? Does it ever argue that *all* are driven by fear, honor, and interest, and, therefore, that justice is the will of the stronger?

Does contemporary American foreign policy ever suggest that "whether for evil or for good" the United States "must force every sea and land to be the highways of our daring?" What is the common good to which American foreign policy is directed? What are the ends toward which honor and valor are to be directed? What is the politics of American policy makers?

In 1985, an American statesman, who, like Pericles, directed the foreign policy of his nation, gave a speech. George Shultz, U.S. secretary of state, addressed the National Committee on American Foreign Policy on the importance of realism in the conduct of America's external relations. "A foreign policy based on realism," he said, "cannot ignore the importance of either ideology or morality. But realism does require that we avoid foreign policies based exclusively on moral absolutes divorced from political reality."[17] What is important, according to Shultz, is that the United States must realize that foreign policy takes place in the real world, and in the real world our ideals and our interests are intimately related. After calculating our interest in a particular instance—for example, South Africa or Nicaragua—we can also arrive at the salutary conclusion that our ideals can be a source of strength rather than a paralyzing albatross or myopic lens that distorts the living field of interest and power. "Our ideals have a concrete, practical meaning today. They not only point the way to a better world, they reflect some of the most powerful currents at work in the contemporary world. The striving for justice, freedom, progress, and peace is an ever-present reality that is today, more than ever, impressing itself on international relations."[18]

The speech is a noble-sounding paean for an approach to foreign policy which is based on an enlightened realism. As such, it is the heir to the Funeral Oration of Pericles. Shultz appeals to the American pathos, its craving to exist and be admired. And,

---

17. George Shultz, "Morality and Realism in American Foreign Policy." Speech given to the National Committee on American Foreign Policy, 1985.

18. Ibid.

just as in the Periclean paean, power is the ultimate source of Athenian glory or American "values." Like the Thucydidean encomium, Shultz makes prudence the highest moral principle of politics. Prudence never overreaches the limits of national power; prudence never underestimates the capabilities of potential enemies; prudence sleeplessly husbands scarce national resources; and prudence never fails to include considerations of a nation's principles as integral elements of national morale.

The troubling thought arises, though, that the speech is a camouflage for the same forces that resulted in the destruction of Athenian order and gave rise to a city whose principle of pragmatic action was pure injustice. In the case of Pericles, the causes of the deformation were the concupiscent desire for power and glory set off by the Athenians' success in the Persian War and the elimination of the tension between power and justice by the Sophists.

Is there some relation between the rhetoric of Shultz's speech and the teaching behind it that would help us understand the meaning behind the words—that is, is there a teacher like Anaxagoras standing somewhere in the wings? In the case of the secretary of state, the intellectual power behind the speech is Hans Morgenthau. As Shultz put it, "Hans Morgenthau was a pioneer in the study of international relations. He, perhaps more than anyone else, gave it intellectual respectability as an academic discipline. His work transformed our thinking about international relations and about America's role in the postwar world. In fundamental ways he set the terms of the modern debate, and it is hard to imagine what our policies would be like today had we not had the benefit of his wisdom and the clarity of his thinking."[19]

Reading that passage another anamnestic experience occurs. First, I remember Morgenthau as the great teacher of the postwar elites and those coming of age in the 1950s, '60s, and '70s.

19. Ibid.

Politics among Nations[20] was, and still is, an elegant work that uses history as an approach to politics to produce what, at least then, appeared to be the final word on the subject. I remember reading it for the first time as an undergraduate and recall the feeling of euphoria as Morgenthau unrolled his lucid, cogent, well-written presentation of "political realism." It was as if the temple veil had been rent, the cave had been transcended, and the soul had achieved its *periagoge*.

Morgenthau's elegant formulation goes something like the following. Humans are driven by deep-seated bio-psychological urges: to live, to procreate, to dominate. From this essential human nature we derive our definition of politics as the struggle for power that takes place at all levels of life. The key to understanding politics is the concept of interest defined in terms of power. At the level of international relations, nations must pursue their national interest, which must avoid the irrationalities of ideology or popular passion. The highest principles of politics are prudence, the art of aligning interest and capabilities, and the maintenance of an equilibrium that works *with* the forces of human nature rather than *against* them (a balance of power). Ethics, morality, and law are human artifacts that emerge from the same elemental forces that build society and give us our definition of politics. Ultimately, the criterion for right action is success in the contest between power units (e.g., democracies are better than totalitarian states because they can marshal national energy in the pursuit of objectives more efficiently).

But the second half of the memory sets off alarm bells. To reach a reasonably clear understanding of reality in the 1950s and '60s a young man or woman had to avoid taking two things really seriously: John Wayne movies and *Politics among Nations*. Emulating John Wayne could get one killed very quickly in the wars of

---

20. Hans J. Morgenthau, *Politics among Nations: The Struggle for Peace and Power*, 6th ed. (New York: Alfred A. Knopf, 1985).

containment, and *Politics among Nations* could pull one into the quicksand of realism. Essential to answering this question is Morgenthau's reading of Thucydides.

Thucydides is incorrectly cited as an early thinker who recognized the permanence of interest as the key to an understanding and practice of politics. (As a mildly amusing, and very revealing, side note, the book went through at least six editions with a mistranslation of the Melian Dialogue, to wit "of the gods we know and of men we believe.") Morgenthau writes, "Thucydides' statement, born of the experience of ancient Greece that 'identity of interests is the surest of bonds whether between states or individuals,' was taken up in the nineteenth century by Lord Salisbury's remark that 'the only bond of union that endures' among nations is 'the absence of all clashing interests.' "[21] But surely it was not Thucydides who made the statement; rather it is from a speech of the Corinthians to their allies. And we are also aware that Thucydides accurately reported the war and recorded the decomposition of order that turned all of Hellas into a *kinēsis* where former principles of injustice became pragmatic principles of order. Morgenthau seems to miss the fact that Thucydides' words contain the shudder of both realization and incomprehension about the monster that Athens had become. Unfortunately, an important piece of Morgenthau's argument rests on this misconception. Reading Thucydides this way leaves the reader wondering whether Morgenthau teaches illusion as certainly as did Pericles.

The Athenian claim of identity of interests finds its parallel both in the dynamics of Cold War thinking about politics and in current notions of global governments and new world orders. Post-war American foreign policy assumed that identity of interests would result in a kind of like-mindedness. The Soviets were motivated by two things, Marxist ideology and Russian national interest. The trick was to contain Soviet power until its leaders

21. Ibid., 10.

could be "housebroken" to think like our elite, that is, in terms of political realism. Meanwhile politics as the struggle for power and interest must go on; balances of power must be maintained; and national interest and national power must be prudently adjusted.

In contemporary international relations the dangers of warfare mean that the struggle for power must be modified. World government is necessary and the prelude to world government must be the formation of a "world community." One assumes that this world community must seek slowly to overcome a variety of religious and political nationalism in favor of a regime which serves the material interests of all to the extent necessary to maintain relative peace at the same time that some global enforcement mechanism is put in place with the support of the strongest nations to make sure that the system is maintained. This mirrors the last part of Morgenthau's book in which he made a powerful argument that realism based on nation-states had not worked well and that the ultimate goal of a transnational elite of realists was the creation of a world government, a global federalism, or at the least some kind of new world order.

With this formulation in mind we can see that Morgenthau and Shultz are involved in the same intellectual exercises that resulted in the reduction of existence to the level of biological life and the shift from a belief that prudence was making righteous policy to prudence as a calculation of power relations. As a participant in one of the small balance-of-power wars that rumbled like distant summer thunder against the blaring, bustling, rock 'n' roll commercial republic, it took a long time to realize that *realism* was the source of that strange feeling of unreality described earlier. Realism is not real, because to perform the realist operation the thinker must do several things that distort or deny the relationship between *ananke* and *dike*.

First, he must remove the soul from its primordial community of being: God and man, world and society. He does so by reducing the essence of a human to bio-psychological urges. That, in turn, enables us to see ethics, morality, and law as the creation of these same primeval drives rather than as reflections of an objective moral order. God, and man as the image of God, are replaced by man as an organism in an environment which requires the invention of the gods.

The operation continues by sledgehammering the soul to its *libido dominandi*. From this drive we arrive at the realist definition of politics, which in turn requires mauling it as well. When Aristotle said that "man is a political animal" he meant that man is a creature whose nature is to live in a polity, thus preserving the word's etymological relation to the Greek *politeia* (meaning "citizenship" or "government," and being a variant of *politēs*, "citizen") as well as to its more ominous Indo-European parent *pelē*, "high fortified place."

Third, the theorist (or philodoxer) must elevate the notion of "national interest" to the position of a sacred symbol. One need not notice either that the symbol is an opaque one, without spiritual or practical substance, or that it is capable of meaning just about any darn thing you want. Or, to add oxymoronic profundity to the "concept" (itself a jargon word), add the words *vital* national *security* interest.

Finally, he must mutilate an ancient text. As our readers know, *Thucydides* did not make the speech about interest being the strongest bond between men and nations, the *Corinthians* did. And if the Melian Dialogue is supposed to be a model for the conduct of international relations, those relations must take place in the shadow of chaos and a revolt against God.[22]

The logic of realism worked its way out in the whole range of Cold War praxeology. The language of nuclear deterrence (both MAD and NUTs) revealed a murderous willingness to actually use atomic weapons—a willingness negated by the sheer fear that lurked behind the "strategic terminology." A vocabulary of "limited war" was worked out that classified war by the weapons or

22. Donald Kagan, *On the Origin of War* (New York: Doubleday, 1995).

level of violence attained, not from the perspective of justice and injustice. A complete theory of "nation-building" was developed to cope with the threat of "revolutionary warfare." Traditional structures and functions of "underdeveloped" nations would be transmuted by the alchemy of economic technical assistance into modern structures and functions. And to protect this process "counterinsurgency" forces would meet the bearers of "guerrilla war" on their own ground—the mountains, jungles, and cities of traditional societies, whose loss would upset the balance of power.

Recently, a cruel book was published that vividly illustrates the blindness of American foreign policy since World War II. In a way it rivals the speeches of Cleon and Alcibiades for its lack of sharp vision under stress. It is *In Retrospect: The Tragedy and Lessons of Vietnam.*[23] The author is Robert S. McNamara, secretary of defense under Kennedy and Johnson. The true irony of the book is its subtitle: . . . *Tragedy . . . of Vietnam.* Over and over the author bemoans the fact that he didn't step in and have a knock-down-drag-out fight with the service chiefs over doctrine; that he didn't help construct a super coordinating body for Vietnam; that we never understood the North Vietnamese, the Democratic Republic of Vietnam, or the Vietcong; and that we could never explain the war aims to our own people. The irony of the title is that in the ethics of tragedy (e.g., Aeschylus, *Suppliants*) the essence of right action is deep diving to find *dikē* against forces that might even physically destroy you—even if you find the righteous thing to do.[24] Failure to attempt the agonizing search is just as much a sin as the conscious decision to do evil. And the essence of McNamara's memories is its endless litany of "Why didn't I do that?"

Here we see McNamara caught in the same deadly trap as the

23. Robert S. McNamara, with Brian VanDeMark. *In Retrospect: The Tragedy and Lessons of Vietnam* (New York: Times Books, 1995).

24. Aeschylus, *The Suppliants* in *The Complete Greek Drama*, vol. 2, ed. Whitney J. Oates and Eugene O'Neill, Jr. (New York: Random House, 1938).

Athenians at Melos. Because of the Athenian thesis they *must* act in a way that will increase their credibility. To back down or just ignore the neutral Melians is *not* an option for the masters of the sea. In the same way, the logic of realism, which starts with the definition that politics is the struggle for power, inclined an American leadership intoxicated by the aromas arising out of the alembic of limitless power and heady success, to view Vietnam in terms of the definition. The insertion of armed forces into Vietnam was not an inexorable deduction from the premises of realism, but in the heady years of the early 1960s there was little to suggest that real men ought really to think of *dikē* first. If *dikē* is only a human artifact, why should it complicate the first task of realist politics—the calculation of relations of power?

Bill Clinton also must have read the second half of Morgenthau's *Politics among Nations* because he finds himself trapped in the new world order paradigm. We *must* establish our credibility as the leader of a new world order. Just as President Bush was impelled to take on Iraq in the name of a new world order (and to prove that a resuscitated U.S. military could still pound people to blood pudding), so must Clinton establish our credibility in snake pits of disorder like Somalia, Haiti, and Bosnia.

In conclusion, the modern project of America begins to look more and more like the ancient project of Periclean Athens. In the beginning of *The Republic,* Socrates and Glaucon are pictured as going down to the Piraeus to witness a religious procession to the goddess Bendis. Down in space, they are walking the four and a half miles from the city to the naval base. Down in time, they are also walking the sixty years between the Athens of Marathon and the Athens of the nightmare of imperial sea power.[25]

To where is the United States "going down"? Did my going down, and that of 1,400 other marines, to the seaport in San Diego, California, foreshadow the gentle vision of an America working its heart out to achieve Morgenthau's ultimate vision of

25. Voegelin, *Plato and Aristotle.*

a world order or world government run by rational practitioners of political realism? Or did it presage the gradual descent into the world of dream and illusion, represented by the Melian Dialogue, in which the order of Zeus is banished from Athens to be replaced by the order of necessity defined solely as power? Are not both visions of America in the world simply different versions of a desire to escape the reality of existence under God, with its terrifying demand of finding *dikē* in the crucible where sin, faith, power, and justice are all thrown in and heated with the fires of the divine-human encounter?

The reduction of human life to its *libido dominandi* seems to have resulted in an eerie inability of the Athenians to make rational calculations between means and ends in the field of pragmatic action, and even about rational ends themselves. The result was "imperial overstretch," military disaster, and eventual defeat at the hands of Sparta and her allies. Could it be that the power upon power that is the United States is immune to such miscalculations? American foreign policy needs to re-orient itself towards consideration of what ends are worth the valor and sacrifice of a Vietnam.

CONTRIBUTORS

STEVEN FORDE is Associate Professor of Political Science at the University of North Texas. His work covers the history of political philosophy and includes a book on Thucydides, *The Ambition to Rule: Alcibiades and the Politics of Imperialism in Thucydides*.

W. DANIEL GARST is author of "Thucydides and Neorealism" (*International Studies Quarterly*). His current work focuses on the social origins of democratic institutions in late nineteenth- and early-twentieth-century Europe.

LOWELL S. GUSTAFSON is Chair of the Political Science Department and Associate Professor at Villanova University. He is author of *The Sovereignty Dispute over the Falkland (Malvinas) Islands*, co-editor of *The Religious Challenge to the State*, and editor of *Economic Development and Democracy: Neoliberalism in Latin America*.

MARGARET HREZO is Assistant Professor of Political Science at Radford University. Published work includes "W. E. B. DuBois" in Sidney A. Pearson's *The Constitutional Polity* and "Civility or the Culture Wars in Politics and Religion" (with Melinda Bollar Wagner) in *Cultural Wars in American Politics*, edited by Rhys Williams. Forthcoming is "Composition on a Multiple Plane: Simone Weil's Answer to the Rule of Power" in *Feminist Approaches to Social Movements, Community, and Power*, edited by Robin Teske and Mary Ann Tetrault.

LAURIE M. JOHNSON BAGBY is an Associate Professor of Political Science at Kansas State University. She received her Ph.D. from Northern Illinois University. Her area of specialization is political philosophy. She is author of *Thucydides, Hobbes, and the Interpretation of Realism* and several articles on Thucydides and international relations.

CLIFFORD ORWIN is Professor of Political Science at the University of Toronto and the author of numerous books and articles on Thucydides, including *The Humanity of Thucydides*.

NICK PAPPAS is Professor of Political Science at Radford University. He is author of numerous book chapters and articles in such journals as the *Air University Review* and *The Naval War College Review*. *Vietnam* magazine published "The Strategic Dreamworld of the Vietnam War" in October 1999.

JACK RILEY is an Associate Professor of Politics at Coastal Carolina University. He has written extensively on the political thought of Thucydides and has published translations of the Funeral Oration of Pericles and the Melian Dialogue in *The Quest for Justice*. He also has a translation of *The War of the Peloponnesians and the Athenians*, forthcoming.

CRAIG WAGGAMAN is an Associate Professor of Political Science at Radford University. He is author of "Milton Friedman" in Mark J. Rozell and James F. Pontuso, eds., *American Conservative Opinion Leaders*, and other articles and book chapters.

INDEX